AMERICAN SECURITY IN A CHANGING WORLD

Issues and Choices

Edited by

Joseph Richard Goldman

UNIVERSITY
PRESS OF
AMERICA

LANHAM • NEW YORK • LONDON

Copyright © 1987 by

University Press of America,® Inc.

4720 Boston Way
Lanham, MD 20706

3 Henrietta Street
London WC2E 8LU England

Printed in the United States of America

British Cataloging in Publication Information Available

Library of Congress Cataloging in Publication Data

American security in a changing world.

Bibliography: p.
1. United States—Foreign relations—1981-
2. United States—National security.   I. Goldman,
Joseph Richard, 1943-
E876.A487   1986   327.73   86-24588
ISBN 0-8191-5706-6 (alk. paper)
ISBN 0-8191-5707-4 (pbk. : alk. paper)

All University Press of America books are produced on acid-free
paper which exceeds the minimum standards set by the National
Historical Publication and Records Commission.

Acknowledgments

A book like this incurs many debts and much gratitude on my part towards everyone associated with it directly or indirectly. The contributors deserve all the credit for their willingness to write an essay; however, all the support and friendship given by a lot of other people from the very beginning of this project must be recognized even though words do not seem enough.

I want to thank W. Phillips Shively, Virginia Gray, Frank Sorauf, and the rest of my colleagues in the Department of Political Science for the opportunity to teach and research at an exciting place. Cathy Duvall and especially Mary Ellen Otis were instrumental in the manuscript preparation; I am grateful.

A special thanks to the publisher and editorial staff at the University Press of America is in order. Their enthusiasm, assistance, and effort contributed to the preparation of this book.

To my family and friends who listened and were there during the time it took working on this book, thank you.

I bear the responsibility for any shortcomings that might be in this book.

Joseph Richard Goldman
University of Minnesota

TABLE OF CONTENTS

Introduction

In the 1980s Americans are increasingly aware that the world beyond U.S. borders can affect their individual and collective well-beings. Mention the arms race, the deficit, the Western alliance, oil and the Middle East, for example, and nearly everyone asked will offer an opinion along with some pointed criticism. In an uncertain time, American security is something that experts and non-experts can debate and disagree, opine and criticize. To be sure, all Americans know that the ongoing arms race with Russia poses a real danger to national survival. So do mounting federal deficits. And certainly the diversion of more scarce capital away from social welfare-- caused by an ever enormous defense budget -- cannot continue for long without harming future American security. Taken together, when the president addresses Congress and the public about a particular policy abroad or at home that affects the well-being of millions of individuals and costs more billions of dollars, the issues and choices presented are usually things which shape our security.

This book is about important issues and choices and American security. But a few words are in order as to the book's purpose. Works with titles like this presumably deal with foreign policy or defense policy, and also they could be generalized texts or specialized readers. There is no doubt that American foreign policy and defense policy are subjects here, however so is political economy. The politics and economics of distribution (and, in some cases, redistribution) with respect to national interests and security are important, too. The conduct of foreign policy and the management of defense policy cannot be so readily divorced from today's marketplace where business, industry, and the public depend on their government to help make the world secure for Americans. In turn, the government requires resources to accomplish this objective--especially when interacting with foreign powers over difficult problems, or mobilizing American strength to maintain peace by being prepared for war. Consequently, the issues and choices involved demand better understanding. That is the purpose of our book.

The essays here are grouped basically (but certainly not rigidly) by categories. The categories are political economy, national security, and international security; however, their ideas may cross

1

boundaries since we seek to present a wide range of
views and perspectives. Also, the reader's attention
is called to the fact that there is no substantive
answer to the question of which relationship (domestic-
foreign or foreign-domestic) always and forevermore
drives policy first; this "chicken-and-egg" question
can bedevil discourses on security affairs as becomes
evident. For example, Aldrich-Duvall-Weldes (chapter
one) raise questions which contrast those put forward
by Ostrom-Simon (chapter three) of how things are
decided, and the ones addressed by Holland-Hoover
(chapter four) challenge decisionmaking theory to
explain local and national relationships. In the area
of arms control nationally and internationally,
Hopmann-Anderson (chapter five) advance a distinct
proposal very different from the one Russett (chapter
seven) advocates; while Boulding (chapter two) and
Sibley (chapter eight) aim at the heart of the problem
with provocative options to present-day U.S. arms
control policies. When we turn to American interests
in Europe and the Persian Gulf, other areas of
controversy appear on the horizon. Ravenal (chapter
six) pushes quite openly for an American departure from
NATO and any continuing "foreign entaglements" which do
nothing to promote US security. On the other hand,
Berkowitz (chapter nine) argues that if Europe is
integral to American security, are we prepared for the
real costs should war break out? Cole and Lockwood
(chapter ten) explain that American security has a
definite European definition, too; one which Americans
on this side of the Atlantic should appreciate with
regard to the Alliance's overall benefit. And Sampson
(chapter eleven) points out that the Persian Gulf poses
challenges to American ingenuity. With the purpose and
plan of this book now in mind, we hope that the
following essays will stimulate thought and encourage
debate among everyone concerned with international
relations, American politics, foreign policy and
national security.

POLITICAL ECONOMY

     In "The Costs of National Security: Spending for
Defense and Spending for Welfare in the United States,
1948-1983", John Aldrich, Raymond Duvall, and Jutta
Weldes explore the relationship between budgetary
politics and trade-offs affecting national security
commitments and social welfare programs. Since 1945
these public policy functions are the product of
political choices stemming from decisions made among
presidents, Congress, and constituencies (i.e.,

bureaucratic players, special interest groups, the general public). The authors present a model that identifies the critical policy variables involved, on the one hand, and then they show how to measure these relationships, on the other. In essence, the dynamics of trade-offs between "guns" and "butter" issues really are not dichotomous as most people think. Aldrich, Duvall, and Weldes confirm that there is a shared pattern underlying defense and social welfare expenditures, and that these trade-offs are not necessarily at opposite sides of the budgetary spectrum if one asks the right questions based on evidence.

With "An Economic Assessment of Unilateral National Defense", Kenneth Boulding approaches the issue of guns versus butter and American security somewhat differently. He states that the war industry which services national defense does so on the basis of political--not market--demand. These businessmen develop, manufacture and sell weapons to the Pentagon in the first place because of the political choices made by those officials in government responsible for national defense. The same decisionmakers then provide these industries with much of their capital to operate from, and it is the "public grants economy" which supports those private enterprises doing business with the government. For their part, the industries claim that they provide jobs in return, which benefit the local and national economies, while simultaneously contributing to American security in times of peace or war. He suggests that this dependency relationship is both politically based and politically perpetuated for reasons having little to do with economic rationality. Were the laissez-faire marketplace really allowed to determine national defense in terms of costs-to-benefits, the choices might be different and the economic savings generated would contribute to American security. One of Boulding's conclusions is this: since politics created the present defense system, politics can change it. The choice is apparently political, but it cannot be left to politicians alone. In regard to this choice, the American people must also participate effectively and profoundly.

NATIONAL SECURITY

Speaking of American politics, in "Defense Policymaking Unmasked: Three Recent Cases of Weapons Procurement", Lauren H. Holland and Robert A. Hoover focus on military policy, and they argue that its formulation and implementation are not necessarily

3

different from domestic policy dealing with other issues or choices. Both authors are interested in the machinations of procurement policy, and whether the bureaucratic politics paradigm is enough to explain why the defense department's policymaking process operates as it does. Holland and Hoover point out that national security policy still is explained in the literature by one model which predominates so many over others: the bureaucratic politics model. While it holds paradigmatic status, the bureaucratic politics model is based on a questionable assumption that somehow defense policy is made in ways which are usually distinctive from the processes involved with domestic policy. In their judgment, it appears that several factors common to domestic policymaking are equally present in national security policymaking; these are: socioeconomic considerations and political interests, the electoral and lobbying processes, and concerns among actors over broader societal impacts of policy choices.

Procurement policy is a combination of choices about what national security requires. The decisions to develop, test, deploy and maintain weapons systems such as the MX, for instance, could be explained as an outcome of bureaucratic politics. However, political and technical decisions also are derivatives of the social, economic, and political milieux of American public life. Holland and Hoover examine three weapons systems' (ABM, ELF, MX) decisions in terms of national-local group interactions, and how the issues and choices involved go beyond agency walls, routines, or personality power plays. Their findings strongly suggest the separation between national security policy and domestic policy is artificial. When the evidence is properly evaluated using socio-political and socio-economic dimensions, linkages appear which join national security policy and domestic policy in ways that the bureaucratic paradigm cannot detect nor make. While they are not repudiating the bureaucratic paradigm as a tool of analysis, Holland and Hoover are forcing us to think at many levels of behavior more relationally (and rationally) about national security and American politics.

In "The President and the Politics of Military Force", Charles W. Ostrom, Jr. and Dennis M. Simon examine presidential decisionmaking and public approval. While looking at presidential war powers as an issue area of constitutional, institutional, historical, political, and behavioral developments, the

4

president himself is scrutinized as an individual responsible for the shaping of a successful foreign policy--besides orchestrating favorable public opinion--when national security calls for the use of force. Ostrom and Simon offer a model to explain presidential decisionmaking; one which is based on their conceptualizations of presidential power, the president as foreign policy leader, and presidential foreign policy decisionmaking. The research hinges on an understanding of how presidents decide in terms of their structural environment and, more importantly, that environment's imprint on any presidential mind. This cognitive-cybernetic model posits a new interpretation of the president as a decisionmaker and how information, perception and decision interact. They proceed to offer ten propositions on which their theory can be explicated and tested. The argument that the exercise of war powers is directly connected (and contingent upon) the structure of domestic politics is clear enough. Then Ostrom and Simon go on to re-examine some policy issues and choices presidents since Franklin Delano Roosevelt through Ronald Reagan have managed as individuals, but from the perspective of these leaders' political sensitivity to public opinion. And in times of uncertainty, both believe that a closer look is needed at who a president is and how public support plays a role in national security policy; especially if Americans are to understand better their relationship with the White House.

In "Vulnerability, Uncertainty, and Priorities for Strategic Arms Control", P. Terrence Hopmann and J. Edward Anderson examine some underlying assumptions shared by many strategists about US nuclear doctrine, force capability, and the arms race-arms control symbiosis; and both offer different explanations which questions these assumptions. They first look at some of the technical problems of ICBM operability and dependability which can occur outside of simulated laboratory conditions and controlled downrange testing. Hopmann and Anderson argue that during a nuclear exchange, politics gives way to physics and mechanics. In the "fog of war", Murphy's Law can take effect as multiple nuclear detonations from ground level upwards, weapons systems malfunctions from pre-launch to re-entry, and the like come into play which wreak the best laid strategies of warplanners owing to "technical difficulties". To counter Murphy's Law, testing is one way of doing away with as many technical difficulties as possible; however testing is one factor driving the arms race which both superpowers are engaged in because

of deterrence and defense. They contend that as
nuclear weapons become technologically reliable (hence,
operable and dependable in war under any
circumstances), instead of increasing security for one
side or the other, increased insecurity will accompany
the United States and the Soviet Union as testing drags
them faster to Armageddon. If the US and USSR halt
testing now and link arms control to deterrence,
perhaps American (and Soviet) security will be enhanced
through this approach. The choice between testing and
racing or halting and controlling is by no means simple
for the governments themselves to make, but the issue
here is mankind's survival for years to come.

With "Maintaining Strategic Nuclear Stability",
Earl C. Ravenal takes a critical look at the issues of
strategic defense and crisis stability in terms of
possible choices coming open to American policymakers.
As this country continues to modernize its strategic
defenses, the question inevitably arises of how
modernization influences--either positively or
negatively--crisis stability between the United States
and the Soviet Union. He presents arguments which
challenge both conventional strategists' and anti-
nuclear advocates' notions with what Ravenal calls the
"logic of incentives," and he then proffers a new set
of strategic ideas based on this logic.

Ravenal argues that American nuclear strategy
today must convince the Soviets it is not in their
interest during a crisis ever to use nuclear weapons.
To accomplish this in part, the US must do several
things differently--and soon. In his opinion, the
concept of strategic defense goes beyond relying on
enough nuclear weapons to retaliate against a Russian
first strike. Counterforce strategy is more than tiers
of ICBM's sequentially launched to punish the USSR
after American society is destroyed. Strategic defense
is another form of counterforce strategy, and it could
broaden the choices available to a president in the
midst of a confrontation with Moscow. As a combination
of new technologies (some existing, others possible)
appear, strategic defense will prompt new policies
likewise. Thus strategic defense and offense will
support American security objectives.

But these objectives must be practical. Ravenal
puts forward an alternative strategy based on
incentives which requires more self-reliance, less
commitment to the nuclear security of other states, and
non-intervention. This strategy is calibrated to

6

events rather than the automatic American lock-step "do-this-when-the Soviets-do-that" course of collision politics. Also, the United States must develop a "finite essential deterrence" approach to national defense instead of the wasteful and costly international defense based on "infinite deterrence" which cannot be attained anyway. Additionally, this country has to apply its power more selectively and realistically in a crisis with the Soviet Union, and a credible deterrence might make the difference between peace and war. In the area of arms control, he suggests that one incentive after another offered to the Soviets in exchange of counterincentives made by them may push the arms race towards disarmament providing that we try a new strategy. From his point of view, the choices are now up to the United States while time is still on our side, and a strategy using the logic of incentives holds more promise than what is being done currently.

In "Sensible Deterrence as Arms Control", Bruce Russett tackles the subject of deterrence from the angle of arms control. After reviewing some standard interpretations of deterrence theory and its relationship to national security, he attacks the suppositions and opinions operating to convince American security managers that the Kremlin accepts the nuclear stalemate exactly as we do. A reliance on the military dimension of deterrence simply is not enough; in fact, it is dangerous in the ongoing arms race with the Russians. Because deterrence is essentially psychological and political, Russett suggests that diplomacy in addition to weaponry must be effective for deterring war. He then surveys the history of various nuclear strategies this country has developed and modified since the early 1950s, and through them the relations both superpowers have. What is being argued is that arms control happens to be a form of deterrence, too. The problem, therefore, centers on restraints. Each side sees dangers and pursues its security objectives without real concern for what the other superpower does (or does not). The present method of pressuring by endangering American (or Soviet) security is, in Russett's thinking, decidedly unproductive and threatening as the arms race demonstrates. He suggests that it is in American interest to use arms control not for matching weapons, but for applying "sensible restraint" on our part as a signal to the Soviets they should. Matching proposals is safer, Russett contends, and arms control with the

Soviets should move the nuclear stalemate from confrontation to cooperation if both sides really try.

Mulford Q. Sibley's "Thinking the Unthinkable: Unilateral Disarmament" addresses the role of military power to American security, and he finds that this power is irrelevant. Sibley argues that the United States has the largest military force in its history--which is expensive and expansive; ironically, this force cannot really defend the people against a nuclear holocaust, nor deter a nuclear war if the Soviet Union unilaterally initiates a conflict. In this age of nuclear arms buildups and the ever-increasing likelihood of Armageddon, more stockpiling of arms, more expenditures for these arms, and more military power to appease the twin Molochs of deterrence and defense makes no sense. Another approach to all this futility is disarmament; one that is unilateral, unconditional, unlimited, and rapid.

The logic of this strategy is quite clear. According to Sibley, unilateralism is a power which cuts two ways: it can begin arms races and initiate wars because of a nation's single-handed acts, or it can terminate arms races and refuse to fight wars also for the same reason. If peace is what American security really wants, then it is better to sacrifice military things than human beings. Thus unilateralism inherently is a challenge-response policy; and if disarmament is a means to promote peace, then America must take the lead and challenge the Russians to respond this way. But Americans as a people must first change their values favoring military power and support unilateral disarmament, otherwise nothing will happen. Once convinced and behind this side of unilateralism, Sibley argues, the resources freed from the military and its servant appendages (the CIA, defense industries, the service academies, etc.) can be used differently for this country's and the world's peaceful development. The choice of which unilateralism to follow is still open to the United States.

INTERNATIONAL SECURITY

Bruce D. Berkowitz's "Making Choices on the North German Plain" discusses the US commitment to West European defense in the 1980s, and the costs involved for maintaining this international security obligation. The critical question for the United States in avoiding a nuclear war in Europe is: "what will it cost Washington in dollars and manpower to have the

8

conventional strength capable of deterring a Soviet attack, or--if that form of deterrence fails--fight successfully without resorting to first use of nuclear weapons and world war three?" Berkowitz points out a dilemma in this case: it is one thing to make the choice in favor of greater conventional military force over nuclear weaponry as a means to meet the Soviet threat; however, it is another issue to raise defense spending and impose the draft here at home (staggering burdens which the American public must bear).

Berkowitz proposes alternatives for meeting the financing of European defense, and he gives the strategic pros and cons of each option. While NATO allies are doing more and contributing to the international security of themselves and America, this country must continue to provide its share even--if larger than others--because there is little choice except withdrawal. Several ways for the US to cover these costs are possible. First, the Administration can increase spending levels as far as the political system allows. Second, the Administration can continue promoting whatever technological and tactical innovations which will give NATO a greater conventional edge. In any case, American and West European international security is at stake; and no matter how expensive the choices are for peacekeeping, after a conflict begins the choices for warmaking are more expensive.

In "U.S. Public Policy toward a Consensus on NATO", Paul M. Cole and Dunbar Lockwood study the roles that the media and public play in NATO affairs. The issues generally troubling the Atlantic Alliance of late are particularly sharp in American-German relations, and their intensity will have an impact on NATO at large for some time to come. However, instead of analyzing these issues purely as diplomatic or strategic differences concerning governments, Cole and Lockwood treat them in terms of media and public interests, too. The authors explain some of the ways in which the American public is influenced by the media's coverage and interpretation of NATO policies, and the same explanation is given for the German counterparts. Issues like who pays more for NATO, who has more forces ready to fight, who will first face a Soviet attack, etc, also affect public perceptions of the Alliance; and in the democracies composing, NATO perceptions translate into votes at election time. Cole and Lockwood look at public opinion data to gauge what Americans and Germans actually think about the

9

NATO partnership. Their findings indicate that alliance strategy is not merely a matter of adequate military planning, economic burden-sharing or political leadership working in tandem for NATO objectives, it is equally a factor of mass support and strong loyalty by Western publics. In the last analysis, Cole and Lockwood demonstrate that any understanding of national security qua government to government is much too limited and inaccurate. It has to include public-to-public relations as well with respect to mutual security.

Martin W. Sampson presents an entirely different picture of the world with his essay "Rapid Deployment in Lieu of Energy Policy?"; today it is one to which we must pay close attention. In his assessment of current energy problems and the military policy to handle them, Sampson shows how persistent dependency of foreign energy sources--especially Middle Eastern oil form the Persian Gulf regions--still threatens American security. Various presidential strategies from Nixon to Reagan to reduce this dependency have produced little effective action for almost 20 years. The perception that in 1986 the energy crisis has passed (or as the Reagan Administration often likes to do when confronted by complex issues and harsh realities it chooses not to face--banish by belief) remains neither realistic nor a substitute for an effective independent energy policy.

He discusses the role that the U.S. military is expected to play in keeping the oil flowing; in reality, this represents another form of dependency. Furthermore, in Sampson's view, the West Europeans and the Japanese (who are far more dependent on Persian Gulf supplies) are doing little militarily, and they seem quite pleased to let America shoulder that burden of defense for them as well. Therefore, the American strategy concerning energy security gives our allies a "free ride" in guaranteeing their oil, and thus it still leaves this country vulnerable with respect to having enough oil for our needs.

The Carter legacy to Reagan in terms of a national policy for energy security is the Rapid Deployment Force (now called Central Command). What Sampson sees is that energy dependency is complemented by a dependency on the military to keep oil access open for American consumers. The departure Reagan makes in what passes for US energy security is a reliance on market mechanisms to control prices, supplies and doubts. Whereas Carter used governmental intervention when necessary to manage both producer-created oil shortages

10

and market (seller)-oriented shortages, Reagan simply does nothing with governmental power in that regard. Instead he lets the private sector work its will on the constituency this president is sworn to protect: the American public. Consequently, American security is still in jeopardy because of the lack of a comprehensive, effective energy policy. While the issues are quite clear on the dangers of continued dependency by this country and the West on Persian Gulf oil, so far the choices made are not very satisfactory compared to those which could be--both market-wise at home and military-wise abroad.

THE COSTS OF NATIONAL SECURITY:
SPENDING FOR DEFENSE AND SPENDING FOR WELFARE
IN THE UNITED STATES, 1948-1983*

John Aldrich   Raymond Duvall   Jutta Weldes

More than any other peacetime period in American
history, the last two years of Carter's term and the
entire Reagan presidency have been marked by a rapid
increase in military expenditures. As of June, 1986,
House-Senate conferees had agreed on a Defense
Department budget of $279.2 billion for fiscal 1987, a
figure that represents an approximately 78% increase
over the $156.9 billion DoD budget of 1982, the first
fiscal year of the Reagan presidency, only five years
earlier. During the same period, Mr. Reagan committed
himself to a vocal campaign to reduce the federal
budget, targeting domestic non-defense expenditures for
reductions. Even if those reductions serve only to
slow projected rates of growth, they have been
sufficiently pronounced as political issues to have
earned the label "the Reagan revolution" in some
circles.

This period contrasts starkly with the decade of
the 1970s. From fiscal 1970 to fiscal 1979 (the second
year of the Carter presidency) the budget of the
Department of Defense increased by only approximately
50%, from $75.4 billion to $113.4 billion, a rate that
was substantially below the roughly 87% inflation for
the same decade. By contrast, the "safety net" of the
American "welfare state" grew rapidly during the 1970s,
even in real terms (i.e., corrected for inflation).
For example, in the 10 years from fiscal 1970 to fiscal
1979, federal income maintenance programs increased
some 278%, from $43.8 billion to $165.6 billion.
Similarly, the federal government's expenditures for
health and medical programs grew by approximately 343%,
from $13.0 billion to $57.4 billion. Because total
national income increased by only 143% (from a GNP of
$993 billion in 1970 to $2414 billion in 1979), these
high rates of social welfare expenditure growth meant
that, even as a relative share, the governmentally
provided "social wage" was expanding rapidly in the
American economy (see Bowles and Gintis, 1982; Hibbs
and Dennis, 1985).

Where the Reagan years give the impression of
defense increases at the expense of domestic

non-defense (particularly "safety net" welfare) expenditures, the 1970s seem, in retrospect, to have been an era of welfare growth at the expense of defense (a retrospective assessment that has certainly been invoked to support Reagan's attempts to reverse budgetary trends). Impressions such as these lead quite naturally to the conclusion that a fundamental feature of budgetary politics in the post-World War II era is a trade-off between military "defense" commitments-- which, following Yergin (1977), we prefer to call national security commitments -- and social welfare programs. Each can increase only at the expense of reductions in the other.

Yet, if we focus our attention on absolute expenditures rather than on relative rates of change, the picture appears to be much more one of mutual growth throughout virtually the entire post-war period. Figure One is illustrative; it presents the yearly expenditures for one summary measure each of national security commitments and social welfare programs. (The measures are described in detail below.) The data in Figure One indicate little apparent competition between defense and welfare, as both seem to exhibit essentially exponential growth trajectories in recent years. Both therefore appear to confirm the conventional wisdom that the public economy is a rapidly growing sector in advanced capitalist societies in the late 20th century.

The question raised by these contrasting images is, to what extent and in what ways, if any, do budgetary politics in the United States involve a trade-off between national security commitments and social welfare programs? Is defense spending increased only at the expense of welfare, or are trade-offs an illusion? It should be apparent from the materials presented above that there is no simple or direct answer to this question. Rather, the answer is dependent on how one approaches the problem -- how one conceptualizes the issue of trade-offs, and against what background one assesses budgetary changes. In short, a determination of the extent and form of trade-offs is dependent on assumptions, perspective and methods.

In this chapter we address some of those conceptual and methodological issues toward the objective of assessing systematically the trade-offs between national security commitments and social welfare programs in the American political economy

13

**Figure 1a: Expenditures for National Security,
1948-1983[*]**

(In millions of current dollars)

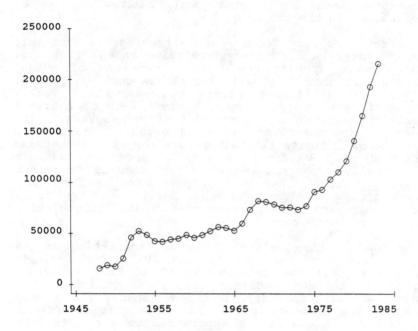

*Source: U.S. Government Budgets, 1950-1985.
Actual expenditures for a given year are
presented in the official budget published
two years later. Expenditures are coded
according to the categories described below,
in the section "Measuring National Security
and Social Welfare Expenditures".

Figure 1b: Expenditures for Social Welfare, 1948-1983*

(In millions of current dollars)

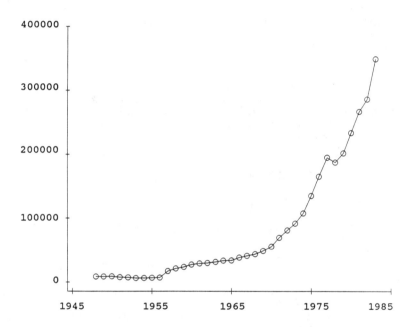

*Source: U.S. Government Budgets, 1950-1985. Actual expenditures for a given year are presented in the official budget published two years later. Expenditures are coded according to the categories described below, in the section "Measuring National Security and Social Welfare Expenditures".

15

since World War II. We do not offer an estimation of those trade-offs, per se, here. Instead, we deal only with the necessary conceptual and methodological preliminaries. In particular, the paper has two main sections. The first is devoted to the conceptualization of the trade-off problem; in it we ask how and at what level one should approach the determination of the form and extent of trade-offs between national security commitments and social welfare programs. The second section is directed to the identification of the structure of change in each of the two respective variables in the trade-off problem. This section, in turn, is in two parts. First we discuss how we measure the two variables in terms of federal budgetary categories; second we model the structure of these expenditure time-series for the 36 year period, fiscal 1948-1983. The time-series modeling of the two separate variables leads us to some initial conclusions about the budgetary process in each of these two broad areas of governmental concern separately, and, on that basis, to some inferences about the possibilities for a trade-off relationship between the two.

CONCEPTUALIZING THE PROBLEM OF TRADE-OFFS

What, exactly, would it mean to say that military "defense", or national security, commitments come at the expense of social welfare programs (or vice versa)? We argue that it can and does mean four different things, depending on which of four distinct conceptions of trade-offs is held. Accordingly, it is imperative that those four different conceptualizations be understood clearly and that their distinct implications and logics be kept in mind in analysis. Unfortunately, as we try to make clear below, such has not been characteristic of published literature on the subject of "guns-butter" trade-offs. Instead, the trade-off problem has often been conceptualized rather crudely and ambiguously.

The four conceptions derive from two variable features, or dimensions, of the arenas in which trade-offs potentially occur. At the generic level, budgetary trade-offs mean that expenditures for one program come at the expense of other desiderata; they entail opportunity costs in the sense that governmental commitments to one category of expenditures reduce the ability to accomplish other outcomes.[1] This general notion implies that, at some level, there are

16

(resource) constraints on the ability to pursue and accomplish objectives; in the absence of constraints, all programmatic objectives could be pursued simultaneously to the fullest. The two dimensions that lead to four distinct conceptualizations follow from this general notion of trade-offs. They are: (1) the character of the opportunity costs; and (2) the level at which the effective constraints operate.

In terms of the first of these dimensions, the opportunity costs of a particular governmental expenditure are of two types. One type is direct opportunity costs; an expenditure means forgone opportunities to allocate resources to other expenditure categories and, hence, to achieve the unique programmatic objectives of those other categories. The second type is indirect opportunity costs; expenditures produce unintended effects and/or effects that are not unique to the programmatic expenditure category, and these "externalities", which can be either positive or negative, are different for various expenditure categories. Indirect opportunity costs involve the relative net positive weight of the externalities of different programmatic expenditures. A particular allocation of resources means forgone opportunities to experience the positive externalities of alternative allocations of those resources.[2]

The second relevant dimension involved in the conceptualization of trade-offs is the level at which the effective constraints operate. Three levels of constraint are logically distinguishable and can be identified in terms of different choice problems. (See Mosley (1985:32-35) for a closely related, but somewhat different, presentation of the three levels of constraint.) At the narrowest, most restrictive level the problem is choice within a given budget-- allocating a defined, or "fixed", set of resources. Here, the effective constraint is the given current budget at the time of allocation. If that constraint is relaxed, a second, broader choice problem emerges; this is a matter of setting the size of the budget, given a "fixed" resource pool from which the government extracts or derives its budgetary resources. The notion here is that the budget (within which the more narrowly constrained choice is made) is alterable over time as the government increases (or decreases) the rate at which it extracts resources from society for its programmatic uses. At this second level, the effective constraint is the given current resource pool (politically and technologically) available to the government for resource extraction; it is represented, roughly, by the government's budget (or an expenditure category) as a proportion of the national economy.[3] If, in turn, the constraint of a given current resource pool is relaxed, a third, and very broad, choice problem exists, which is choice about the size of the future resource pool, given the "technology" or "production function" according to which current governmental expenditures generate an expansion (or shrinkage) in the size of the future available resource pool.[4] Here, the notion is that through economic multiplier, factor productivity, and other effects, governmental expenditures of different types effect relatively greater or lesser rates of growth of the national economy; some expenditures move the economy closer to its growth potential, while others are less efficient in that respect. At this third, and broadest, level the effective constraint is the production possibility frontier for growth of the national economy, given the current technological production function for economic growth as it is affected by governmental expenditures of different types.

Combining these two dimensions -- the three levels of effective constraints and the two forms of opportunity costs -- yields six logically possible conceptions of budgetary trade-offs, which are represented in Figure 2. Of those six possible conceptions, two do not seem to be internally consistent, and, hence, are not conceptually meaningful. The two illogical conceptions are: 1) indirect opportunity costs of expenditure externalities from allocation choices under a fixed budgetary constraint; and 2) direct opportunity costs of forgone expenditures under the very loose constraint of the production possibility frontier for future national economic growth. The first of these two is internally inconsistent, and thus illogical, because, the choice problem is a matter of allocating a fixed budget to alternative programmatic objectives, and the trade-off must therefore be in terms of the direct opportunity costs of forgone objectives, not the indirect costs of the external effects of various different allocations among programs. Similarly, the second conception is illogical, because, if there are no effective current constraints (i.e., neither a fixed budget constraint nor a fixed resource pool constraint), then trade-offs cannot exist in the form of direct opportunity costs of one expenditure coming at the expense of another expenditure category; instead, they can only exist as

18

Figure 2: Alternative Conceptions of Budgetary Trade-Offs

Level of Constraint on Choice

Nature of Opportunity Costs	Given current budget	Given current resource pool for budgetary extraction	Given "technological" limits on future growth of resource pool
Direct, as forgone expenditures and programmatic objective	Trade-offs as competing budgetary allocations under fixed budget	Trade-offs as competing budgetary allocations from resource pool	✕
Indirect, as forgone external effects of expenditures	✕	Trade-offs as relatively more or less negative external effects of expenditures in fixed resource pool	Trade-offs as relatively more or less positive external effects of expenditures in affecting future growth of resource pool

indirect opportunity costs. If we are correct in this, there are _four_ distinct and meaningful conceptions of budgetary trade-offs:

1) Direct expenditure trade-offs under a fixed budget constraint;

2) Direct expenditure trade-offs under the constraint of a given total national economic resource pool;

3) Trade-offs in terms of the indirect, external effects of expenditures under the constraint of a given total national economic resource pool;

4) Trade-offs in terms of the indirect, external effects of expenditures under the constraints of the production possibility frontier for future national economic growth.

We maintain that an adequate, comprehensive assessment of "guns-butter" trade-offs must entail a consideration of all four conceptualizations. It would hardly be definitive to demonstrate that national security commitment increases come at the expense of social welfare programs in terms of one conception if, in another conception, the two are unrelated or even complementary. Such, unfortunately, is the state of the literature on the trade-offs, for precisely the reason that each contribution typically cuts into the problem from the perspective of one conception of trade-offs or another without regard to the comprehensive, complex picture of multiple conceptualizations. In the remainder of this section, we comment on that literature as we describe each of the four conceptualizations in turn.

Trade-offs within a Fixed Budget

The first and most direct way in which to perceive a budgetary trade-off is in terms of the relative size of expenditures for two or more programs within the total current budget. At this level, one treats the total budget as if it were fixed and views the separate components -- national security commitments, social welfare programs, and others -- as proportions of the total. Here, the question is to what extent an increase in the proportion of the total budget allocated to defense purposes comes at the expense of the proportion devoted to welfare efforts, and vice versa.

The theoretical imagery underlying this most basic perspective on the trade-off problem is that of conscious choice by the government among alternative goods (in this case, governmental programs) under rigid constraint, and hence this conceptualization has its foundations in the traditions of microeconomics and the extensions of the latter in welfare economics. That is, the trade-off problem at this level is essentially a social choice issue. The President and Congress are faced with the necessity of choosing a basket of goods (including, but not limited to, national military security and social welfare) under a set budget constraint in order to maximize some aggregate measure of societal (or governmental) welfare. Since, in composing this basket of goods, the President and Congress must forgo some amount of one good in order to realize a particular level of another good, the issue of trade-offs is posed very starkly.

This perspective is represented, at least implicitly, in much of the popular political discussion about governmental programs. The debates about trade-offs of welfare for defense in the Reagan years and the converse trade-offs said to have marked the 1970s -- the examples with which we began this paper -- are illustrative. In a similar vein are those hypothetical scenarios regularly offered by advocates of a reduced military budget who point to the potentials for improved education or employment security if the government were only to forgo the MX missile system or some equivalent and spend the savings on one or another welfare program.[5] Also illustrative is the spirit underlying recent Congressional budget reforms, according to which, by law, Congress must first pass a budget ceiling and then, secondarily, decide how to allocate that total. The Gramm-Rudman-Hollings legislation emphasizes the constraining role of these reforms by mandating a particular budget ceiling for each year. In all of this, the thinking implicitly is in terms of proportional allocation within a fixed budget, of governmental choice under a set budget constraint (Ferejohn and Krehbiel, 1985).

In spite of the conventional, popular appeal of this perspective, the direct, simple formulation that it affords of the trade-off problem, and the potentially powerful theoretical foundations on which it rests, this conceptualization has not much informed

21

the scholarly literature on either military defense budgeting or the extent of trade-offs between national security commitments and social welfare programs (Lyttkens and Vedovata, 1984). Some students of the trade-off problem pay only lip service to this perspective as they set up or introduce their respective empirical analyses with a discussion of direct opportunity costs, but then fail to structure those analyses in terms of conscious choices under fixed budgetary constraint (e.g., Eichenberg, 1984; Russett, 1969, 1970). Many ignore this perspective altogether as they prefer to focus on "budgetary dynamics" (examples are discussed below). To our knowledge, only a handful of empirical analyses have been published which study the trade-off problem in terms of this first conceptualization of trade-offs (Verner, 1983; Peroff and Podolak-Warren, 1979; Peroff, 1977; Dabelko and McCormick, 1977; Ames and Goff, 1975; and, to a limited extent, Hayes, 1975). In those studies (except Hayes, 1975), the effort is to determine the impact of changes in the proportion of the total budget (national government or national, state, and local governments combined) allocated to defense expenditures on simultaneous changes in the proportion of the budget devoted to specific and narrowly defined welfare programs -- health, public aid, housing, and education. For these particular programs, trade-offs were not found to be especially strong or pronounced in any of the studies. On this basis, one might conclude that a government's basket of goods is sufficiently complex that an increase in the relative amount of one good (even one as important as military defense) does not directly and simply mean a reduction in the relative amount of any other single good. The trade-offs, which <u>have</u> to exist at some level given a fixed budget constraint, may be spread widely over a broad set of expenditure categories, at least within certain ranges of their relative sizes. But too little literature exists within this perspective to enable us to draw any definitive conclusions. One reason that analysts appear to shy away from this first conceptualization of the trade-off problem is that it implies an examination of budgetary proportions (or some equivalent means of dealing with choices under a fixed budget constraint), and many social scientists are reluctant to conduct analysis in terms of ratio variables (see, e.g., Domke, Eichenberg, and Kelleher (1983), who attempt to assess trade-offs in terms of actual dollar expenditures). In our judgment, this is an unfortunate instance of letting technical issues in statistical analysis predominate over the conceptual and theoretical formulations that should take the lead. We will address this issue further below, but it is worth emphasizing that in one sensible conceptualization the problem of trade-offs _is_ an issue of direct opportunity costs under fixed budgetary constraint, and hence any comprehensive assessment of "guns-butter" trade-offs must be attentive to this conceptualization. Accordingly, primary consideration should not be given to the technicalities of analyzing ratio variables but rather to the recognition that conceptually the appropriate measure _is_ a proportion (for this particular conception).

Trade-offs as Competitive Expenditures within a National Resource Pool

Security-welfare trade-offs do not involve solely the set of choices governments make within the context of a fixed budget constraint. On the contrary, we must recognize the possibility of trade-offs in the larger political economy that result from the government's changing rate of extraction and utilization of resources for the (potentially) competitive objectives of national security and social welfare. In this perspective, the government's budget constraint is not fixed, but is instead expanded or contracted as the government increases or decreases its rate of extraction of resources from society (under the constraints of a given current national resource pool from which to extract). Here, both national security commitments and social welfare programs may be increased simultaneously, even while all other governmental programs are also increasing. This is the picture presented by Figure 1 above, a picture that is quite familiar to students of the expanding size and role of the public economy in advanced capitalist countries since the middle of the 20th century. It leads comfortably to the conclusion that national security commitments and social welfare programs may not be competitive goods, per se, but rather that both may change together as manifestations of the government's basic disposition toward its own expansion or limitation.[6] This conclusion is drawn by Otto Eckstein:

> "I think that historical experience has been that governments are either stingy or they're spenders, and if they're stingy about defense, they're stingy about everything. I

23

would say that the historical record suggests that the association between civilian spending and military spending is positive, not negative." (Eckstein, 1963: 1012)

In short, when one accepts that governments are able to alter their effective budget constraints, at least within limits, one is forced to recognize that the trade-off problem is different, if only in being less direct and less simple than is the necessity of choice among competing goods under fixed budgetary constraint (see Frey and Schneider, 1979, and, in response, Alt and Chrystal, 1983).

What, then, is the trade-off problem in this perspective? It appears to us that it is the conceptualization that has been most extensively represented in the scholarly literature: While both national security commitments and social welfare programs may be increased as the scope of the public economy is expanded (the government's extraction and utilization of resources is increased relative to the size of the national resource pool), the increase in one is likely to come at the expense of a relatively reduced rate of increase in the other.[7] This conception underlies those studies that cast their analysis of expenditure trade-offs in terms of either absolute expenditures[8] or expenditures standardized by some measure of the income pool from which the government extracts resources (e.g., Gross National Product), rather than in terms of expenditures as a proportion of a total budget. Most of the literature on "guns-butter" trade-offs is of this type (Griffin, Devine, and Wallace, 1985, 1983, 1982; Hicks and Mintz, 1985; Jencks, 1985; Eichenberg, 1984; Mintz and Hicks, 1984; Swank, 1984; Domke, Eichenberg, and Kelleher, 1983; Griffin, Wallace, and Devine, 1982; Russett, 1982, 1970, 1969; Kelleher, Domke, and Eichenberg, 1980; Pluta, 1978; Caputo, 1975; Wilensky, 1975; Hollenhorst and Ault, 1971; Pryor, 1968). In effect, then, the vast bulk of the scholarly literature on trade-offs between national security commitments and social welfare programs rests on a conception of trade-offs as relative rate-of-increase issues. While we recognize that any effort to assess "guns-butter" trade-offs comprehensively would be inadequate if it overlooked this conception in terms of relative growth rates (indeed, some of the analysis we report below is in terms of expenditures relative to GNP and hence is in line with this conception), we think it an overly

24

narrow perspective to stand as _the_ way in which trade-offs are to be analyzed.

The principal problem with the literature that approaches budgetary trade-offs solely in these terms is that it rests on a loose set of poorly articulated "theoretical" principles. Those principles appear to include some general cognizance of budgetary limits, but not in explicit fashion. None of the analysts of expenditure processes, to our knowledge, claims that the expansion of the scope of the public economy (relative to the total national resource pool) is limitless -- otherwise there would be no trade-off problem of any kind. But neither are the limits dealt with at all explicitly. Instead, the operative assumption seems to be that a variety of forces propel the expansion (or contraction) of programmatic expenditures (and, in turn, the expansion -- or contraction -- of the scope of the public economy), and that those forces are held in chech by rough limits on the ability of the government to expand (or contract) its expenditures (Alt and Chrystal, 1983).[9] Those rough limits, then, force something of a trade-off, at the margins, as the more rapid expansion of one area of expenditures reduces the ability of another area to grow as quickly.

With this conception, the trade-off problem is viewed as implying the necessity of including expenditures (especially changes in expenditures relative to GNP) for one program (e.g., national security commitments) among the set of explanatory variables in a model of the determinants of expenditures in another area (e.g., social welfare programs). To represent the hypothesized trade-off, a negative coefficient is expected for the explanatory expenditure. Three recent articles provide prominent illustrations. Griffin, Devine, and Wallace (1982) regress U.S. military expenditures as a percentage of GNP (yearly, 1949-76) on a set of variables that represent features of the U.S. economy, international political/security conditions, domestic political processes, and two broad (trade-off) "constraints" -- civilian expenditures and total revenues as percentages of GNP.[10] Domke, Eichenberg, and Kelleher (1983) estimate a three-equation model of the impact of international political conditions, domestic political and economic conditions, and other budgetary commitments on yearly percentage changes in real defense expenditures, welfare expenditures, and total governmental expenditures for the U.S., Germany,

Britain, and France for the period 1957-76. And Russett (1982) estimates two equations -- one each for yearly percentage changes in U.S. government expenditures for education and for health, 1941-79 -- by regressing these variables on a set of demographic, economic, domestic political, and international political variables, plus several budgetary variables, including percentage change in military expenditures, taxes, and housing expenditures.

These studies, and others in this tradition of research on trade-offs, share several important features in common, although they differ from one another in a number of obvious respects -- the dependent variable is different (sometimes "guns", sometimes "butter"; here expenditures as a percentage of GNP; there percentage changes in absolute expenditures), the exact set of explanatory variables is different, the statistical estimation procedures vary somewhat, etc. The most relevant similarity, in our judgment, is that they all approach the problem of trade-offs from the perspective that a competing expenditure program is simply another determinant -- a broad constraint serving to limit the rapidity with which the expenditure category in question can expand -- among the set of factors that explain expenditure growth. There is no explicit theory underpinning the research; plausible hypotheses are offered to justify the examination of possible determinants, and competing expenditure programs are included apparently on the assumption that there are some loose budgetary limitations acting as loose constraints on expenditure increases. Accordingly, the research is structured as a conventional regression estimation problem, in which the objective is to determine the explanatory power of one expenditure category on another, controlling for a set of factors that ostensibly propel expansion of the latter. In this sense, the regression model seems to drive the conception of trade-off dynamics more than the other way around.

The conclusion that is frequently drawn in these studies is that the "guns-butter" trade-off is weak, at best; the parameter estimates for the explanatory budgetary category often turn out to be insignificant when controlling for the effects of other determinants of the expansion of some particular component of the government sector (Griffin, Devine, and Wallace (1982) is an important exception). This has led at least some analysts to infer that the trade-off between national security commitments and social welfare programs is

26

only an "Illusion of Choice" (Domke, Eichenberg, and Kelleher, 1983). But due to the general absence in this tradition of explicit conceptual and theoretical foundations for examining trade-offs, and given the problems inherent in treating expenditure dynamics and trade-offs as conventional regression model issues, we are not yet prepared to accept this conclusion. Even in terms of this, the most widely employed, conception of the "guns-butter" trade-off problem, more work is required before anything close to a definitive answer is available. In particular, models need to be developed which incorporate the relevant constraints on choice more explicitly; if there is not a fixed budget constraint, but, instead, choice among expenditure categories is made by the government only under the less direct and immediate constraint of a given current national resource pool, then the ways in which those less direct constraints operate to effect opportunity costs in terms of forgone increases in one expenditure category because of increases in another expenditure category need to be explicitly theorized and modeled. To our knowledge, at this point in time such theories and models are absent from the scholarly literature on "guns-butter" trade-offs.

Trade-offs as Negative Externalities of Expenditures in a Given Resource Pool

The problem of trade-offs can be approached and conceptualized in an alternative way within the framework of a loose and expanding budget constraint. One does not need to think of it only as a matter of competitive rates of increase among expenditure categories, controlling for the determinants of programmatic expansion. Instead, the trade-offs may be somewhat less direct, expressing themselves as different "external" programmatic consequences of expansion (or contraction) in one or another budgetary category. For example, as a greater (or lesser) portion of societal resources is extracted by the government and allocated to national security commitments, are social welfare outcomes, such as employment or price levels, adversely affected (or enhanced) on net? If adverse welfare conditions result, then a trade-off is involved in this sense: Increasing governmental expenditures for national security make the <u>costs</u> of social welfare programs more expensive by setting back welfare outcomes and hence by creating a larger burden on a given welfare budget. It would cost more to stay even. Similarly, one would

27

ask, if a greater portion of societal resources is extracted by the government and allocated to social welfare programs, is national security reduced? Again, if so, then a trade-off is involved. In this conception, the trade-offs would not need to be symmetric -- expenditures for national security commitments, for example, might reduce welfare outcomes by stimulating inflation or unemployment, while social welfare program expenditures might be irrelevant to or even strengthen national security.

The research strategy implied by this conception of the trade-off problem is quite different than that found in most of the literature, and described above. In this case one does not regress welfare expenditures on security expenditures, but rather one attempts to ascertain the impact of security expenditures on welfare outcomes (or welfare expenditures on national security outcomes).

To date, not a great deal of systematic empirical research has been directed to this conception of trade-offs, and the literature that does exist is focused entirely on the welfare effects of security expenditures. Presumably this imbalance is due to the recognition of the possible asymmetry in trade-offs mentioned above and to the assumption that the welfare effects of security expenditures are apt to be much more pronounced than are the security effects of welfare expenditures. Certainly there is a substantial literature, often highly critical of the role of the military in advanced capitalist societies, that offers a number of hypotheses about the alleged welfare effects of military expenditures (see, e.g., Mosley, 1985; Gansler, 1980; Melman, 1978, 1974). But relatively few have picked up on these arguments and begun to investigate them systematically. The empirical studies that do exist focus primarily on the employment-(or unemployment-)generating effects of national security expenditures (Chan, 1984; Dunne and Smith, 1984; Ball and Leitenberg, 1983; Griffin, Wallace, and Devine, 1982; Krell, 1981; Nincic and Cusack, 1979; Best and Connolly, 1976; Anderson, 1975; Bezdek, 1975; Chase Econometric Associates, 1975; Szymanski, 1973; and Leontief, 1965). While the conclusions to be drawn from these studies are not entirely clear, due to the fact that most of the analysis is at a very high level of aggregation and most of the studies are flawed on methodological grounds (Mosley, chap. 5; for an exception, see Dunne and Smith, 1984), the evidence seems to indicate fairly

28

strongly that defense expenditures may come at the opportunity cost of greater unemployment. But one would certainly not want to be too bold in asserting this as a definitively established relationship.

Beyond studies of the employment effects of national security expenditures, empirical research on the social welfare externalities of defense commitments is in its infancy, if that. Chan (1984), Starr, Hoole, Hart and Freeman (1984), and Ball and Leidenberg (1983) offer preliminary analyses of the impact of defense expenditures on inflation, which generally operates as an income redistribution process from the poor to the rich. No clear relationship is apparent from these studies. Some years ago, Russett (1970, 1969) examined effects of defense expenditures on personal consumption levels, but, to our knowledge, this line of analysis has not been actively pursued since that time. And other important aspects of social welfare -- such as effects on income distribution or human capital/ training -- have been virtually ignored in empirical research on the negative welfare externalities of national security expenditures.

It seems fair to conclude that for this conception of "guns-butter" trade-offs the work of careful empirical research is just beginning. The causal processes through which national security expenditures have external effects on such aggregate economic outcomes as unemployment, inflation, income distribution, and personal consumption (if they do at all) must be more clearly specified and more carefully studied, and these aggregate outcomes need to be more fully disaggregated.

Trade-offs in an Expanding Economy

If the second level of perspective on effective constraints relaxes the assumption of a fixed budget to focus on the expanding extraction of resources from the total societal resource pool, the third level of effective constraints relaxes the assumption of a fixed pool of societal resources. Here, one considers the government's use of resources -- programmatic expenditures -- as a possible stimulant to increased national wealth; its programs may expand the resource pool from which it, in turn, extracts resources for further programmatic growth.[11]

Making this kind of assumption, it might seem, would lead to the conclusion that trade-offs are not at issue. If governmental expenditures stimulate economic growth, what are their trade-off costs (other than the types we have identified above)? Our response is that, while opportunity costs are only very indirect in this perspective, there is nevertheless a conceptualization of trade-offs that is both sensible and important. In this conceptualization, if other governmental or private sector uses of the resources would stimulate greater growth than is stimulated by the use to which they are actually put, then those governmental expenditures, while contributing to an expansion of societal wealth, come at an opportunity cost in terms of potential future social welfare. If the resources were used in an alternative way that generated greater growth than is generated by their current use as governmental expenditures of one form or another, then their current use constitutes an effective reduction in the size of the potential total resource pool from which the government will be able in the future to extract resources to pursue the same objectives at the same level. In that way, the trade-off is in terms of future programmatic opportunities.

The empirical assessment of trade-offs in this sense is a difficult task. It requires ascertaining the relative growth stimulating effects of alternative uses of various governmental expenditures. We doubt that this is possible in any definitive sense without a full, complete, and highly accurate model of the entire political economy. Short of that, however, a less-than-perfect strategy can provide some understanding of trade-offs at this level. That strategy is to investigate the impact of expenditures on economic outcomes with data on savings and investment rates, research and development efforts, or even simply national economic growth. This strategy is similar to the third conception of trade-offs described above, which involved the estimation of deleterious impacts of expenditures in one governmental program for outcomes relevant to another program, in that both focus on economic effects of aggregate expenditures. But there are differences. For one thing, of course, the kinds of economic impacts that are investigated are different -- things like unemployment and inflation that are adverse to social welfare for the previous conceptions versus economic expansion for the third. More importantly, however, the underlying logic is different. The potential asymmetry that is a feature of the previous conception of trade-offs enables the investigator to focus on the putative adverse effects of one category of governmental expenditures in isolation. By contrast, the fact that here the conception is in terms of _relative_ growth- stimulating effects of alternative uses of resources means that the assessment of trade-offs _requires_ that the investigator focus explicitly on the effects of alternative uses of governmental resources as well as the programmatic category in question. To put it more concretely, if one were interested in the social welfare trade-off costs of national security commitments, one could not examine the growth-stimulating impact of defense expenditures alone; what is relevant is the magnitude of that impact _relative_ to the growth-stimulating effects of alternative expenditures, such as those for social welfare programs.[12]

Levels of Aggregation in the Conceptualization of Trade-offs

To this point, our discussion of the conceptualization of budgetary trade-offs has not dealt explicitly with the level of aggregation at which trade-offs are to be assessed. We have approached the four conceptions implicitly at a relatively high level of aggregation; broad expenditure categories and aggregate, macroeconomic outcomes set the tone of the discussion. But that is not necessary, since the conceptions of trade-offs are independent of the level of aggregation involved. Each of the four conceptions could have been described in terms of disaggregated expenditures and/or micro-level economic outcomes.

Nevertheless, the level of aggregation is directly relevant to the actual assessment (although not the conceptualization) of trade-offs. For example, in terms of the first or second conceptions, the more disaggregated the expenditure categories are defined to be, the less likely it is that a strong trade-off effect will be apparent. However, the level of aggregation takes on a special significance for the assessment of trade-offs in terms of the third and especially the fourth conceptions. The difference lies in the fact that a simple probabilistic expectation of the kind just stated for the first and second conceptions cannot be stated at this level. Disaggregated expenditure items can have very pronounced trade-off effects (through negative externalities, multipliers, and spin-offs) in terms of micro-level economic outcomes, which may or may not be

31

apparent at the aggregate level. So, whereas trade-offs should be less apparent as expenditures are disaggregated in the first or second conceptions, they may be either stronger or weaker under disaggregation in the third and especially the fourth conceptions. This gives a special status to the desirability of including a disaggregated version of the third and fourth conceptions in any effort to assess trade-offs comprehensively.

For the fourth conception, the strategy involves moving down from aggregate expenditures and aggregate macroeconomic outcomes to investigate the particular multiplier and spin-off effects of individual expenditure items. Again, trade-offs, per se, can be assessed through this strategy only by comparing the relative multiplier effects of all alternative expenditures, but here the comparison of relative effects is at a more microsopic level. Aggregate expenditure categories such as national security commitments are disaggregated into particular expenditure items and the multiplier effects of those individual items are traced (through their impact on human capital, on technological innovation, and on demand and supply stimulation).

We are aware of no comprehensive, systematic study of this type, although some pieces of the puzzle have been and are being addressed. For example, there is some work on national security research and development expenditures (e.g., Vayrynen, 1983; Kaldor, 1981), defense expenditures to and performance in particular industrial sectors, such as the aerospace industry (e.g., Mason and Muldoon, 1984), and the infrastructural development consequences of military technology acquisition policies (e.g., Neuman, 1979), to mention just a few topics of concern at this disaggregated, more microscopic level. At this point, however, all that can be said is that such a strategy for approaching the "guns-butter" trade-off problem remains an important, but not yet realized, component of the broad conceptualization of such trade-offs under the assumption of an expanding national economy (or resource pool for governmental programs).

A Summary Statement on the Conceptualization of Guns-Butter Trade-offs

Approaching the issue of trade-offs between national security commitments and social welfare

32

programs through two abstract dimensions of the generic notion of trade-offs -- the character of the opportunity costs (direct or indirect through externalities, multiplier effects, etc.) and the level of constraints (fixed budget, fixed resource pool, or fixed production function for expansion of the resource pool) -- we have identified four distinct conceptions of the trade-off problem:

1) Competitive proportions of a given budget;

2) Competitive increases of expanding programmatic expenditures in a given resource pool;

3) Deleterious impacts of expenditures on outcomes that are basic to the costs of other programs;

4) Relative growth stimulating or depressing effects of alternative programmatic expenditures.

We argue that any effort to assess "guns-butter" trade-offs comprehensively and definitively must be attentive to all four conceptualizations. Otherwise, only part of the picture, at best, is dealt with.

In a larger project, we are engaged in an attempt to develop such a comprehensive assessment of "guns-butter" trade-offs for the U.S. government in the post-World War II era. At this point, like most other analysts, we are directing our attention to aggregate expenditures and hence to the four conceptualizations of the trade-off problem enumerated above at the aggregate level. Conceptualizations in terms of disaggregated expenditures and micro-level economic outcomes, especially the fourth conception, will be addressed in the future. However, even in terms of the analysis of aggregate expenditures and the trade-offs they entail, our project differs from other published work. For one thing, to our knowledge no one addresses all four conceptualizations. Additionally, our work rests on a somewhat different methodological foundation than is employed in most, if not all, other research on "guns-butter" trade-offs, or on the consequences of defense expenditures.

In particular, our methodology is different than most research in two important respects. First, we do not simply accept conventional departmental or

33

administrative categories of expenditures, but rather we work with a variety of alternative definitions of each expenditure category in terms of functional, programmatic objectives. Hence, for the United States, for example, we do not limit our analysis of national security commitments solely to "defense expenditures," defined as DoD appropriations, as do most other analysts. Instead, we approach national security commitments conceptually and devise a set of alternative measures of aggregate expenditures for it defined more or less broadly, more or less restrictively.[13]

Second, virtually all systematic empirical research on "guns-butter" trade-offs employs either a simple tabular presentation of basic data or some form of a general linear (regression) model for which the model structure is stipulated by loosely defined, but plausible, hypothesized relationships. In this sense, regression models are used as hypothesis-testing devices to investigate whether some trade-off effect can be detected. By contrast, we are constructing our analytical models of trade-off dynamics as well-specified representations of the results of prior model-building tests of the kind recommended by Sargent (1979) and summarized by Freeman (1983). These tests are of two broad types: tests designed to establish the precise temporal structure underlying observed time-series processes; and tests designed to determine exogeneity or causal directionality between and among seemingly interdependent time-series. On the basis of those tests, the analytical, regression models that we estimate are not simply stipulated structures for the conduct of hypothesis-testing research. Instead, they are vehicles for the estimation of parameters of precisely specified and empirically well-grounded causal structures of trade-off dynamics.

In the remainder of this paper, we discuss and illustrate some of these methodological procedures as they underpin our project. In particular, we first describe our alternative measures for both national security commitments and social welfare programs. We then present the results of our analyses of the structures of each of these two time-series expenditure processes. These analyses, by themselves, do not address the issue of trade-offs. But they are an integral component of the effort to assess trade-offs, as they lead directly to the specification of appropriate temporal structures in analytical models of trade-off dynamics.

IDENTIFYING THE STRUCTURE OF CHANGE IN
NATIONAL SECURITY AND SOCIAL WELFARE EXPENDITURES

Measuring   National   Security   and   Social   Welfare
Expenditures

Many students of budgetary processes approach
their study as if appropriate expenditure categories
were already established by administrative or organizational criteria. This is particularly true of students
of U.S. "defense expenditures", who often define the
latter simply in terms of the budget of the Department
of Defense (see note 13 above). We do not believe that
this approach is either necessary or desirable. First,
and most importantly, neither the departmental budget
nor the functional expenditure categories used in the
federal budget adequately captures the programmatic
objectives of U.S. government. They therefore do not
provide accurate measures of national security and
social welfare commitments. The budget of the
Department of Defense, for example, includes not only
U.S. defense expenditures narrowly construed (e.g., the
maintenance and expansion of military personnel and
hardware), but enormous expenditures for military
pensions as well. Conversely, this budget excludes
various defense-related expenditures, most notably the
defense-related atomic energy expenditures included in
the budget of the Atomic Energy Commission. While the
functional expenditure categories used in the federal
budget partially solve this problem for any given year,
these categories have undergone repeated revision and
thus do not provide measures of defense and welfare
expenditures that are consistent over time. Finally,
restricting the measurement of national security and
social welfare to departmental budgets or functional
federal budget categories is unnecessary since more
detailed summaries of U.S. government expenditures are
available in each yearly budget.

In order to create measures of defense and welfare
expenditures that more accurately reflect programmatic
commitments and are, as well, consistent over time, we
constructed a new set of functional expenditure
categories. (An example of these categories for
federal government expenditures for fiscal 1982 is
presented in the Appendix.) The categories were
defined quite narrowly to facilitate flexibility in the
construction of more or less restrictive measures of
defense and welfare expenditures through aggregation of

35

the individual categories. These narrow expenditure categories were then used to create four successively more inclusive measures of national security expenditures and three increasingly broad measures of social welfare expenditures. The measures are described below, with particular attention to those used in the time-series modeling discussed in the next section.

Measurement of National Security Expenditures

Our most restrictive measure of national security commitments includes only military expenditures per se; that is, it is limited to those expenditures directly concerned with the maintenance and expansion of active-duty military personnel and hardware. It thus includes the "defense" category (see Appendix), which encompasses expenditures of the U.S. armed forces and defense-related atomic energy expenditures, as well as military assistance to foreign governments. It does not, however, include military pensions, since these do not contribute directly to national defense. Our second measure of national security commitments adds to the first measure expenditures for some aspects of economic assistance to foreign governments. Since this second measure is used in the statistical analysis presented later, it will be discussed in a bit more detail below. Our third measure again expands the conception of national security commitments to include expenditures by both the Arms Control and Disarmament Agency and the space program. Finally, our most inclusive measure of national security commitments encompasses what might be called "supporting activities", such as expenditures for veterans' services and benefits, military pensions, and the conduct of foreign affairs (the largest portion of which is allocated to the Department of State).

Our second measure of national security commitments, which includes expenditures for the purchase of current military goods and services, military assistance, and some forms of economic assistance, is used in the time-series analysis presented below. This measure captures those expenditures that lie at the heart of, and are most directly related to, national security commitments. The inclusion of current "defense" expenditure seems to us unproblematic and, hence, not in need of justification; similarly, the addition of military assistance to foreign governments is conceptually

36

straightforward. The inclusion of some forms of economic and financial assistance to foreign governments, however, requires some explanation. Much of the economic and financial assistance given to foreign governments, to "friendly" nations whether allies or potential allies, is, in effect, a substitute for more direct military assistance and not simply a philanthropic activity undertaken for purely humanitarian reasons. Illustrative are the post-World War II Marshall Plan expenditures, which were intended as much as anything else to strengthen Western Europe in the face of potential threats of Communist take-over. The economic assistance variable, then, adds to the national security measure (especially in the immediate post-war years) such budget categories as "International recovery and relief" and "Philippine war damage and rehabilitation". On the other hand, those economic assistance programs that are motivated more apparently by humanitarian concerns (e.g., "Food for Peace") were excluded from this measure of national security expenditures.

Measurement of Social Welfare Expenditures

Our most restrictive welfare measure is limited to those expenditures aimed at the maintenance of minimum income levels. This measure includes expenditures for "income security" as well as for veterans' benefits and services. The "income security" variable includes, among others, those public assistance programs that are (or were) federally funded, as well as retirement and disability insurance (e.g., Social Security), unemployment compensation, and food and nutrition assistance. The "veterans service and benefits" variable includes not only income security for veterans, but education, rehabilitation, health and housing benefits as well.

Again, it is our second, somewhat more inclusive, welfare measure that is used below in the time-series analysis. It augments the first measure with federal expenditures for "manpower", which include job training and employment programs as well as "area and regional development" programs designed to increase employment in economically depressed regions. Although this is a relatively small addition ($9 billion as compared to $252 billion for income security), it is closely related to governmental commitments to the maintenance of some minimum level of income. Our final and broadest welfare measure can be mentioned very briefly.

37

It includes not only basic federal government expenditures for income maintenance, but also expenditures for
housing and community development, health care and
research, and revenue sharing.

Modeling the Time Series of Welfare and Security Expenditures

Having established appropriate measures of welfare
and security expenditures, we examine these
expenditures for the 36 year period, fiscal 1948-
1983.[14] In this paper, we look at the two variables as
separate, or univariate, time-series, and analyze their
time dynamics via the Box-Jenkins or "ARIMA" (Auto-
Regressive Integrated Moving Average) method.

The General Strategy ARIMA modeling is basically
an inductive procedure that attempts to discern just
what is systematic in a time-series and what is random
or non-systematic. In our use of it here, we do not
test theoretically derived hypotheses directly.
Instead, we make the assumption that the systematic
components we uncover have, in turn, systematic
explanations. Because our ultimate concern is the
(potential trade-off) relationship between the two
expenditure processes (for national security
commitments and social welfare programs), we ask not
just what is "driving" welfare and what is "driving"
security expenditures in post-World War II America as
individual budgetary processes, but we also ask how
similar the two "driving" forces are. Again, this is
not done directly, but rather through the determination
of the structures of the two time-series expenditure
processes. If the two have quite similar structures,
the plausibility of a similarity or relatedness in
underlying causal, driving forces is enhanced. If, for
instance, both budgets are set by the pluralistic
interplay of Presidents, bureaucracies, Congress, and
interest groups, we would expect that the two time-
series would have quite similar forms. To the extent
that they differ, the implication is that different
forces, such as different goals, ideologies, groups,
and external (e.g., the USSR) or contextual (e.g.,
unemployment) factors, are important in explaining --
and differentiating -- the two time-series.

The analysis proceeds in two steps. The first
step is to transform the variables so that each has as
close an approximation as possible to a constant mean
and constant variance over time. For reasons we will

38

detail shortly, this first step, obtaining "homogeneity and variance stationarity" as it is called, is necessary for further modeling. In addition, it is an important first step substantively, for it requires accounting for the pattern of growth or decay in each of the two variables over time. We then turn to the estimation of the parameters for the ARIMA models themselves, a process that proceeds via tentative model identification, estimation, diagnosis, and, perhaps, repetition of this cycle.

ARIMA models are based on the assumption that there are three basic systematic factors potentially involved in a time-series. The first is the systematic growth or decline (and its variance counterparts) already described in terms of (lack of) stationarity. Secondly, the time-series may have one or more auto-regressive components (the "AR"), commonly modeled in government budgetary processes (notably in the pioneering work by Davis, Dempster, and Wildavsky (1966)). Formally, this means that current expenditures are a linear function of last year's and possibly preceding year's expenditures. Even in the simplest case of one AR lag, such models induce a longer-term "memory", since this year's expenditures are a function of last year's, which in turn are a function of the preceding year's, and so on. In the Davis, Dempster, and Wildavsky interpretation, for example, last year's budget sets a base line for this year's budget, so that this year's expenditures may be last year's plus, say, 5 percent more (the latter growth increment, of course, entailing non-stationarity). Thirdly, there may be one or more moving average terms (the "MA"). In this case, the past has a non-linear effect, rather than a linear effect as in an AR model. For example, in a one-period MA process, only the last period's value affects this year's, while in a two-period MA process, the average of the last two year's values affect the current year's expenditures, and so on. In an MA process, there is no longer-term memory. The MA terms affect or "shock" the current year's expenditures -- and then their impact is gone. One could easily imagine that the two-year con-gressional or four year presidential election calendar could induce a moving average process in expenditures. For U.S. national security spending decisions, the five-year Soviet plans likewise could induce a moving average process, if some form of bilateral reactive arms-race logic applies. In ARIMA modeling, these three basic components of a time-series structure are summarized by the notation (p,d,q), which represents an

39

AR of lag p, a "differencing" to achieve homogeneous stationarity of order d, and an MA of lag q.

There are also possible seasonal variations of each component; these are especially important in economics. Quarterly sales of toys, for example, are regularly largest in the fourth quarter of the year. Such regular seasonal cycles might appear in any of the three basic components in ARIMA modeling, but we do not treat them here because there are no clear, a priori reasons to expect such seasonal cycles, nor are any apparent empirically. We do, however, note the minor exceptions as they arise.

The general strategy we follow is called "model overfitting" (McCleary and Hay, 1980, p. 101). To illustrate the procedure, let us say that the model that seems best involves two auto-regressive lag coefficients. Then, by fitting models with one, two, three, and possibly more coefficients, the plausibility of the two-lagged model can be judged comparatively. The estimated model with one lag should not provide a good fit, while that with three (or more) lags should either show that the additional lag is not significant, that the fit of the model is actually made worse (the "overfitting" part), or, commonly, both. In other words, by "overfitting", the best structure in that class of models can be discerned.

This procedure allows comparisons between four possible models. First, it is of course possible that there remains nothing systematic in the time-series once stationarity is achieved. That is, there are no auto-regressive or moving average components to the series. Secondly, there will be a best-fitting auto-regressive model. Thirdly, there will be a best-fitting moving average model. Finally, there may be a fully integrated model containing all three terms: This latter, due to the well-known "parameter redundancy" effect, according to which these more complex models can often be shown to be nearly equivalent to simpler models, should, in general, be considered suspect. In ARIMA notation, then, the four possible models to be compared in terms of goodness of fit and other tests are (1) (0,d,0); (2) (p,d,0); (3) (0,d,q); and (4) (p,d,q). In this paper, however, we examine closely only the first three for the reason just given.

Time-Series: Stationarity The first step in analyzing any time-series is to ensure that any

40

systematic change in the level of the series, so obvious in the growth of welfare and security expenditures presented in Figure One above, is removed. This is a crucial first step methodologically, because failure to do so will result in spurious systematic patterns, typically "unstable" estimates of explosive growth, being "found" in those residuals.[15] In the statistical literature, this step is called establishing "homogeneous stationarity" (or, more exactly, specifying a form in which the assumption of constant expectation with time can be reasonably approximated).

As neutral as this step sounds when presented in methodological jargon, there are important theoretical issues here. For example, there is an obvious explanation for the rapid growth in absolute expenditures for both welfare and security, namely, that inflation affects both variables, even if differently. The theoretical point is that such sources of increasing welfare and security expenditures are not due to decisions about welfare or security, per se, or even to their joint production by the government (and any possible trade-off between them). Instead, such sources of growth are attributable to some third factor or set of factors. The methodological "detrending" to ensure homogeneous stationarity is designed to remove these "external" causes of expenditures so that we can focus exclusively on their own "internal" dynamics. In short, systematic growth or decline suggests that the univariate time-series models are misspecified, while the "detrending" is designed to make the specification assumption tenable.

Several procedures for "detrending" are available. Economists, for example, often take a logarithmic transformation. However, simply log-transforming the expenditure variables does not produce homogeneous stationarity, as it often does in economic variables. On the contrary, for these two expenditure series it actually increases non-stationarity, which further detrending then exacerbates. Alternatively, inflation could be corrected by using constant dollars, but this correction has several problems. First, constant-dollar expenditures make surprisingly little progress in "detrending", and they induce non-stationarity variance problems comparable to those introduced by the logging procedure. Second, constant dollars make little difference when expenditures are measured as a proportion of total net government expenditures and even less when expenditures are measured as a

41

proportion of GNP -- both of which are important
measures given our conceptual discussion of trade-offs
above -- since both proportions are already in a form
that, in effect, "controls" for inflation. Finally, we
want to be able to model inflation and its impact on
government decision-making, as well as the impact of
government expenditures on inflation, an analysis made
impossible by "correcting" for inflation at the outset.
A third approach not employed here would be to express
expenditures as some non-linear function of time. This
can be accomplished adequately with a third degree
polynomial (!), but it presents some considerable
problems. For one thing, the residuals from the
polynomial, which would be the stationary time-series
to be analyzed, contain much less than ten percent of
the variation in the original expenditure data; this
raises severe questions about removing the "real"
variance to be explained. In addition, the third
degree polynomial is an ad hoc formulation, since we
lack any theoretical explanation for that particular
functional form.

The detrending procedure we use, therefore, is to
take first, second, or third differences of the time-
series.[16] This procedure specifies the "d" in the
expression (p,d,q). The question, then, is how many
differences are necessary to achieve homogeneous
stationarity.

Absolute expenditures for both welfare and defense
require two differences (d=2). The first difference
retains a strong trend pattern (correlation with time
of .71 for welfare and .49 for security). The time-
series of second differences exhibits some non-
stationary growth, indicating a tendency for changes in
the rate of expenditure increases themselves to
increase over time, but for neither expenditure series
is this trend significant or very large (e.g.,
correlations with time of .20 and .22, respectively).
Further, inspection of the time-series (via the
autocorrelation function and partial autocorrelation
function discussed below) reveals none of the tell-tale
signs of significant non-stationarity. The four
proportion measures (each expenditure as a proportion
of total budget and as a proportion of GNP) require
only a first differencing (d=1), implying in effect
that one degree of differencing of actual expenditures
is accounted for by taking the ratios. For all six
expenditure series measures, then, we conclude that the
assumption of homogeneous stationarity is supported at
the specified level of differencing, but is not

42

supported, even as an empirical approximation, at a lower degree of differencing. Further differencing yields no improvement, but instead shows signs of over-differencing, just as the model overfitting strategy would suggest.

Homogeneous stationarity is a necessary condition for analyzing any time-series, but not a sufficient condition. The variance of the time-series should also be stationary over time (equivalent to the homoskedasticity assumption of regression). Visual inspection of our expenditure series suggests that there is some degree of heteroskedasticity in both sets of variables. For the welfare series, the last six years, 1978 to 1983, appear to have greater dispersion than the rest of the series about the first or second differences, probably reflecting the heightened political attention given during the Carter and Reagan administrations to the growth of the American welfare state. The first few years of the security series, 1948 to 1954, also appear to have greater dispersion. This is not surprising given the post-World War II demobilization, the birth of the Cold War, and the fighting of the Korean War, all of which occurred during that period. With so few observations, formal testing of these visual patterns is not practical. However, we are fortunate that these observations are the at ends of the time-series, because this means that some diagnosis is possible. Specifically, we are able to repeat the time- series analysis on the shorter time-series where no heteroskedasticity is visually apparent (in what is reported below we refer to these as the shortened or "truncated" time-series). Thus, the robustness of the full time-series analysis can be tested.

In sum, by second differencing the absolute expenditures and first differencing the ratio expenditure variables, it is reasonable to assume that the various time-series are stationary. This seemingly irrelevant conclusion does have some significance for the study of "guns-butter" trade-offs. That both the national security and social welfare expenditure variables required exactly the same detrending in each of the three measurement forms (i.e., as absolute expenditures, as proportions of GNP, and as proportions of total government expenditures) lends credence to the proposition that they are subject to trade-offs. In the methodological jargon, "third" forces apparently act on the dynamics of welfare and security expenditures in a similar fashion in the United States, at least from 1948 to 1983. Decision-makers are apparently confronted by similar constraints or opportunity costs for the two kinds of programmatic expenditures at each of the three levels.

Time-Series Analysis: Identification, Estimation, and Diagnosis The six expenditure variables, once stationary, are ready to be analyzed over their univariate time-series by the Box-Jenkins, ARIMA, procedures. The first step is to examine the autocorrelation function -- the correlation of each variable with its sequence of lagged values (hereafter the ACF) -- and the comparable partial autocorrelation function (the PACF). As is often the case, relatively simple patterns are found in these two functions, and reasonably simple ARIMA models are indicated. But, as is also usually the case, the empirical ACF's and PACF's do not conform exactly to their pure, theoretical counterparts.

1) Absolute welfare expenditures

The absolute welfare expenditure variable yields an ACF with four early lags of relatively large autocorrelations (lags 1,2,4, and 5), but only lag four is considered statistically significant (i.e., twice its standard error). The PACF has no significant lags, but lags 1, 2, and 4 are relatively large. These visual patterns suggest five possible models. The first is one with no auto-regressive or moving average terms at all -- a simple (0,2,0) model -- while the others include one or two auto-regressive or moving average terms. Three of these models are viable. A second-order auto-regressive model is clearly better than the first-order because both parameters are significant and all diagnostic statistics are improved. The second-order moving average model, however, is not an improvement on the first-order model, as the additional coefficient is neither statistically significant nor substantial.

The three models that remain as candidates to represent the structure of the absolute social welfare expenditure time-series, then, are the pure second differences process, (0,2,0), a second differences, second-order auto-regressive process, (2,2,0), and a second differences, first-order moving average process, (0,2,1). We report the parameter estimates for the (0,2,1) and (2,2,0) models in Table 1, along with relevant diagnostic information on all three models. In comparison with the (0,2,0) model, both of the

44

Table 1

Welfare Expenditures, 1948-83 fiscal (Nominal Dollars)

Model (0,2,1) = 1106 - .753 MA(1)
    (s.e.)   (531) (.167)
    (t)   2.08   -4.50

                           Resid. Var.=.102 E+09

Model (2,2,0) = 2734 - .440 AR(1) - .464 AR(2)
             (1880) (.204)   (.212)
             1.45 -2.16   -2.19

                           Resid. Var.=.111 E+09

| Q-Statistic* | Lag(6) | (12) | (18) |
(Prob. of Q**)			
(0,2,0)***	11.59	12.75	13.23
	(.08)	(.39)	(.78)

                         Var. = .131 E+09

(0,2,1)	3.48	4.47	5.04
	(.481)	(.924)	(.996)
(2,2,0)	6.59	7.17	7.40
	(.086)	(.619)	(.946)

  * Box-Ljung (small sample) Q, which is distributed as a chi-square under the null hypothesis, is reported in all tables.

 ** Degrees of freedom are found by subtracting the number of coefficients estimated (including the constant) from the number of lags tested (6, 12, or 18).

*** The Q and probability statistics for all (0,d,0) models were calculated by the authors, with probabilities interpolated from published chi-square tables.

others show clear improvements in the residual variance, with the (0,2,1) model yielding about a ten percent further improvement over the (2,2,0) model in that measure. The relevant parameter estimates in both models are significant as well, suggesting that both are improvements over (0,2,0). The moving average representation appears superior, finally, to the auto-regressive form in terms of the "bottom-line" criterion for ARIMA models: Are the residuals "white noise" (i.e., consistent with the hypothesis that they are independently and identically randomly distributed)? The Q-statistic to test that hypothesis is uniformly better in the (0,2,1) model, and visual inspection of the residual autocorrelations or RACF (an ACF treating the residuals as a univariate time-series) on which the Q-statistic is based supports that inference, since it is quite flat. Moreover, in the (2,2,0) model there is one nearly significant residual lag. Thus, we take the (0,2,1) model as the best representation of the process, a so-called IMA model (i.e., ARIMA with no significant auto-regressive coefficients). This model is both parsimonious and, in terms of the criteria used to evaluate the structure of time-series models, quite good.

We noted earlier that there was a potential problem of variance non-stationarity, indicated by a large spread of observations in the last six years. Dropping those six observations and re-estimating the ARIMA models indicates strongly that the (0,2,0) model fits that period best (see Table 3A, below). Most noticeably, the shortened-series ACF is really very flat.

These results suggest that the relevant "action" generating the (0,2,1) process is contained in the last six years, roughly the Carter and the Reagan administrations. Given the high inflation of the Carter years and its impact on welfare measures with automatic cost of living adjustments, the domestic spending cuts of the Reagan years, as well as the rapid drop in inflation (countered only in the very last observations by increases in expenditures due to the recession and welfare-entitlement programs), the larger variation in welfare and the necessity of a moving average coefficient to represent the effect of these exogenous "shocks" seem sensible.

Thus, we are led to three conclusions. First, the (0,2,1) model is the best representation of the full time-series for absolute welfare expenditures. Only the future will tell us whether the pure (0,2,0) process is the best generic description of social welfare expenditure processes, as it appears to have been for most of the post-World War II period. Thus, the second conclusion is that (0,2,0) may in fact be the best model if the last years of the current series are only passing exceptions. Third, the (2,2,0) model is not a bad approximation. This conclusion is important for later work, not reported here, that relies on regression procedures. That is, regression procedures that employ two lagged welfare terms can be taken as a reasonable approximation of the absolute welfare expenditure series.[17]

2) Absolute security expenditures

The comparable absolute security expenditure series presents a slightly different picture in terms of model identification. Here the first lag in the ACF and the PACF is very close to zero while the second lag is approximately significantly negative in both.

Empirically, the strongest candidate ARIMA models are (3,2,0) and (0,2,2). They are reported in Table 2. For the (3,2,0) model, none of the three coefficients is very large, and the AR(1) coefficient is especially small (-.162) and far from significant. For the (0,2,2) model, while the MA(2) coefficient is large (-.508) and significant, MA(1) is small (-.139) and insignificant. The diagnostics present a mixed picture. The residual variance is almost 20 percent smaller in the (3,2,0) model, and it clearly does a better job of eliminating problems in long-term lags in the RACF. On the other hand, the (0,2,2) model does a better job with respect to the short-term lags. Finally, both yield substantial reductions in the remaining residual variation compared to (0,2,0).

Nonetheless, the (0,2,0) model is judged superior here, primarily due to the very small first lag in the ACF and PACF (e.g., the Durbin-Watson coefficient from a regression of security spending on time is 2.05!), and its consequent impact on the rather small magnitude and degree of statistical significance of many of the coefficient estimates. Moreover, the diagnostic statistics imply that (0,2,0) cannot be rejected on statistical grounds. Basically, therefore, we believe that the second lag coefficient in the ACF and PACF, which is nearly significant but not very large (-.309), can be considered a statistical artifact (i.e., a chance event), since the pattern is inconsistent with

47

Table 2

Security Expenditures, 1948-83 (Nominal Dollars)

Model (3,2,0) = 540 - .162 AR(1) - .284 AR(2)
    (s.e.)   (1056)   (.165)   (.153)
    (t)   0.51   -0.98   -1.85

                        -.259 AR(3)
                         (.160)
                         -1.62

                              Resid. Var.= .333 E+08

Model (0,2,2) = 480 - .139 MA(1) - .508 MA(2)
                (420)   (.154)   (.163)
                1.14   -0.90   3.11

                              Resid. Var.= .369 E+08

Q-Statistic   Lag(6)   (12)   (18)
  (Prob. of Q)

    (0,2,0)   7.82   10.75   22.01
                   (.26)   (.55)   (.24)

                              Var. = .442 E+08

    (3,2,0)   3.77   7.31   13.96
                   (.152)   (.504)   (.453)

    (0,2,2)   3.46   6.40   16.23
                   (.327)   (.699)   (.367)

Table 3

Welfare and Security Shortened Series (Nominal Dollars)

Table 3.A: Welfare: 1948-77

Welfare (0,2,1) = 1062 - .0867 MA(1)
 (s.e.)   (642)   (.189)
  (t)   1.65   0.46

Resid. Var.= .137 E+08

Q-Statistic (Prob. of Q)	Lag(6)	(12)	(18)
(0,2,0)	2.17 (.90)	4.14 (.95)	12.78 (.80)
			Var. = .138 E+08
(0,2,1)	2.16 (.706)	3.91 (.951)	13.06 (.668)

Table 3.B: Security: 1955-83

```
Security (3,2,0) = 1385   - .188 AR(1)  - .194 AR(2)
         (s.e.)    (1226)    (.202)         (.204)
         (t)       1.13      -0.93          -0.95

                        - .237 AR(3)
                          (.205)
                          -1.16

                                Resid. Var. = .325 E+08

      (0,2,2)   =  854 -.258 MA(1) -.251 MA(2)
                  (547)   (.188)       (.204)
                  1.56    1.37         1.23

                                Resid. Var. = .295 E+08
```

Q-Statistic (Prob. of Q)	Lag(6)	(12)	(18)
(0,2,0)	5.31 (.50)	7.69 (.81)	13.76 (.74)
			Var. = .322 E+08
(3,2,0)	3.21 (.201)	6.71 (.569)	11.52 (.645)
(0,2,2)	2.96 (.397)	7.27 (.610)	12.56 (6.36)

any of the pure, theoretical cases [(3,2,0), (0,2,2) or even (2,2,0)]. The truncated time-series results, reported in Table 3, further support the (0,2,0) model, as, for example, its ACF is very flat.

We therefore conclude that absolute defense expenditures follow a (0,2,0) model, and thus have essentially no systematic pattern once detrended.[18] We further suspect, as tentative as this conclusion may be, that in modeling the series to include terms to capture war expenditures for Korea and Vietnam, the time-series will contain even less systematic regularity.

Finally, we hasten to add that the structures of the absolute welfare and security expenditure models are actually quite similar. Even for the welfare expenditure process, the (0,2,0) model could not be rejected easily. However, what systematic pattern there is in the detrended series shows only slight differences across the two expenditure processes. The most important of these differences is the prominence of lag 1 in the welfare variable autocorrelation function and its total absence in the defense measure (or, alternatively, the prominence of the single lag 2 for security and slightly greater structure in the short-term lags of welfare expenditures). In either case, the choice boils down to a pure second difference versus a moving average representation.

3) Welfare and security expenditures as proportions of government expenditures

We can cover the results for welfare and security as proportions of net government expenditures quickly. Both are well represented as (1,1,0) models.

For welfare, the ACF and PACF are approximately similar, with the first three lags fairly large, positive and close to significant, and with a nearly significant, negative fifth lag. This suggests a (0,1,0), (1,1,0) or (0,1,1) model; the latter two turn out to be clearly better than higher-order alternatives, which suggests that the addition of any more terms overfits the series (see Table 4). The (1,1,0) model yields a nearly significant coefficient of .251, and in this sense, as well as in terms of all other measures, it uniformly, if slightly, out-performs (0,1,1). We believe that (1,1,0) is a better model than (0,1,0) because the auto-resgressive coefficient is large and the model yields good diagnostic

51

Table 4

Welfare as Proportion of Net Expenditures, 1948-83

```
Model (1,1,0)        = .00569  +  .251 AR(1)
      (s.e.)           (.00526)   (.166)
        (t)             1.08       1.51

                            Resid. Var. = .924 E-03

Model (0,1,1)        = .00542  +  .236 MA(1)
                       (.00641)   (.170)
                        0.85       1.38

                            Resid. Var = .954 E-03

Model (1,1,0)(0,0,5) = .00726 + .132 AR(1) -.355 SMA(5)
                       (.00358)  (.166)      (.167)
                        2.02      .79       -2.13

                            Resid. Var. = .821 E-03
```

Q-Statistic (Prob. of Q)	Lag(6)	(12)	(18)
(0,1,0)	12.76 (.05)	17.75 (.13)	24.45 (.15)

Var. = 1.01 E-03

	Lag(6)	(12)	(18)
(1,1,0)	6.49 (.165)	8.14 (.615)	14.65 (.550)
(0,1,1)	6.86 (.143)	11.28 (.336)	17.36 (.363)
(1,1,0)(0,0,5)	3.06 (.383)	5.29 (.808)	11.65 (.705)

statistics. Moreover, when estimating the "truncated" model (i.e., dropping the last six years) to see if the apparent heteroskedasticity produces inefficient estimates, the (1,1,0) model is found to be significant with a slightly larger auto-regressive coefficient estimate, just as we would expect from non-constant variance (see Table 8, below).

We should note that the fifth lag in the welfare ACF is nearly significant and fairly large. None of the simple models is able to reduce that "spike" to white noise in the residual ACF. While we believe the "spike" can be ignored as a statistical artifact, for purposes in which it is necessary to have pure, "white-noise", residuals the (1,1,0) model with a fifth-term seasonal moving average parameter [i.e., (1,1,0)(0,0,5)] is an appropriate representation. The five-year seasonal moving average coefficient estimate of .35 is significant, the RACF and related diagnostics are very good, and the residual variance is noticeably reduced.

The time-series of security expenditures as a proportion of net government expenditures is about as close to a pure AR(1) process as the real world provides. The ACF shows a significant, positive lag one correlation and a smaller, insignificant second lag, while the PACF shows lag one significant and lag two almost zero. As Table 5 indicates, the (1,1,0) model fits very well, with a healthy and significant AR(1) coefficient (.402). The Q-statistic and RACF are also very good. In short, the (1,1,0) model is accepted, out-performing (0,1,1), and noticeably improving upon (0,1,0). Finally, the (1,1,0) model estimated on the shortened time-series yielded virtually the same results, clearly indicating its robustness.

That a (1,1,0) model fits both welfare and security expenditures as a proportion of net government expenditures is not surprising. There is a long tradition of theoretical and applied research on the budgetary process in the U.S. government which argues that, over the long haul, most expenditure decisions are made incrementally when set in the context of a given budgetary constraint. The Lindblom (1965; 1959) and Wildavsky (1964) arguments about bounded rationality and bureaucratic politics, drawn from the more general theories of March and Simon (1958), suggest that changes in budgetary proportions are made at the margin, as relatively small increments or

53

Table 5

Security as Proportion of Net Expenditures, 1948-83

Model (1,1,0) = -.00332 + .402 AR(1)
     (s.e.)   (.00683)   (.157)
        (t)   -0.49   2.56

                              Resid. Var. = .156 E-02

Model (0,1,1) = -.00455 - .369 MA(1)
                    (.00901)   (.157)
                    -0.51   -2.35

                              Resid. Var. = .154 E-02

Q-Statistic   Lag(6)   (12)   (18)
   (Prob. of Q)

   (1,1,0)   3.74   5.65   13.62
                        (.442)   (.844)   (.627)

   (0,1,1)   5.50   7.84   14.35
                        (.240)   (.644)   (.573)

decrements to the proportional size of last year's budgetary breakdown. The perspective of the complexity of pluralistic and bureaucratic-presidential-congressional infighting leads to a similar conclusion about outcomes. Empirical work, such as the pathbreaking studies of Davis, Dempster and Wildavsky (1966), provides strong evidence in support of this formulation. Thus, that both welfare and security budgeting in terms of proportions of total budgets follows this pattern of "bureaucratic politics" (as used, for example, by Ostrom (1978) and Marra (1985) in the context of defense spending) is not surprising. Indeed, these particular measures of welfare and security expenditures (i.e., as proportions of net expenditures) are where the "marginalist" hypothesis is most descriptive and, hence, where a (1,1,0) model could be expected to be found. This was the point made earlier, of course, about the narrowest conceptualization of trade-offs. Measuring expenditures in actual dollars or as proportions of the nation's wealth implies a different perspective on choice under constraints that might -- and does -- suggest different formulations. In this light, we turn to expenditures as proportions of GNP and do indeed find different systematic components to their univariate series.

4)   Welfare and security expenditures as proportions of GNP

   Welfare expenditures expressed as a proportion of GNP are modeled very well as a (0,1,1) process. The ACF is a nearly perfect example of this model, with a first lag autocorrelation coefficient of some size and about twice its standard error, and with lags 2 and 3 very close to zero. The PACF is not a perfect example, however. While the first lag is nearly significant and positive, the second lag is of moderate size, but negative. Nonetheless, the (0,1,1) model performs very well, as seen in Table 6, and it clearly outperforms its closest competitor, (1,1,0). Second lags in both cases are insignificant. The only tiny wrinkle is that, in the RACF, lag 21 remains relatively large (it is of some size in the welfare/net government expenditures measure, as well). Again, for those cases in which the hypothesis of completely random residuals is crucial, we present estimates of an (0,1,1) model with a seasonal moving average, lag 21, to pick up the "spike". While the "spike" is clearly very large and significant, we reject such a model as a statistical artifact, especially given the length of that lag in comparison to the length of the time-series.

55

Table 6

Welfare as Proportion of GNP, 1948-83


```
Model (0,1,1)   =   .00209   +   .481 MA(1)
      (s.e.)          (.00144)    (.154)
        (t)           1.45        3.13
```

                                        Resid. Var. = .340 E-04

```
Model (1,1,0)   =   .00145   +   .333 AR(1)
                    (.00108)     (.169)
                    1.34         1.97
```

                                        Resid. Var. = .366 E-04

```
Model (0,1,1)(0,0,21)=.00209 + .408 MA(1)+ .775 SMA(21)
                      (.000846) (.160)        (.202)
                      2.47      2.55         -3.83
```

                                        Resid. Var. = .240 E-04

Q-Statistic (Prob. of Q)	Lag(6)	(12)	(18)
(0,1,1)	2.11 (.716)	3.67 (.961)	6.60 (.980)
(1,1,0)	3.32 (.505)	5.20 (.878)	8.33 (.938)
(0,1,1)(0,0,21)*	2.01 (.570)	3.48 (.942)	7.67 (.936)

* The SMA coefficient was included to correct for
  large residual autocorrelations beginning at lag
  21, beyond the periods over which the Q-statistics
  reported here are calculated.

The national security expenditure series as a proportion of GNP appears to be best modeled as a (2,1,0) model. In its ACF, lags one through three are fairly large, with lag one positive and lags two and three negative. In the PACF, Lags one and two remain so, while lag three is near zero. The (2,1,0) model is clearly the best of the AR forms, as (0,1,1) is of the MA forms. As Table 7 suggests, the choice between them is not clear. However, the diagnostic statistics indicate that the AR formulation performs uniformly, if only slightly, better than the (0,1,1) model.

Table 8 reports the selected models for the four ratio variables as they are re-estimated on the shortened time-series. In each case, the results are only marginally different, at best, strongly implying that the selected models are robust in the face of potential heteroskedasticity.

CONCLUSION

We close by stressing the two most important conclusions drawn from this analysis of the structures of expenditure processes.

First, the ARIMA models identified as the best representations of the structures of welfare and security expenditure time-series are remarkably similar to one another for each of the three measurement formulations of those time-series. The different measurement formulations correspond to, and are directly implied by, different conceptions of the trade-off problem of choice under constraint. In particular, as we argued above, if trade-offs are viewed as a matter of choice between competing alternative programmatic objectives under fixed budgetary constraint, then the implied measure of expenditures is as a proportion of the net budget. Similarly, if trade-offs are conceptualized in terms of direct expenditure opportunity costs under the constraint of a given resource pool from which the government extracts resources, then the implied measure involves expenditures as a ratio of some appropriate indicator of the size of that resource pool (e.g., GNP). When trade-offs are conceptualized in terms only of indirect opportunity costs (whether as negative externalities in a given resource pool or as relatively less positive multiplier and spin-off effects in a potentially expanding resource pool), the absolute

Table 7

Security as Proportion of GNP, 1948-83

Model (2,1,0)   =   .0000887   +   .488 AR(1) - .386 AR(2)
      (s.e.)   (.00186)   (.154)   (.153)
        (t)   0.05   3.16   -2.53

                                    Resid. Var. = .114 E-03

Model (0,1,1)   =   -.00113   +   .595 MA(1)
                        (.00299)   (.136)
                         0.38   4.36

                                    Resid. Var. = .127 E-03

Q-Statistic   Lag(6)   (12)   (18)
  (Prob. of Q)

    (2,1,0)   2.89   4.10   7.14
                     (.408)   (.905)   (.954)

    (0,1,1)   4.83   7.18   11.17
                     (.305)   (.708)   (.799)

Table 8

Welfare and Security as Proportions of
Net Expenditures and of GNP, Shortened Series

Table 8.A: Welfare: 1948-77

Expenditures Model (1,1,0) = .00677 + .373 AR(1)
                  (s.e.)   (.00540)   (.171)
                  (t)   1.25   2.19

                                  Resid. Var. = .774 E-03
                                        Var. = .942 E-03

Q-Statistic	Lag(6)	(12)	(18)
(Prob. of Q)			
	6.25	7.51	12.59
	(.181)	(.677)	(.703)

GNP Model (0,1,1) =   .00239 + .630 MA(1)
                       (.00151)   (.145)
                       1.59   -4.34

                                  Resid. Var. = .260 E-04
                                        Var. = .329 E-04

Q-Statistic	Lag(6)	(12)	(18)
(Prob. of Q)			
	4.93	7.44	12.69
	(.295)	(.683)	(.695)

Table 8.B: Security: 1955-83

Expenditures Model (1,1,0)   =   -.00761   +   .382 AR(1)
                                 (.00536)   (.179)
                                 -1.42   2.13

                                      Resid. Var. = .596 E-03
                                             Var. = .677 E-03

Q-Statistic   Lag(6)   (12)   (18)
 (Prob. of Q)
                  1.93   9.51   12.71
                  (.748)   (.484)   (.694)

GNP Model (2,1,0) = -.00134 + .439 AR(1) - .367 AR(2)
                    (.00105) (.182)   (.188)
                    -1.28   2.41   -1.95

                                      Resid. Var. = .248 E-04
                                             Var. = .307 E-04

Q-Statistic   Lag(6)   (12)   (18)
 (Prob. of Q)

                  2.65   6.31   12.25
                  (.449)   (.708)   (.660)

(i.e., unstandardized) magnitude of the expenditures is called for. Hence, the similarity of time-series structure between national security and social welfare expenditures at each of these three measurement levels can be discussed in terms of structural similarities (of expenditure processes) within the framework of different respective conceptualizations of trade-offs. Figure 3 illustrates this by presenting the ARIMA model structures in a format that is identical to that presented in Figure 2 above, in which the four alternative conceptions of trade-offs were identified.

Our position, you may recall, is that any conception of a "guns-butter" trade-off rests on the presumption that national security and social welfare expenditures are set in and affected by a joint, or common, context of constraints. There is no reason to assume an identical basis for reaching collective decisions about welfare and defense spending levels (or proportions), so the precise parameters of the time-series models need not be identical (as Tables 1 to 8 reveal they are not), but there must be some reflection of a common set of constraints and choice environments. This is the significance of the similarity of the general structure of expenditure processes for both welfare and security in each of the cells in Figure 3: The similarity is consistent with the conceptual foundations of a trade-off dynamic, namely that there should be similar dynamic forces driving the two series. Our data analysis provides strong evidence that there is a common dynamic pattern underlying welfare and security expenditures.

Our second and more important argument also concerns the conceptualization of trade-offs. We have argued that a comprehensive notion of trade-offs must include multiple levels of analysis, and, in particular, we presented four basic conceptions at different levels relevant to the study of "guns-butter" trade-offs. This multi-level conceptualization permits one to expect quite different trade-off dynamics across different levels. Our empirical results conform closely to that expectation. The narrowest perspective looks at expenditure choices under a fixed budget constraint. Here, our empirical analysis supports the standard view of "incrementalism" in budgeting for both welfare and security expenditures. This relatively standard result is equivalent to the marginalist perspective in which trade-offs, made at the margin, are seen most commonly. Looking at welfare and security expenditure processes in a larger perspective,

61

Figure 3: Best Fitting ARIMA Models of Expenditure Processes
(by Conception of Trade-off)

Level of Constraint on Choice

Opportunity Costs	Given current budget	Given current resource pool for budgetary extraction	Given "technological" limits on future growth of resource pool
Direct	welfare: (1,1,0) security:(1,1,0)	(0,1,1) (2,1,0)	✕
Indirect	✕	[[	(0, 2, 0)] (0, 2, 0)]

62

whether in terms of absolute expenditures or as a proportion of societal resources (here measured as GNP) provides quite a different view of the dynamics of expenditure patterns. The analysis of a "guns-butter" trade-off therefore requires a different theory in all three cases.

In conclusion, in this paper we have offered a conceptual framework for the study of expenditure trade-offs between welfare and security in the United States. We have analyzed the dynamic pattern or time-series structure of welfare and security expenditures from 1948-1983. The results of this analysis are consistent with the theoretical conceptualization of the general problem of trade-offs, and they present a positive first step in that analysis. The analysis does not prove whether there has or has not been a trade-off between "guns and butter" in the post-World War II United States, but it does lay the groundwork necessary for seriously studying this important macro-policy question.

APPENDIX: An Example of Expenditure Categories, 1982

Federal government expenditures for fiscal 1982 are found in the U. S. Government Budget for Fiscal Year 1984 (pp. 9-20 to 9-31).

Measures of National Security Commitments

```
    SECURE1 = Defense + Military Assistance
  *SECURE2 = SECURE1 + Economic Assistance
    SECURE3 = SECURE2 + ACDA + Space Program
    SECURE4 = SECURE3 + Veterans Services + Residual
```

Measures of Welfare Commitments

```
    WELFARE1 = Income Security + Veterans Services
  *WELFARE2 = WELFARE1 + Manpower
    WELFARE3 = WELFARE2 + Housing + Health + Revenue
               Sharing
```

Categories of Actual Expenditures for Fiscal 1982
(These are gross expenditures calculated prior to the deduction of offsetting receipts.)

Defense: $184,558,000,000

    051   Department of Defense-Military (excludes
           "retired military personnel")
    053   Atomic energy defense activities
    054   Defense-related activities (e.g., CIA,
           Selective Service, etc.)

Military Assistance: $15,492,000,000

    152   International security assistance
    155   International financial programs: "funds
           appropriated to the President" only

Economic Assistance: $4,217,000,000

    151   Foreign economic and financial assistance

Arms Control and Disarmament Agency: $16,000,000

    153   "ACDA" only

Space Program: $5,980,000,000

    251   General science and basic research - "Energy
            activities" only
    253   Space flight
    254   Space, science, applications and technology
    255   Supporting space activities

Residual Defense Expenditures: $22,924,000,000
    051   "Retired military personnel" only
    153   Conduct of foreign affairs - excluding ACDA
    154   Foreign information and exchange activities
    155   International financial programs - excluding
            "funds appropriated to the President".

Income Security: $252,296,000,000

    506   Social services
    601   General retirement and disability insurance
    602   Federal employee retirement and disability
    603   Unemployment compensation
    605   Food and nutrition assistance
    609   Other income security

Veterans Service and Benefits: $24,615,000,000

    701   Income security for veterans
    702   Veterans education, training and
            rehabilitation
    703   Hospital and medical care for veterans
    704   Veterans housing
    705   Other veterans benefits and services

Manpower: $9,072,000,000

    452   Area and regional development
    504   Training and employment
    505   Other labor services (for example, NLRB)

Housing and Community Development: $16,069,000,000

    371   Mortgage credit and thrift insurance
    451   Community development
    453   Disaster relief and insurance
    604   Housing assistance

Health: $92,204,000,000

    551   Health care services
    552   Health research
    553   Education and training of health care work
           force
    554   Consumer and occupational health and safety

Revenue Sharing: $9,141,000,000

    851   General revenue sharing

Agriculture: $14,882,000,000

    351   Farm income stabilization
    352   Agricultural research and services

Natural Resources: $23,577,000,000

    271   Energy supply
    272   Energy conservation
    274   Emergency energy preparedness
    276   Energy information, policy and regulation
    301   Water resources
    302   Conservation and land management
    303   Recreational resources
    304   Pollution control and abatement
    306   Other natural resources

Commerce and Transportation: $23,837,000,000

    372   Postal service
    376   Other advancement of commerce
    401   Ground transportation
    402   Air transportation
    403   Water transportation
    407   Other transportation

Education: $13,290,000,000

    501   Elementary, secondary and vocational
           education
    502   Higher education

Culture: $2,144,000,000

    251   "National Science Foundation" only
    503   Research and general educational aids

General Government: $24,521,000,000

    751   Federal law enforcement activities
    752   Federal legislative and judicial activities
    753   Federal correctional activities
    754   Criminal justice assistance
    801   Legislative functions
    802   Executive direction and managment
    803   Central fiscal operations
    804   General property and records management
    805   Central personnel management
    806   Other general government

Total Interest: $119,207,000,000

    901   Interest on the public debt
    908   Other interest

Total Gross Federal Expenditures: $844,616,000,000

    Sum of all preceding categories

Net Governmental Expenditures: $728,375,000,000

    "Total"   p. 9-31

* The authors are grateful to the Department of Political Science of the University of Minnesota for providing financial support for the research reported here, and to John R. Freeman for his very helpful comments on an earlier draft. We also want to thank Mary Ellen Otis for her skillful secretarial support.

1. The trade-offs problem is not equivalent to the question of who benefits from or who pays for a particular expenditure or budgetary decision. That question, which was posed explicitly by Russett (1969, 1970) as part of his pioneering work on the trade-offs problem, is, we recognize, a very important question. But it is conceptually distinct from the issue of trade-offs. To know, for example, that military defense expenditures constitute an inter-regional, inter-generational, or inter-class redistributive mechanism is to know something of considerable significance, but it is not to know directly the implications of an allocative choice (in this case, for defense expenditures) for the ability of the chooser to accomplish other, competing objectives. Trade-offs are in terms of the desired objectives of the chooser. In that sense, one can talk sensibly of "guns-butter" (or other) budgetary trade-offs if, but only if, one assumes that the government (or its budgetary agencies) makes choices among competing objectives.

2. Precisely because these externalities involve unintended and non-unique effects, they may not be easily recognized or well-understood, particularly by those responsible for making the allocation choices. Indirect opportunity costs, while complex, are nevertheless an important aspect of the governmental expenditures trade-off problem.

3. We recognize that this abstract conceptualization of budgetary choice constrained by the size of the resource pool is less than perfectly applied to real political systems. In particular, governmental budgets are not effectively constrained by the current resource pool if deficit financing is employed to a significant extent. Where the government is able to run a large budgetary deficit (and, hence, to borrow against the future), the choice problem at this second level still concerns the extent to which societal resources should be extracted for governmental purposes, but the relevant resource pool from which

68

extraction is to occur is less sharply defined because of future uncertainties. The choice problem, then, is less a matter of determining how much of society's current resources to allocate to governmental (rather than non-governmental) uses of various kinds than it is a matter of determining how much to extract from future societal resources for current governmental uses. We recognize the real importance of this intertemporal transfer dynamic in contemporary budgetary processes, but we do not believe that it alters, in any fundamental sense, the basic conceptualization at this second level of constraint. The problem is still a matter of choice under the constraint of the (current and, perhaps ill-defined, future) resource pool from which resources are extracted for governmental programs.

4. There should be no implication in this discussion that budgetary decision-makers are aware of, or have any substantial knowledge about, the "production function" that converts current governmental expenditures into future expansion (or contraction) of the national economy. To pose this third level as a choice problem is not meant to suggest that decision-makers choose a rate of economic growth for the future and then allocate current expenditures in such a way as to effectuate that future growth. On the contrary, it is simply to make explicit the recognition that current budgetary allocations are choices (whether conscious or not) that have significant impact on (and, hence, are "about") future national economic conditions.

5. In March 1985, President Reagan complained about those who wanted to cut his proposed defense budget "merely" to increase domestic spending, instead of using the reductions to reduce the deficit. Interestingly, from our perspective, his complaint was cast in terms of two distinct conceptions of the trade-off problem simultaneously: expenditures under fixed budget constraint (the "merely" part); and expenditures under the constraint of a given national resource pool (the "instead of" part -- where the conception is extended to include the possibility of deficit financing according to our discussion in footnote #2 above).

6. Ignoring effective budget constraints, and hence ignoring the necessity of trade-offs in the direct opportunity cost sense discussed above, leads many scholars to the conclusion that they can sensibly

69

and adequately analyze budgetary processes in one or another major expenditure area in isolation. The implicit assumption seems to be that the government's ability to move its budget constraint outward is so limitless that the determinants of expenditures in that programmatic area do not include trade-off considerations for other programs -- hence the reasonableness of investigating one area of expenditure while ignoring others. For major expenditure programs, such as national security commitments and social welfare programs in the United States in the middle and late 20th century, this seems to us to be an unfortunate and ill-advised assumption. In our judgment it is a serious flaw in much of the work on defense expenditure processes, including most empirical arms race modeling efforts. In such studies, the explanatory model and statistical analysis typically include variables representing the international context of national security pursuits, the domestic American socioeconomic environment, and national political processes, but do not consider trade-offs with other governmentally desired programmatic objectives, except in the highly general "fatigue" coefficient of the Richardson formulation. As a result, otherwise important studies are weakened (Marra, 1985; Berry and Lowery, 1984; Ward, 1984; Ward and Mahajan, 1984; Majeski, 1983; Nincic, 1982; Cusack and Ward, 1981; Majeski and Jones, 1981; Moll and Luebbert, 1980; Lambelet and Luterbacher with Allan, 1979; Nincic and Cusack, 1979; Ostrom, 1978, 1977).

    7. In this discussion we ignore the possibility of "money illusion" increases that are matched or outstripped by inflation (i.e., real constancy or real declines in programmatic expenditures that are increasing in current dollar terms, but not as rapidly as is inflation). Such increases do not affect the conceptual discussion importantly, but repeated mention of them would complicate the presentation. Our discussion, then, assumes real expenditure increases.

    8. If direct expenditure trade-offs are assessed in terms of absolute expenditures rather than in terms of expenditures relative to national income or expenditures as a proportion of the budget, and if the size of the national resource pool (e.g., GNP) is not incorporated directly into the model of the absolute expenditure process, then the implicit assumption is that the given current size of the national resource pool constitutes no effective constraint at all on the

increase in governmental expenditures. We believe that to be a generally indefensible assumption.

9. Recently, some interesting literature has begun to appear about the contraction of the scope of the public economy in advanced capitalist states. Most analysts, however, continue to focus on the expansion rather than the contraction of government expenditures. For those who do address contraction, the logic of this conception comes close to converging with the first conception of the trade-off problem as being a matter of choice under a fixed budget constraint. The trade-off problem in the face of governmental contraction is addressed explicitly and in an interesting way in Tarschys (1984), and is illustrated in a recent set of country case studies: Aberbach and Rockman (1985); Anton (1985); Ashford (1985); Campbell (1985); Esping-Andersen (1985); and King (1985).

10. This article was the subject of reanalysis and criticism in a series of articles: Griffin, Devine, and Wallace (1985); Hicks and Mintz (1985); Jencks (1985); Mintz and Hicks (1984).

11. Of course, the possibility should be recognized that governmental expenditures are purely and simply a net drain on the economy -- that, on net, they have no positive multiplier or spin-off effects. Note that this is not the same thing as the frequently heard critical charge that governmental programs are less efficient than the private sector, because in that charge there is typically an implicit assumption that governmental expenditures contribute to economic expansion to some degree, if only through the multiplier effects of demand stimulation. The charge, whether right or wrong, is that their contribution to growth is simply less than that of private sector expenditures, not that governmental programs constitute a dead loss to the economy. If they were a dead loss, this conceptualization would reduce to the second and/or third conceptions of trade-offs described previously.

12. In our judgment, this is a nearly fatal flaw with those several studies that have offered an assessment of "guns-butter" trade-offs in terms of the aggregate investment effects or the aggregate economic growth effects of defense spending. Such studies rarely, if ever, make an explicit comparison with the effects of alternative expenditures. They limit their attention, instead, to a comparison of growth (or

71

investment) rates under conditions of high defense
spending with those that are found under conditions of
lower defense spending (often controlling for a few
other variable determinants of growth -- or investment
-- through the vehicle of a multiple regression model).
If that comparison yields an inverse, or negative,
correlation -- higher growth is associated with lower
defense expenditures and vice versa -- then a trade-off
is concluded to exist (see Biswas and Ram, 1986; Ball,
1985, 1983; Frederiksen and Looney, 1985, 1983, 1982;
Cappelen, Gleditsch, and Bjerkholt, 1984; Chan, 1984;
Faini, Annez, and Taylor, 1984; Mahler and Katz, 1984;
Rasler and Thompson, 1984; Deger and Sen, 1983; Deger
and Smith, 1983; DeGrasse, 1983; Huisken, 1983;
Leontief and Duchin, 1983; Lim, 1983;; Smith, 1980;
Benoit, 1978, 1973: Chester, 1978; Nardinelli and
Ackerman, 1976; Lee, 1973; Rothschild, 1973; Szymanski,
1973; Hollenhorst and Ault, 1971; Russett, 1970, 1969).
Such a conclusion is not well-founded; nor is the
converse. The _relative_ effects must be addressed by
considering alternative uses explicitly.

Good commentaries are available on the literature
that examines the impact of national security
expenditures on economic growth. See, especially, Chan
(1985), Mosley (1985), Lindgren (1984), and Kennedy
(1983).

13. We do not want to imply that others have not
grappled seriously with the issue of how best to
measure the government's expenditures for national
security, or defense, programs. On the contrary, there
is very active disagreement among scholars on that
issue. (The disagreement is summarized, in part, by
Mosley (1985: Chapters 2 and 3) and by Kennedy (1983:
Chapter 3).) However, the vast majority of literature
addressed to one or another of the four different
conceptions of trade-offs between national security and
social welfare expenditures described above does employ
the conventional administrative category, DoD
expenditures. Even in this "guns-butter" trade-offs
literature, however, there are some exceptions (e.g.,
Clayton, 1976; Cypher, 1974).

14. Actual expenditures, as opposed to
appropriations or authorizations, are reported in the
official budget of the U.S. government for the second
fiscal year after the year in which they were spent.
The fiscal 1983 expenditures, then, were reported in
the official budget presented by the President to
Congress for fiscal 1985. Because the analysis

reported in this paper was conducted in 1985, figures for fiscal 1983 were the most current available to us.

15. It is important to note that by imposing homogeneous stationarity on the entire 36 year expenditure time-series, we are implicitly assuming that the series is produced by, or represents, a single, structurally stable process. This, of course, is a potentially inappropriate assumption (e.g., the national security expenditure process might have had a very different structure in the era of massive retaliation than it does in the period of mutual assured destruction). In the end, it is an assumption that stands or falls only on grounds of theoretical and substantive appropriateness, and not on technical, methodological bases.

16. The first difference is given by $X_{t+1} - X_t$. A time-series of first differences, then, is a series of raw magnitudes of change in the original time-series. Similarly, the second difference is given by $(X_{t+2} - X_{t+1}) - (X_{t+1} - X_t)$, which is the difference between successive first differences. A time-series of second differences is a series of changes in rates of change.

17. It can be shown that the (2,2,0) and (0,2,1) models do not differ greatly in their algebraic form, suggesting not that they are interchangeable but that they are reasonable approximations of one another.

18. For those who feel that any significant coefficient implies that the analyst should reject the assumption of no systematic effects, we recommend inclusion of an MA(2) parameter in a non-linear model, and three auto-regressive parameters in a linear regression model, thereby certainly eliminating any systematic pattern in the residuals. These formulations would represent the (0,2,2,) model and the (3,2,0) model respectively.

BIBLIOGRAPHY

Aberbach, J. D. and Rockman, B. A. 1985.
"Governmental Responses to Budget Scarcity: The
United States." Policy Studies Journal 13(3), pp.
494-505.

Alt, J. E. and Chrystal, K. A. 1983. Political
Economics. Berkeley: University of California
Press.

Ames, B. and Goff, E. 1975 "Education and Defense
Expenditures in Latin America: 1948-1968," in C.
Liske, et al., eds., Comparative Public Policy:
Issues, Theories, and Methods. Beverly Hills: Sage
Publications, pp. 175-197.

Anderson, M. 1975. The Empty Pork Barrel: Unemployment
and the Pentagon Budget. Lansing: Public Interest
Research Group.

Anton, T. J. 1985. "Governmental Responses to Budget
Scarcity: Sweden." Policy Studies Journal 13(3),
pp. 525-533.

Ashford, D. E. 1985. "Governmental Responses to
Budget Scarcity: France." Policy Studies Journal
13(3), pp. 517-524.

Ball, N. 1983. "Defense and Development: A Critique
of the Benoit Study." Economic Development and
Cultural Change 31(3), pp. 507-524.

Ball, N. and Leitenberg, M., eds. 1983. The Structure
of the Defense Industry: An International Survey.
New York: St. Martin's Press.

Ball, N. 1985. "Defense Expenditures and Economic
Growth: A Comment." Armed Forces and Society
11(2), pp. 291-297.

Benoit, E. 1973. Defense and Economic Growth in
Developing Countries. Lexington, Mass.:
Lexington Books, D. C. Heath and Co.

Benoit, E. 1978. "Growth and Defense in Developing
Countries." Economic Development and Cultural
Change 26(2), pp. 271-280.

74

Berry, W. D. and Lowry, D. 1984. "Disaggregating United States Government Growth: 1948-1982." Paper prepared for the annual meeting of the American Political Science Association, Washington, DC, August 30-September 2.

Best, M. H. and Connolly, W. 1976. The Politicized Economy. Lexington, Mass.: D. C. Heath and Co.

Bezdek, R. 1975. "The 1980 Economic Impact -- Regional and Occupational -- of Compensated Shifts in Defense Spending." Journal of Regional Science 15(2), pp. 183-197.

Biswas, B. and Ram, R. 1986. "Military Expenditures and Economic Growth in Less Developed Countries: An Augmented Model and Further Evidence." Economic Development and Cultural Change 34(2), pp. 361-372.

Bowles, S. and Gintis, H. 1982. "The Crisis of Liberal Democratic Capitalism: The Case of the United States," Politics and Society 11(1), pp. 51-93.

Campbell, J. C. 1985 "Governmental Responses to Budget Scarcity: Japan." Policy Studies Journal 13(3), pp. 506-516.

Cappelen, A., Gleditsch, N.P., and Bjerkholt, O. 1984. "Military Spending and Economic Growth in the OECD Countries." Journal of Peace Research 21(4), pp. 361-373.

Caputo, D. A. 1975. "New Perspectives on the Public Policy Implications of Defense and Welfare Expenditures in Four Modern Democracies: 1950-1970." Policy Sciences 6(4), pp. 423-446.

Chan, S. 1984. "Defense Spending and Economic Performance: Correlates Among the OECD Countries." Paper prepared for the annual meeting of the International Studies Association, Atlanta, March 27-31.

Chan, S. 1985. "The Impact of Defense Spending on Economic Performance: A Survey of Evidence and Problems." Orbis 29(2), pp. 403-434.

Chase Econometric Associates, Economic Impact of the B-1 Program on the U.S. Economy. Bala Cynwyd, Pa.

75

Chester, E. 1978. "Military Spending and Capitalist Stability." Cambridge Journal of Economics 2(3), pp. 293-298.

Clayton, J. 1976. "The Fiscal Limits of the Warfare-Welfare State: Defense and Welfare Spending in the United States Since 1900." Western Political Quarterly 29(3), pp. 364-383.

Cusack, T. R. and Ward, M. D. 1981. "Military Spending in the United States, Soviet Union and the People's Republic of China." Journal of Conflict Resolution 25(3), pp. 429-469.

Cypher, J. 1974. "Capitalist Planning and Military Expenditure." Review of Radical Political Economics 6, pp. 1-19.

Dabelko, D. and McCormick, J. M. 1977. "Opportunity Costs of Defense: Some Cross-National Evidence." Journal of Peace Research 14(2), pp. 145-154.

Davis, O. A., Dempster, M. A. H., and Wildavsky, A. 1966. "A Theory of the Budgetary Process." American Political Science Review 60(3), pp. 529-547.

Deger, S. and Sen, S. 1983. "Military Expenditure, Spin-off and Economic Development." Journal of Development Economics 13, pp. 67-83.

Deger, S. and Smith, R. 1983. "Military Expenditures and Growth in Less Developed Countries." Journal of Conflict Resolution 27(2), pp. 335-353.

DeGrasse, R. W. 1983. Military Expansion, Economic Decline: The Impact of Military Spending on U.S. Economic Performance. Armonk, N.Y.: Council on Economic Priorities/M. E. Sharpe.

Domke, W. K., Eichenberg, R. C., and Kelleher, C. M. 1983. "The Illusion of Choice: Defense and Welfare in Advanced Industrial Democracies, 1948-1978." American Political Science Review 77(1), pp. 19-35.

Dunne, J. P. and Smith, R. P. 1984. "The Economic Consequences of Reduced UK Military Expenditure." Cambridge Journal of Economics 8, pp. 297-310.

Eckstein, O. 1963. <u>Public Finance</u>. Englewood Cliffs, N.J.: Prentice-Hall.

Eichenberg, R. C. 1984. "The Expenditure and Revenue Effects of Defense Spending in the Federal Republic of Germany." <u>Policy Sciences</u> 16(4), pp. 391-411.

Esping-Andersen, G. 1985. "Governmental Responses to Budget Scarcity: Denmark," <u>Policy Studies Journal</u>, 13(3), pp. 534-546.

Faini, R., Arnez, P., and Taylor, L. 1984. "Defense Spending, Economic Structure, and Growth: Evidence Among Countries and Over Time." <u>Economic Development and Cultural Change</u> 32(3), pp. 487-498.

Ferejohn, J. and Krehbiel, K. 1985. "The Budget Process and the Size of the Budget," manuscript, Stanford University and California Institute of Technology, August.

Frederiksen, P.C. and Looney, R.E. 1982. "Defense Expenditures and Economic Growth in Developing Countries: Some Further Empirical Evidence." <u>Journal of Economic Development</u>, July, pp. 113-125.

Frederiksen, P. C. and Looney, R. E. 1983. "Defense Expenditures and Economic Growth in Developing Countries." <u>Armed Forces and Society</u> 9(4), pp. 633-645.

Frederiksen, P.C. and Looney, R.E. 1985. "Defense Expenditures and Economic Growth in Developing Countries: A Reply." <u>Armed Forces and Society</u> 11(2), pp. 298-301.

Freeman, J. R. 1983. "Granger Causality and the Time Series Analysis of Political Relationships." <u>American Journal of Political Science</u> 27(2), pp. 327-358.

Frey, B. S. and Schneider, F. 1979. "An Econometric Model with an Endogenous Government Sector." <u>Public Choice</u> 34, pp. 29-43.

Gansler, J. 1980. <u>The Defense Industry</u>. Cambridge: MIT Press.

77

Griffin, L. J., Devine, J., and Wallace, M. 1982. "Monopoly Capital, Organized Labor, and Military Expenditures in the United States, 1949-1976." American Journal of Sociology 88(Supplement), pp. S113-S153.

Griffin, L. J., Wallace, M., and Devine, J. 1982. "The Political Economy of Military Spending: Evidence From the United States." Cambridge Journal of Economics 6(1), pp. 1-14.

Griffin, L. J., Devine, J., and Wallace, M. 1983. "On the Economic and Political Determinants of Welfare Spending in the Post-World War II Era." Politics and Society 12(3), pp. 331-372.

Griffin, L. J., Devine, J., and Wallace, M. 1985. "One More Time: Militarizing the U.S. Budget: Reply to Jencks." American Journal of Sociology 91(2), pp. 384-391.

Hayes, M. D. 1975. "Policy Consequences of Military Participation in Politics: An Analysis of Trade-offs in Brazilian Federal Expenditures," in C. Liske, et al., eds., Comparative Public Policy: Issues, Theories, and Methods. Beverly Hills: Sage, pp. 21-52.

Hibbs, D.A., Jr. and Dennis, C. 1985. "Partisan Eras and the Distribution of Net Income." Paper delivered at the annual meeting of the Midwest Political Science Association, Chicago.

Hicks, A. and Mintz, A. 1985. "Theoretical Insights and Oversights in 'Methodological Problems'." American Journal of Sociology 91(2), pp. 379-384.

Hollenhorst, J. and Ault, G. 1971. "An Alternative Answer to: Who Pays for Defense?" American Political Science Review 65(3), pp. 760-763.

Huisken, R. 1983. "Armaments and Development," in H. Tuomi and R. Vayrynen, eds., Militarization and Arms Production. New York: St. Martin's Press, pp. 3-25.

Jencks, C. 1985. "Methodological Problems in Studying 'Military Keynesianism'." American Journal of Sociology 91(2), pp. 373-379.

Kaldor, M. 1981. The Baroque Arsenal. New York: Hill and Wang.

Kelleher, C. M., Domke, W. K., and Eichenberg, R. C. 1980. "Guns, Butter and Growth: Patterns of Public Expenditures in Four Western Democracies, 1920-1975," in Defense of Politics of the Western Alliance. Edwin H. Fedder, ed., New York: Praeger, pp. 153-188.

Kennedy, G. 1983. Defense Economics. New York: St. Martin's Press.

King, A. 1985. "Governmental Responses to Budget Scarcity: Great Britain," Policy Studies Journal 13(3), pp. 476-493.

Krell, G. 1981. "Capitalism and Armaments: Business Cycles and Defense Spending in the United States, 1945-1979." Journal of Peace Research 18(3), pp. 221-240.

Lambelet, J. C. and Luterbacher, U. with Allan, P. 1979. "Dynamics of Arms Races: Mutual Stimulation vs. Self-stimulation." Journal of Peace Science 4(1), pp. 49-66.

Lee, J. R. 1973. "Changing National Priorities of the United States" in B. Russett and A. Stepan, eds., Military Force and American Society. New York: Harper and Row.

Leontief, W. 1965. "The Economic Impact -- Industrial and Regional -- of an Arms Cut." Review of Economics and Statistics 47(3), pp. 217-241.

Leontief, W. and Duchin, F. 1983. Military Spending: Facts and Figures, Worldwide Implications, and Future Outlook. New York: Oxford University Press.

Lim, D. 1983. "Another Look at Growth and Defense in Less Developed Countries." Economic Development and Cultural Change 31(2), pp. 377-384.

Lindblom, C. E. 1959. "The Science of Muddling Through." Public Administration Review 19(2), pp. 79-88.

Lindblom, C. E. 1965. The Intelligence of Democracy; Decision Making Through Mutual Adjustment. New York: Free Press.

79

Lindgren, G. 1984. "Review Essay: Armaments and Economic Performance in Industrialized Market Economies." Journal of Peace Research 21(4), pp. 375-387.

Lyttkens, C. H. and Vedovata, C. 1984. "Opportunity Costs of Defence: A Comment on Dabelko and McCormick." Journal of Peace Research 21(4), pp. 389-394.

Mahler, V. A. and Katz, C. J. 1984. "The Impact of Government Expenditures on Growth and Distribution in Developed Market Economy Countries: A Cross-National Study." Paper prepared for the annual meeting of the American Political Science Association, Washington, D.C., August 30-September 2.

Majeski, S. J. and Jones, D. C. 1981. "Arms Race Modeling: Causality Analysis and Model Specification." Journal of Conflict Resolution 25(2), pp. 259-288.

Majeski, S. J. 1983. "Mathematical Models of the U.S. Military Expenditure Decision-Making Process." American Journal of Political Science 27(3), pp. 485-514.

March, J. G. and Simon, H. A. 1958. Organizations. New York: John Wiley.

Marra, R. F. 1985. "A Cybernetic Model of the U.S. Defense Expenditure Policy-Making Process." International Studies Quarterly 29(4), pp. 357-384.

Mason, W. L. and Muldoon, J. P. 1984. "Politics and High Technology in the European Community: A Study of Joint Ventures in the European Aerospace Industry." Paper prepared for the annual meeting of the International Studies Association, Atlanta, March 27-31.

McCleary, R. and Hay, R. A. 1980. Applied Time Series Analysis for the Social Sciences. Beverly Hills: Sage Publications.

Melman, S. 1974. The Permanent War Economy: American Capitalism in Decline. New York: Simon and Schuster.

80

Melman, S. 1978. "Inflation and Unemployment as Products of War Economy." Peace Research Reviews 7, pp. 17-52.

Mintz, A. and Hicks, A. 1984. "Military Keynesianism in the United States, 1949-1976: Disaggregating Military Expenditures and Their Determination." American Journal of Sociology 90(2), pp. 411-417.

Moll, K. D. and Luebbert, G. M. 1980. "Arms Race and Military Expenditure Models." Journal of Conflict Resolution 24(1), pp. 153-185.

Mosley, H.G. 1985. The Arms Race: Economic and Social Consequences. Lexington, Mass.: Lexington Books.

Nardinelli, C. and Ackerman, G. B. 1976. "Defense Expenditures and the Survival of American Capitalism: A Note." Armed Forces and Society 3(1), pp. 13-16.

Neuman, S. G. 1979. "Arms Transfers and Economic Development: Some Research and Policy Issues" in Arms Transfers in the Modern World, Stephanie G. Neuman and Robert E. Harkavy, eds., New York: Praeger.

Nincic, M. and Cusack, T. R. 1979. "The Political Economy of U.S. Military Spending." Journal of Peace Research 16(2), pp. 101-115.

Nincic, M. 1982. The Arms Race. New York: Praeger.

Ostrom, C. W. 1977. "Evaluating Alternative Foreign Policy Decision-Making Models: An Empirical Test Between an Arms Model and an Organizational Politics Model." Journal of Conflict Resolution 21(2), pp. 235-266.

Ostrom, C. W. 1978. "A Reactive Linkage Model of the U.S. Defense Expenditure Policy-Making Process." American Political Science Review 72(3), pp. 37-49.

Peroff, K. 1977. "The Warfare-Welfare Trade-off: Health, Public Aid and Housing." Journal of Sociology and Social Welfare 4(3-4), pp. 366-381.

Peroff, K. and Podolak-Warren, M. 1979. "Does Spending for Defense Cut Spending for Health?" British Journal of Political Science 9(1), pp. 37-49.

Pluta, J. E. 1978. "National Defense and Social Welfare Budget Trends in Ten Nations of Post-war Europe." International Journal of Social Economics 5(1), pp. 3-21.

Pryor, F. L. 1968. Public Expenditures in Communist and Capitalist Countries. Homewood, Illinois: Irwin.

Rasler, K. A. and Thompson, W. R. 1984. "Longitudinal Change in Defense Burdens, Capital Formation and Economic Growth." Paper prepared for the annual meeting of the International Studies Association, Atlanta, March 27-31.

Rothschild, K. W. 1973. "Military Expenditure, Exports and Growth." Kyklos 26(4), pp. 804-813.

Russett, B. 1969. "Who Pays for Defense?" American Political Science Review 63(2), pp. 412-426.

Russett, B. 1970. What Price Vigilance? New Haven: Yale University Press.

Russett, B. 1982. "International Interactions and Processes: The Internal vs. External Debate Revisited." Paper delivered at the annual meeting of the American Political Science Association, September 2.

Sargent, T. J. 1979. "Causality, Exogeneity, and Natural Rate Models: Reply to C.R. Nelson and B.T. McCallum." Journal of Political Economy 87(April), pp. 403-409.

Smith, R. P. 1977. "Military Expenditures and Capitalism." Cambridge Journal of Economics 1(1), pp. 61-76.

Smith, R. P. 1978. "Military Expenditures and Capitalism: A Reply." Cambridge Journal of Economics 2(3), pp. 299-304.

Smith, R. P. 1980. "Military Expenditure and Investment in OECD Countries, 1954-1973." Journal of Comparative Economics 4, pp. 19-32.

Starr, H., Hoole, F., Hart, J., and Freeman, J. 1984. "The Relationship Between Defense Spending and Inflation." Journal of Conflict Resolution 28(1), pp. 103-122.

Swank, D. H. 1984. "The Political Economy of State Defense Spending in Eighteen Advanced Capitalist Democracies, 1960-1980." Paper prepared for the annual meeting of the American Political Science Association, Washington, D.C., August 30-September 2.

Szymanski, A. 1973. "Military Spending and Economic Stagnation." American Journal of Sociology 79(1), pp. 1-14.

Tarschys, D. 1984. "Good Cuts, Bad Cuts: The Need for Expenditure Analysis in Decremental Budgeting." Scandinavian Political Studies 7(4), pp. 241-259.

Vayrynen, R. 1983. "Military R&D and Science Policy." International Social Science Journal 35(1), pp. 61-79.

Verner, J. G. 1983. "Budgetary Trade-offs between Education and Defense in Latin America: A Research Note." The Journal of Developing Areas 18 (October), pp. 77-91.

Ward, M. D. 1984. "Differential Paths to Parity: A Study of the Contemporary Arms Race." American Political Science Review 78(2), pp. 297-313.

Ward, M. D. and Mahajan, A. K. 1984. "Defense Expenditures, Security Threats, and Governmental Deficits." Journal of Conflict Resolution 28(3), pp. 382-419.

Wildavsky, A. 1964. The Politics of the Budgetary Process. Boston: Little, Brown.

Wilensky, H. 1975. The Welfare State and Equality. Berkeley: University of California Press.

AN ECONOMIC ASSESSMENT OF UNILATERAL NATIONAL DEFENSE

Kenneth E. Boulding

"National defense" is a polite synonym for war and the war industry. The very shift from the term "War Department" to the "Department of Defense" is a symptom of the growing illegitimacy of war as an institution, although this growing illegitimacy has not reached the point where war and the war industry are taboo. In fact, at the moment of writing in 1985 there is a good deal of political enthusiasm for them, especially on the part of President Reagan and his followers. The "war industry" may be defined as that part of the economy which produces what is purchased with the military budget or the national defense budget. In this sense the war industry is certainly part of the economy. It originates, however, not in market demand but in political demand. It is financed almost entirely by what might be called the "public grants economy," financed either by taxation or by public borrowing, or by the creation of money by the public sector.

The place of the war industry in the economy of the United States ever since 1929 is shown quite dramatically in Figure I. I call this a "layercake" diagram, as the different layers represent the changing proportions of the components of the gross capacity product, which is a rough measure of the total size of the economy. The gross capacity product here is defined as what the gross national product would have been if the unemployed had been producing at the average level of labor productivity. This is somewhat inaccurate, but as the two major inaccuracies tend to offset each other, it is probably the best measure that we have in the absence of a much more complex information system. The two offsetting errors are, first, that the unemployed probably would be less productive than the employed part of the labor force if they were employed. This is offset, however, by the fact that the unemployment figure itself underestimates the amount of unemployment as it does not include part-time and "discouraged" workers who have left the labor force.

In Figure I, then, unemployment appears as unrealized product in the top layer. The next small layer is net exports, roughly equivalent -- though, again, not very accurate -- to net exports of real capital from the United States to the rest of the world. This has now become negative -- that is, net imports for the rest of the world is in balance sending real capital to us. The third layer is gross private domestic investment, that is, the gross addition to the value of the real capital stock of businesses and possibly some households. The fourth layer is the war industry as measured by the national defense budget, or rather, expenditures. The next layers are federal civilian purchases and state and local government. The last layer is household purchases.

We see the Great Depression, with unemployment reaching 25 percent of the labor force and the economy by 1932 and 1933, largely the result of the virtual collapse of gross private domestic investment and the failure either of government or of household purchases to take up the

84

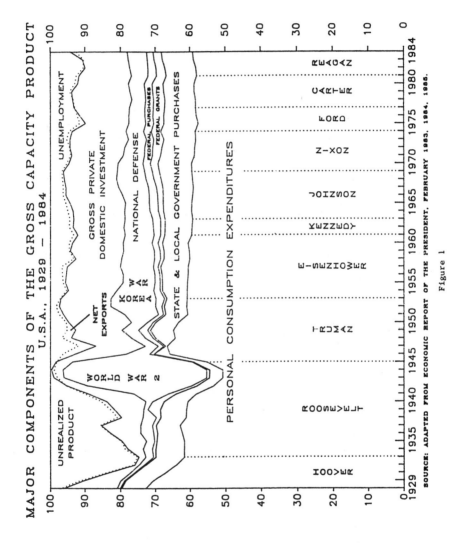

MAJOR COMPONENTS OF THE GROSS CAPACITY PRODUCT
U.S.A., 1929 – 1984

Figure 1

SOURCE: ADAPTED FROM ECONOMIC REPORT OF THE PRESIDENT, FEBRUARY 1983, 1984, 1985.

85

slack. The war industry at this time is very small, in 1929 actually less than 1 percent of the economy. We see what might be called the "civilian recovery" up to 1937, mainly the result of the revival of gross private domestic investment. There was a little depression in 1938, mainly the result of the sudden introduction of Social Security taxes without many payments out of the system. Then from 1938 we see the expansion of the war industry into the Second World War, culminating, of course, in 1944, when it was almost 42 percent of the economy. Then we have the Great Disarmament of 1945-46, when we transferred over 30 percent of the economy from the war industry into civilian industry without unemployment rising much above 3 percent. This was an extraordinary achievement, which oddly enough has not entered our national mythology. There is a national myth that Hitler got us out of the Great Depression, and the evidence shows that he did get us out of half of it, although it is quite likely that if economic policy had been better we could have gotten out of the whole thing by a revival of gross private domestic investment and suitable monetary policy. There is no national myth about the great disarmament, which is strange.

Then we see the beginnings of the Cold War, the Korean War in the early 1950s, when the war industry went to nearly 14 percent of the economy. After that, a long, slow decline in the proportion of the economy occupied by the war industry, a small upsurge in the Vietnam War, which was surprisingly small. Then, of course, the beginning of an upsurge under the Reagan administrations, though this also is not very large. Nevertheless, the war industry has averaged something on the order of 8 to 10 percent of the economy from about 1950 on, as compared with the 1 percent that it was, say, in the 1920s and early 1930s. This is a very marked change and has had a profound effect on the economy.

There is an illusion particularly common among the more politically radical, or even liberal members of society -- by no means unknown among the far right -- that war is essentially an economic phenomenon and that the causes of war are to be found in economic conflict. Hardly any illusion could be further from the truth. War and the war industry are essentially political phenomena, even though they have very profound economic consequences and occasionally economic excuses are given for them. I have suggested that there are three major systems in society which organize the overall patterns of human and social history (Boulding, 1978). One is the threat system, which begins when A says to B: "You do something I want or I will do something you do not want." The dynamics of it then depends on B's response, which may be submission, defiance, flight, counterthreat, or threat-diminution structures or behaviors. The second is the exchange system, which originates when A says to B: "You do something I want and I will do something you want." This leads into trade, the production of goods, business, finance, and so on. The third is the integrative system, which is harder to identify, but which involves such things as perceptions of identity, legitimacy, community, friendship, enmity, and so on. All human institutions actually involve mixtures of all three. Political institutions rest more heavily on threat; economic institutions on exchange; and cultural institutions, like the church and the family, rest more on integrative relationships.

Threat systems are of two kinds, depending on the admixture of integrative, and to some extent exchange, components. We have what we might call internal threat, such as the system of law, criminal justice, taxation, and so on, in which the threats are rather specific on the part of the threatener, such as "If you exceed the speed limit you will be fined fifty dollars," or "If you don't pay your income tax, your property will be constrained, or you may even go to jail." These internal threats are largely accepted as legitimate, with two exceptions: the "saint," for whom the threat of the law may conflict with higher moral obligations; and the criminal, who submits only when the threats of the law actually are carried out. Internal threat is also important in the family, especially in the raising of children. Virtually all organizations appeal to it in some degree.

Then we have what might be described as the external threat system, of which the principal institutional representative is unilateral national defense organizations, like the United States Department of Defense and its equivalents in the other nations. There is a shifting integrative structure in the international system consisting of international law, treaties, diplomats, and a good deal of custom and taboo. But the international system, on the whole, is one of weak integrative structures as compared with domestic law and politics, as the very word "domestic" suggests. Nationalism is a kind of extension of the ethic of the family to national states. The ethic of the stranger outside the family applies to people of other nations.

Each of these three social organizers seems to produce a corresponding set of psychological attitudes, motivations, and ethical patterns. The exchange system, not surprisingly, has a tendency to produce what might be called an "economic pattern" of valuation, decision making, and behavior. In addition, it might almost be called the "accounting pattern" because it always involves something like a "bottom line." Perhaps in part this is because exchange develops a relative price structure, which is a very convenient way of measuring complex evaluation structures. The balance sheet is an economic institution par excellence. It lists assets, which we value positively, and liabilities, which we value negatively. It evaluates these in terms of a monetary unit, it adds up the values of the heterogeneous assets and subtracts the equally heterogeneous group of liabilities, and the result is net worth, the bottom line.

One of the most characterestic institutions of economic life is cost-benefit analysis, in which we evaluate all the diverse heterogeneous items in a situation according to some common "numeraire," such as the dollar. We add the plusses and subtract the minuses and come out with some kind of roughly quantitative answer that we can then compare with alternatives. An economic decision is one in which we contemplate an array of possible futures, evaluate the various components in monetary units, compute the net worth or bottom line for each using discounting for the future or for uncertainty if necessary, and then choose the one that has the highest net worth at the moment of choice. Cost-benefit analysis is even supposed to guide political decisions, as in building a dam, a throughway or a bridge. It also guides personal decisions, although often very roughly, in choosing a spouse, buying a home, taking another job, going to the doctor, or even having children. Many of these bottom lines we evaluate very roughly, like our state of health or the success of our marriage. When the bottom line becomes negative we get really worried.

The test of economic behavior is the question, "Is it worth it?" Economists have a profound conviction that everybody does what he or she thinks is best at the time. This principle (which it seems hard to get people to admit they do not follow) is capable of surprising mathematical elaboration in the theory of maximizing behavior. Economists also tend to favor a marginalist approach: If we do a little bit more of A, this means that we will have a little less of B, and is what we gain in a little more of A worth what we lose in a little less of B? Even the artist in deciding where to put the horizon in painting a landscape follows the economist's equimarginal principle. He puts it where a little more sky isn't worth the loss of a little less land or sea in the picture.

Curiously enough, both the threat and the integrative systems have in them a strong element of rejection of economic behavior. They often advocate a "heroic" rather than an economic ethic. Both the soldier and the saint here have something in common: "To give and not to count the cost, to labor and ask for no reward." There is something of this also in the mountaineer and the rock climber. And we find it generated even in competitive sports. There is an "all or nothing" ethic that denies and despises marginalism, perhaps because it thinks there are infinite values. This is the ethic of "winning" at whatever cost; the fight to death; climbing Mount Everest "because it is there"; the joyful martyr to a noble cause; the crucified Christ — did Jesus do a cost-benefit analysis of that trip to Jerusalem?

War is a very strange mixture of threat and integrative structures, with the economic aspects very much in the background. The hero rejects the economist saying, "Tut, tut, you mustn't go too far," or Adam Smith saying, "Among the civilized nations of modern Europe . . . not more than one hundredth part of the inhabitants of any country can be employed as soldiers, without ruin to the country that pays the expence of their service" (Smith, 1776/1937, pp. 657-658).

There is, of course, another side to the heroic ethic, even in war. Sociological studies of the military suggest that soldiers don't really die for their country; they die for their buddies. The military creates a very close integrative structure under the stress of battle and actual combat. The military indeed tends to be a subculture very much isolated from the rest of society, cut off in camps, reservations, military bases, and so on, almost a nation within a nation. The military organization is much more like a church than it is like a corporation, even though strategy and tactics are not wholly unknown to corporations. The overriding difference, however, between economic organizations and the military arises from the fact that

88

exchange, at least so economists think, is a positive-sum game in which both parties benefit, whereas threat is always a negative-sum game, in which the winner wins less than the loser loses.

Nevertheless, it is hard for an economist not to see human history as an ongoing evolutionary process in which institutions, ideas, and habits of behavior, which do not "pay off" in some sense, have a poorer chance of surviving than those that do pay off. The feudal system did not survive the invention of gunpowder and the efficient cannon, which destroyed the threat-reduction capability of castles and city walls. Duelling did not survive the development of the efficient pistol. The collapse of empire in the last generation is very closely related to the proposition, for which there is a great deal of evidence, that empire did not pay the imperial powers, that it was a brain drain, a capital drain, that it diverted their attention from the real business of getting richer. Sweden, for instance, which was a very poor country in 1860, got richer much faster than Britain and France did between 1860 and, say, 1950, because it stayed home and minded its business well and had a purely defensive war industry that really didn't threaten anybody else. Even Britain and France have gotten richer much faster since they unloaded their empires than they did before. Japan is an even more spectacular case.

There are indeed a good many economic and cultural benefits of defeat in war. Paris became the cultural capital of the world after France was defeated by Germany in 1870. Berlin remained hopelessly provincial. Berlin became an extraordinary cultural center between 1919 and 1932 with the development of the Bauhaus and the great upsurge of art and literature, like the "Blue Riders" and Brecht. There is no doubt that it was Japan and Germany, especially West Germany, who won the Second World War economically, largely because they got rid of the burden of the military and were able to devote an unusually large proportion of their resources to getting richer. Like all attractive propositions, this one has exceptions. Carthage did not do very well after the Punic Wars and Islam never seems to have recovered from the Mongol invasions. But every conqueror who conquered China seems to have perked it up a bit and become Chinese in the process, whereas it was under the native Ming emperors that China stagnated and failed to respond to the rise of science. A good deal of official history here clearly needs to be reexamined.

Whether we should go for an economic or a heroic, romantic approach to national defense clearly has something to do with what a cost-benefit analysis would reveal. In some situations we might very well have a very low or even a negative bottom line, or an excess of costs over benefits, and still feel that considerations of more absolute values or of some heroic and romantic ethic have to be taken into consideration. At some point, however, as costs rise and benefits fall, economics must take over. If the chance of being killed while climbing Mt. Everest were 100 percent, it is doubtful whether anybody would do it. To give and not to count the costs may be fine up to a point, but if giving results in the ruin both of the giver and the recipient, then somebody has to count the costs. If somebody says they would rather be dead than red, this is a legitimate

89

personal privilege. If somebody says they would rather have everybody dead rather than anybody red, then cost-benefit analysis had better come into play.

The development of the nuclear weapon has clearly put the whole institution of unilateral national defense into a situation where the costs are potentially so totally devastating and the benefits so obscure that the heroic ethic simply has to be abandonned and cost-benefit analysis has to be applied. In this case, costs are much easier to estimate than benefits, but there are grave difficulties even in estimating costs. But when the costs seem to outweigh the benefits to such an enormous extent, some attempt must be made to estimate both. The costs of the war industry are not confined to economic costs. There may well be moral costs, social and psychological costs that have to be considered. The economic costs are perhaps the most tractable. Economic costs consist, first, of the potential product of the alternative use of the resources employed in the war industry. If the only alternative use is unemployment, then the economic costs are very low and may even be an economic benefit.

The evidence suggests, however, that there are alternatives to the war industry that consist either in a larger amount of civilian investment, which would make future generations richer, or increased domestic consumption, which makes us richer right away. Comparing the situation of the United States economy as between, say, 1929, when the war industry was less than 1 percent and, say, the situation in the 1960s, when the war industry reached about 7 to 9 percent, the cost clearly can be expressed in terms of the reduction in gross private domestic investment, in civilian government, and in household purchases. Whether these alternatives can be realized, of course, depends on the economic policies and practices, mainly of government but also to some extent of the private sector, but there is every reason to suppose that there is no nonexistence theorem about an economy of this sort being well managed, in which the war industry can be replaced by civilian occupations that make us richer. A sudden reduction of the war industry, of course, would cause some dislocations and redistributions of economic welfare, but the experience of 1945-46 certainly suggests that the American economy at least is extraordinarily flexible and that these adjustments can be made or, if not, can be easily compensated for.

The economic costs of the war industry are not confined to immediate sacrifices in the production of goods for civilian enjoyment which the absorption of resources by the war industry entails. There may also be very important long-run costs that arise through two major sources. One is the fact that the war industry represents an internal "brain drain," which drains out of civilian industry some of the best scientists and engineers, and hence leads to a decline in the rate of increase in productivity in civilian industry. This has been very striking in the United States, where the rate of increase of productivity diminished very sharply in the 1970s, to the point where in one or two years productivity even decreased. The extraordinary economic success of Japan in the last thirty years or so is closely related to the fact that it had virtually no war industry. Hence there was nothing to divert its intellectual resources from the delightful occupation of getting richer. The scientists and engineers in the United States who should have been designing Hondas in Detroit were probably designing missiles for Lockheed.

The other effect of the war industry, well documented by Seymour Melman and others, is that it develops a culture within the war industry firms of extravagance, indifference to costs, and technological wastefulness, inspired by the fact that even quite large mistakes will be covered by increased public expenditures (Melman, 1974). There is some point, of course, at which the political system rears back and says that it has had enough, but it seems to take a long time to reach it. What is worse is that the culture of inefficiency and waste, which is an almost essential concommitant of the war industry, spills over into the rest of the economy in a kind of penumbra and creates a psychological situation that is unfavorable to economy, carefulness, productivity, and development.

Counteracting this there are the spillovers from the technology in the war industry into civilian industry. We would certainly not have had nuclear power if it had not been for the Manhattan Project. Computers would probably have developed a little more slowly had it not been for the war industry. On the other hand, here again, the evidence suggests that the spillovers from the war industry seem to have pathologies of their own (Dumas, 1982). The most striking example of this, of course, is the light-water reactor, which came out of Shippingport and the nuclear submarine. There is little doubt now that this has been an economic disaster for the public utilities. While some excuse might be found for this disaster in overregulation and delays, the Three Mile Island incident showed that breakdowns in nuclear power plants might not be terribly dangerous to the surrounding public, but are enormously expensive. Whether we would have done better by going to civilian-based nuclear power, like the gas-cooled reactor or the CANDU -- that is, the Canadian heavy-water reactor -- is a question that without a good deal of further research is difficult to answer, but at least there is some probability that we might have discovered alternatives to the light-water reactor that are much more economical if we had not been in such a hurry to beats swords into plowshares. The trouble seems to be that swords don't make very good plowshares and if we want plowshares it is much better to make them directly.

Another case in point is the impact of the war industry on sophisticated computerized machine tools, which also seems to have been very unsuccessful (Dumas, 1982). Curiously enough, there is evidence that the National Aeronautics and Space Administration (NASA), even though it has a strong military component, has had much more successful spillovers, which is hardly surprising, because its main business has been to increase human knowledge rather than to develop a capability for enormous destruction.

Estimating the benefits of unilateral national defense is an almost impossible task, and yet it is obviously one that cannot be ignored. There are at least two kinds of war, with very different kinds of benefits. One is

91

the war of conquest, which produces annexation of territory to the victor. The conquest of the indigenous peoples in the Americas and in Australia, New Zealand, etc. is a case in point. Where the technology and culture of the conquerors is such that they have a much larger ecological niche than the conquered (as was certainly the case in the Americas, Australia, and New Zealand) there may be ultimate benefits even for the conquered if they can adapt, which, however, they frequently cannot. Even the Norman conquest of Britain produced more impressive architecture than the Saxons had and may not have impoverished the Saxons much, although it left a political legacy and a class structure that persists to this day.

In the modern world, however, there is nothing much left to conquer. To an extraordinary extent, even in the twentieth century the world has become a total system economically and even socially and conquest has paid off very poorly. About the only war of conquest in the twentieth century was that which led to the foundation of Israel and the human cost of this has been very high, although there are undoubtedly benefits as well. One could visualize a situation in the Middle East in which Israel made all the surrounding countries richer. This could well be the case if there were stable peace in that area. Both Napoleon's and Hitler's attempted conquests of Russia were utter failures. We have noted earlier the collapse of the concept of empire in the last forty years, partly as a result of the realization that empire simply did not pay the imperial powers and that the costs of conquest far exceeded the benefits to the conqueror. It would not be surprising if the Russians and the Chinese also find this out within a decade or two. There is a good deal of evidence that their "empires" impoverish them. Ethiopia is an even more shocking case.

Even if we look at conquest as an attempt to increase the food supply of a society, it seems pretty clear that devoting resources to increasing the yield of crops pays off at a very much higher rate of return than devoting resources to the conquest of new lands. The same goes even for natural resources like oil and minerals. The West clearly decided that it was cheaper to pay tribute to OPEC than it was to try to conquer it, and they were almost certainly right in this. The classic American statement, "Millions for defense, but not a penny for tribute," unfortunately does not stand up to economic analysis, which often reveals that tribute is much cheaper than defense. This could easily be true up to a point in regard to crime. There may come some point indeed at which defense is cheaper than tribute, but to assume that this is always so is a romantic illusion.

The moral and psychological costs of the war industry are harder to estimate, but they may be very real. The problem here arises from the fact that the difference between war and peace is essentially defined by what might be called the position of the "taboo line." Within the possibility boundary, beloved of economists, which divides what we can do from what we cannot do, there is a taboo line which divides what we can do and do not do from what we can do and do do. Peace has two aspects. In one sense it is everything that is not war: plowing, sowing, reaping, manufacturing, getting married, having children, having fun, singing, dancing, practicing the arts, and so on. In another sense, peace is a negative concept. It is refraining from doing things that we have the power to do -- that is, it represents what lies on the near side of the taboo line: In peace we do not bomb cities, we do not invade other countries, the military are not being used for their destructive power. Once war begins, however, the taboo line starts to shift. Sometimes it shifts only a little way and then stops, as in Grenada. Sometimes there is nothing to stop it, and we end up with the taboo line right next to the possibility boundary, doing everything we can do in the way of destruction. The Second World War is a good case in point. It started off with the so-called "phony war," in which there were no civilian bombings; it ended with the roasting alive of 300,000 or 400,000 people in Nagasaki, Hiroshima, and Dresden, which can hardly be called anything but genocide, about the moral equivalent of Auschwitz. Even Hitler's war against the Jews began with the day of broken glass and ended with Dachau and Auschwitz. These are very high moral and psychological costs of the institution of war and we never know when they may have to be paid.

The other source of war is, of course, the breakdown of deterrence. Deterrence is the threat-counterthreat system: You do something nasty to me and I will do something nasty to you. It is the search for deterrence and the theory of mutually assured destruction (MAD) that has persuaded the political structures of both the United States and the Soviet Union to invest so heavily in overkill in nuclear weapons, and to indulge in a very large research and development program that seems to be designed to bring the extinction of the human race a little closer. The truth about deterrence is that it can be stable in the short run, but it cannot be stable in the long run. If it were stable in the long run it would cease to deter. If the probability of nuclear weapons going off were zero they would not deter anybody in the short run. In order for deterrence to operate in the short run, there must be some probability that it will break down. Historically, it has always broken down into war. The First World War was a good example; the Second World War might be cited as a war of failure of deterrence rather than a breakdown, but that is a nice historical point.

There is no doubt in the present situation that there is some positive probability of the nuclear weapons going off, even on a fairly large scale. It is easy to talk about limited nuclear war until one asks, What is the machinery for limiting it? The answer is, none. Just as one can say with a great deal of confidence about the future that San Francisco will be destroyed by an earthquake in X years, so we can also say that if the present system of unilateral national defense continues, the United States and the Soviet Union will destroy not only each other but perhaps the whole human race and bring the evolutionary process to a halt on this planet. If Jonathan Schell (1982) and Carl Sagan (1983) are right about "nuclear winter," as they may well be -- at least there is some probability that they may be right -- then all we have to do is to multiply that probability with the probability of nuclear war to get the probability of human destruction and irrecoverable catastrophe. If we want to calculate the benefits, therefore, of unilateral national defense, we must put it at the present value of the probability of the eventual destruction of the human race. If we value the human race at X quadrillion dollars, whatever it is, then we put minus this amount on the bottom line of unilateral national defense, including the United States Department of Defense. Even unilateral disarmament certainly has a higher bottom line than this. It could even be positive, although perhaps small. We do not even have to go to this extent though. We can develop a national policy for national security through stable peace, which is the only national security now available. The probability that we would get this is by no means 1.0, but it is a positive number, so that the bottom line of such a policy is also a positive number. As between the bottom line which gives a chance, no matter how small, of a positive number and the bottom line which is a certainty of total destruction, the economic choice is for the riskiest chance of real security. We have now gotten to the point where national defense is the greatest enemy of national security. If we don't get rid of it, it will get rid of us.

REFERENCES

Boulding, K. E. (1978) Ecodynamics: A New Theory of Societal Evolution Beverly Hills, California: Sage.

Dumas, Lloyd, ed. (1982) The Political Economy of Arms Reduction: Reversing Economic Decay Boulder, Colorado: Westview Press.

Melman, Seymour (1974) The Permanent War Economy: American Capitalism in Decline New York: Simon & Schuster.

Sagan, Carl (1983) "Nuclear War and Climatic Catastrophe," Foreign Affairs, 62, (2): 257-292.

Schell, Jonathan (1982) The Fate of the Earth New York: Alfred A. Knopf.

Smith, Adam (1776/1937) The Wealth of Nations New York: Random House Modern Library Edition.

THE PRESIDENT AND THE POLITICS OF MILITARY FORCE

Charles W. Ostrom, Jr. and Dennis M. Simon

Introduction

Discussions of the American presidency, in both academic and political circles, commonly emphasize that the "war powers" associated with the office are substantial. For example, President Harry Truman once observed that the military powers of the office "would have made Caesar, Genghis Khan, or Napoleon bite their nails with envy." Nearly thirty years later, historian Arthur Schlesinger, Jr. (1973) argued that "the American President had become on issues of war and peace the most absolute monarch (with the possible exception of Mao Tse-tung of China) among the great powers of the world." The exercise of these war powers has assumed a variety of forms over the past forty years. Presidents have ordered quick military strikes to rescue imperiled American personnel (e.g. Mayaguez), military incursions designed to influence the domestic politics of small countries (e.g. Grenada), mobilization of force to limit the expansion of hostilities (e.g. Mideast War of 1973), the use of air and naval forces in superpower confrontations (e.g., Cuban Missile Crisis), and troops to combat in protracted wars with limited objectives (e.g. Vietnam). Our concern in this paper focuses on presidential decisions to exercise this broad range of war powers. The objective of the discussion is to formulate an explanation of presidential decision making as it pertains to the control, deployment, and use of the military.

The thesis of this paper is that there is a striking uniformity in presidential decisions to exercise the "war powers." We will argue that this uniformity is the result of a domestic political system which requires all modern presidents (Greenstein, 1978) to assume the same role in the foreign arena, to pursue the same foreign policy goals, and to engage in the same struggle to preserve their power and influence over government policy making. These similarities in the structure of the domestic political system and the incentives which it creates makes the use of military action an attractive and, at times, compelling alternative for occupants of the modern office, Presidents Truman through Reagan. Indeed, this uniformity of behavior exists despite the seemingly different personalities of modern presidents and the diverse international situations they faced while in office.

To support this thesis, we will develop four basic arguments. First, there is a strong, institutionalized role which provides the president with the mechanisms, rationales, and discretion for using military force. Second, the development of this role created expectations which impose three specific goals on the conduct of American foreign policy: action, anti-communism, and containment. Third, in order to satisfy these expectations,

95

presidents must acquire and maintain political power; this need for power creates an incentive to use military force. Fourth, there is a reciprocal relationship between presidential power and decision making.

Our explanation will be presented in the following manner. The first four sections of the paper will focus upon the basic elements of the domestic political structure: roles, goals, power, and the reciprocal relationship. In the fifth section, we turn to the task of explaining presidential decisions to use military force. Here, we will rely upon both cybernetic and cognitive theories to develop a model of decision making which includes the reciprocal relationship between power and presidential choice. The next section offers several propositions derived from the model and evaluates these using data on public opinion and the uses of force. The paper then concludes with a discussion of the politics of presidential war making.

Presidential Roles

A role refers to the tasks or set of behaviors that the president is assigned and expected to perform during his tenure in office. These roles define the substantive arenas in which presidents will operate, create vantage points for presidential action, and specify the responsibilities of the president in that arena. These roles are the product of the Constitution, presidential actions, decisions rendered by the Supreme Court, and statutes enacted by the Congress.

The Constitution: An Ambiguous Grant of Power

With respect to the war powers, the most obvious characteristic of the Constitution is ambiguity. The Constitution vests the executive power in the president and designates him as the commander-in-chief (Article 2, Section 2, 2). The president is assigned responsibility for receiving ambassadors and other foreign ministers and shares the power to make treaties and appoint ambassadors with the Senate. This grant of authority is both vague and meager. These characteristics are a reflection of the disputes among delegates to the constitutional convention and the political nature of the document. Because factions opposed to a strong executive possessed the capacity to deadlock the proceedings, compromise was required if any document was to be produced.

From the standpoint of presidential authority, two compromises are important. First, the framers devised a system of separate but competing institutions sharing decision making authority. An independent executive branch was created but its operation would be limited by two competing branches -- congress and the judiciary. Competition over decision making authority would be ensured by a system of checks and balances. Second, because any detailed enumeration of the president's powers threatened to disrupt the convention, silence and ambiguous phrasing were used to preserve an already delicate set of compromises. As a result, the war powers of the national government were left as a vast "gray area". The question of whether the decision to make war belongs to the president (via the commander-in-chief title) or to the Congress (via its authority to declare war) was left unresolved.

This silence provides the president with considerable flexibility. It allows him to lay claim to authority not specifically mentioned in the Constitution. As Pious notes (1979, p. 47), when a president asserts such a claim and acts unilaterally, he is instituting government by prerogative. The consequences of such an action depend not on the Constitution per se but upon the reactions of other decision makers. The Constitution simply puts the president and competing decision makers into the "ring" and leaves it to the political process to determine whether an assertion of prerogative will be accepted or rejected by the coordinate branches.

The Modern Presidency: Preeminence in Foreign Affairs

Beginning with the administration of Franklin Roosevelt, the decisions of both the Supreme Court and the Congress institutionalized a unique and preeminent role for the president in foreign and military policy. The Supreme Court declared the president to be the "sole organ of federal government in the field of international relations" who could exercise authority which "did not depend upon the affirmative grants of the Constitution" (U.S. v. Curtiss-Wright; see Pyle and Pious, pp. 236-238). Moreover, throughout the modern era, the judicial system has been most reluctant to rule against presidential exercises of authority in foreign and military affairs. The courts have upheld the use of executive agreements [U.S. v. Belmont (1937)], dismissed challenges to the exercise of war powers during the Vietnam era (Pyle and Pious, pp. 342-361), and supported the prerogative of presidents to abrogate treaties [Goldwater v. Carter (1979)]. Thus, the judicial system has been instrumental in establishing and maintaining the president's preeminent position in foreign affairs.

The laws and resolutions of Congress also consolidated and expanded the authority of the president. In the National Security Act of 1947, the president was provided with potent organizations and near-monopoly control over information and expertise (e.g. the DOD, NSC, and CIA). Resolutions passed by Congress emphasized that the president was responsible for the deployment and use of the military (e.g. Gulf of Tonkin). The ratification of the treaties which marked the entry of the United States into a system of military alliances multiplied the pretexts for using military force (e.g. NATO).

In sum, the actions of the coordinate branches created a role which far exceeds the enumerated powers given the president by the Constitution. The role provides the president with the mechanisms, rationales, and discretion for exercising military force. It also creates expectations about how that discretion should be exercised.

Expectations and Goals

While the role of Foreign Policy Leader enhances the authority of the office, it also multiplies the demands on the president. The politics which accompanied the development of this role created a variety of expectations about how presidents should behave and the goals they should pursue while in office. Expectations have three prominent characteristics. They are imposed on the president because it is believed that the office provides any incumbent with the authority and the means to satisfy them. These expectations are common in the sense that they are shared by the public at large, opinion elites, rival decision makers, and the president's political opposition. Finally, expectations serve as "perceptual filters" used to select and interpret information about the environment. As such, they identify the elements of the political environment that are important to monitor; they are also used to arrive at judgments about the quality of conditions and events in the environment AND whether the president is performing in a satisfactory manner. It is in this sense that expectations lead to the imposition of the same goals on modern presidents.

In the realm of foreign and military affairs, there are three dominant goals which developed on a parallel track with the modern role of the president: a preference for action, anti-communism, and containment of the Soviet Union. The preference for action is a product of the need to fill a "power vacuum" in the years after 1945 and the historical "lessons" (e.g. Munich) which reversed the isolationist tendency in American Foreign Policy. The goal of anti-communism is based upon three common perceptions of communism -- its diabolic nature, its expansionistic tendencies, and its monolithic structure. Finally, because the American view of communism also recognized Moscow as the "control center" of this international movement, it was believed that the United States must use "any means necessary" to contain Soviet expansionism and prevent the formation of new communist regimes (see Kegley and Wittkopf, 1982, for similar discussion).

The Enduring Nature of the Goals

Although the facts and interpretations underlying these goals have been the subject of much debated, there is overwhelming evidence that these goals were shared by foreign policy decision makers, opinion elites, and the public. Moreover, the goals have endured since 1945. From "massive retaliation" to "counterinsurgency warfare," the strategic doctrines articulated by modern presidents were justified in the political arena as necessary for the achievement of these goals.

The universal and enduring character of these goals is due to a variety of factors. First, they were reinforced by events. The Soviet sphere of influence in Eastern Europe, the Soviet nuclear capability, the fall of China, and the attack of South Korea are among the most prominent. Second, the goals were reinforced by domestic politics. The political damage suffered by the Truman Administration for "fall of China" and the

98

resulting McCarthy movement provided a lesson to all subsequent presidents. As a result, anti-communism became an "acid test" for all aspiring politicians; "soft on communism" remains one of the most dangerous accusations against a political candidate. In sum, domestic politics taught decision makers that to argue or to act against these goals was to invite political challenge and electoral defeat.

As a result, these goals are critical for understanding decision making in the White House. The goals create a predisposition to monitor certain aspects of the environment. They condition certain types of actions and responses as well. Thus, they are a source of continuity for studying presidential decisions to use military force.

Presidential Power

The previous sections have established that the role as Foreign Policy Leader provides the president with discretion for exercising the war powers and that the enduring goals of American foreign policy specify the ends that such exercises are intended to achieve. While important, roles and goals are not sufficient for explaining the decision to use military force. It is also necessary to consider whether the president possesses the political power to act. This section is designed to explain the importance of presidential power as a common goal shared by all modern presidents.

The Need for Power

The general task of modern presidents is to influence the environment by exercising control over the actions and policies of the national government. All presidents must attempt to direct and coordinate the machinery of government to maintain or restore desirable states in the domestic, international, and economic arenas. The need for power arises because of the structure of the government and the resulting character of the policy making process. The primary feature of Washington politics is that formal decision making authority is fragmented among multiple "pockets of power" -- the president, the cabinet, careerists in the bureaus and agencies of the executive branch, congressional committees and subcommittees -- each pursuing their own objectives, each responsible to different constituencies, and each exercising checks upon the authority of other decision makers. The president encounters conflict over the priority of problems, their proposed solutions, and the timing of government action. As a matter of general strategy, the president cannot rely upon command or the assertion of prerogative (see, for example, Neustadt, 1980, pp. 9-23). Instead, he must acquire the leverage and influence needed to cause competing decision makers to act in a manner consistent with his agenda and goals. The need for power arises, therefore, from the president's position in a decentralized system of policy making.

A Definition of Presidential Power

In a widely acclaimed analysis first published in 1960, Richard Neustadt defined presidential power (or influence) as the ability to persuade other decision makers to do what they otherwise would not do. The task involved is to convince decision makers that acting in accord with presidential wishes is the best alternative for pursuing their own self interest. Viewed in this light, power is not automatically conferred upon the occupant of the White House. It is not constant during the tenure of a single president or for different presidents. Rather, power is ephemeral. It is also subjective. The effectiveness of presidential persuasion rests largely upon the perceptions of those who are the potential targets of the president's efforts.

Neustadt's analysis identifies three factors which influence these perceptions. The first are vantage points conferred upon the office by the Constitution and its interpretation, statutes and tradition. Vantage points are associated with the president's ability to act unilaterally. Neustadt's analysis demonstrates that vantage points, while providing the president with bargaining leverage, are not sufficient for the exercise or power.

For Neustadt, reputation and prestige are the needed ingredients (1980, pp. 44-79). Reputation pertains to the judgments of other decision makers about the president's skill as a politician. Such judgments are based upon a willingness and ability to play the "insider" game, to protect and reward allies, and to maximize the political discomfort of adversaries. Prestige refers to the president's standing outside the Washington community, primarily his standing with the American public. The basic measure of prestige is public support, a measure produced by national surveys in which citizens are asked whether they approve or disapprove of the way an incumbent is handling his job as president. As the foremost indicator of prestige, these polls provide an indication of whether "it is wise or foolish to resist presidential persuasion" (Brody and Page, 1975, p. 136).

The Value of Public Support

With respect to presidential power, the significance of public support is tied to its value as a determinant of public and congressional behaviors deemed important by the president. There is considerable evidence for such a connection. Evaluations of presidential performance will exert an impact on the results of both presidential (e.g. Brody and Sigelman, 1983) and congressional (e.g. Tufte, 1978) election campaigns. Consequently, public support is connected to the president's electoral fortunes as well as the party balance in Congress.

Evaluations of presidential performance also exert a direct impact on congressional decision making. Evidence shows that public support is related to roll call support for members of Congress (Edwards, 1980), presidential victories on roll calls (Ostrom and Simon, 1985), and the congressional response to presidential vetoes (Rohde and Simon, 1985). In addition, the history of the modern presidency reveals that the congressional response to presidential claims of "prerogative power" will vary with public support. When public support is high, what Pious (1979, p. 50) terms the frontlash effect is likely. Congress will be inclined to grant broad delegations of authority and not to challenge unilateral presidential actions. However, when public support is low, backlash or its more virulent form, overshoot and collapse, is the probable result (Pious, 1979, pp. 60-69). Attacks on the president become commonplace and congressional investigations exploit his growing vulnerability.

This evidence leads to the conclusion that public support is a valuable commodity for the president. It provides presidents with a resource or form of political currency which can be used, as Neustadt's power discussion implies, to pursue the task of exerting influence on both the government and the environment.

The Perpetual Election and a Common Presidential Goal

Of the three ingredients of power identified by Neustadt, public support is the most important. There are several reasons for this conclusion. First, as noted previously, a strategy which relies solely upon vantage points and the assertion of prerogative is limited. Second, according to Neustadt (1980, p. 165), the distinction between prestige and reputation has eroded; public support is thus an increasingly important consideration in the behavior of rival decision makers. Third, public support is also a more dynamic element than other factors which give the president "an edge" (e.g. election margins, the partisan and ideological composition of Congress). Such factors are fixed or initial conditions and cannot account, therefore, for the substantial variations in the power of the president over the course of the term.

Finally, evaluations of presidential performance stimulate much interest and attention among both decision makers and opinion elites. Presidential performance polls have become "a part of America's unwritten Constitution (quoted in Cantril, 1980, p. 48). The result is a "perpetual election" (Hodgson, 1980, pp. 210-11) wherein presidents are subjected to continuous scrutiny and evaluation. The context created by this perpetual election means that the need for public support is ever-present.

Our consideration of power, public support, and the perpetual election lead to several important conclusions. The operation of public support as a resource creates an incentive for presidents to control how they are evaluated by the public. Presidents must maintain a level of support necessary to preserve their influence over other decision makers. The perpetual election means that this need for public support never abates. It is central to the day-to-day conduct of the office and the ability of the president to satisfy the expectations placed on the office. As such, acquiring the political influence generated by high levels of public support is a COMMON GOAL shared by all modern presidents.

The Determinants of Public Support

To uncover the incentives for using military force created by this need for power and resources, it is necessary to consider the determinants of public support. In general, public support is a function of public expectations, environmental outcomes, and the relative salience of problems (Ostrom and Simon, 1985). The combination of these factors means that citizens hold presidents responsible for maintaining a reasonable quality of life and expect presidents to be astute managers of crises and events. Because of such expectations, public support varies with the following outcomes: unemployment, inflation, battle casualties, actions and rhetoric directed at the Soviet Union, the introduction and passage of domestic programs, scandals, domestic unrest, international crises and diplomatic initiatives.

The Political Incentives to Use Military Force

A comparison of these determinants of public support reveals that the incentives for using military force are particularly strong. Here, we will use as a basis of comparison the three roles of the modern president -- Foreign Policy Leader, Economic Manager, and Domestic Policy Initiator. Let us first consider the ease of presidential action in influencing these determinants. Control of the economy requires the president to exert substantial influence over the Congress whose "power of the purse" grants them jurisdiction over the major components of fiscal policy, taxing and spending. Similarly, domestic program initiation demands that considerable time and resources be directed toward Capitol Hill (Light, 1982). In general, these roles require a legislative strategy. The exercise of war powers, however, does not depend upon a cumbersome legislative process. The president can choose to act unilaterally.

Another comparison pertains to the consequences of presidential action in each arena. Quite often economic management and domestic policy making involve divisive issues of redistribution (e.g. Reagan's budget cuts). When presidents act on such issues, they suffer an immediate penalty; they will trigger a "coalition of minorities" effect and lose the support of those who are opposed to the policy initiative (Ostrom and Simon, 1985; Mueller, 1973). The political benefits of action in these arenas will be substantial and relatively enduring. To gain such rewards, however, the president's proposals must be passed and then work in the sense of improving the environment. Further, there may be a substantial lag time between implementation of the program and its impact on the environment.

Unlike the divisions which are activated when presidents venture into redistributive politics, action in the foreign arena typically generates a "we-they" perspective and a "rally-round-the-flag effect" (Mueller, 1973). As a result, the use of military force typically has two short-term consequences. First, it generates an immediate increase in public support. The use of force, particularly if it is accompanied by harsh rhetoric toward the Soviets, satisfies the expectations of action, drama, anti-communism, and containment. Second, military action diverts public attention from divisive domestic or economic issues and focuses it on the foreign arena. Because of the rally effect and the consensus surrounding the enduring foreign policy goals, public support will increase as the relative salience of foreign policy issues increase.

A final comparison pertains to the costs of inaction. In the domestic and economic arenas, presidents can blame delay and deadlock on either the opposition party, as President Reagan did with the Social Security issue in 1982, or on vested interests, as President Carter did on the energy issue in 1978. In foreign affairs, however, presidents cannot afford this luxury; the role of modern presidents clearly place responsibility for action on the president. Therefore, the costs of inaction are potentially great. This is certainly the lesson derived by presidents since the "fall of China" in 1949.

The political incentive to use force is clear. The exercise of war powers has the potential to generate an immediate increase in public support, divert attention from divisive domestic and economic problems, and create "windows of opportunity" for the passage of policies designed to exert a long-run impact on the environment. There are, however, substantial risks associated with the decision to use force. First, history shows that presidents will incur a loss of support if the use of force is perceived to be unsuccessful (e.g. the Iranian rescue attempt) or if it leads to prolonged hostilities with little evidence of "victory" (e.g. Korea, Vietnam). Second, the use of force is a contested power and involves an assertion of presidential prerogative. For this reason, it may trigger a backlash effect in Congress resulting in criticism and legislation designed to reduce the president's authority and flexibility. Politically, then, the use of force is not cost free. Indeed, as we will show in the next section, the political consequences of using force will depend upon the level of public support.

Power and Decision Making: A Reciprocal Relationship

A final characteristic of the political structure concerns the relationship between presidential power and decision making. Our discussion in previous section reveals that there are a variety of available levers for exercising control over public support. However, there remains the question of the president's ability to "pull" the levers. To influence outcomes or engage in political drama, the president needs the leverage and credibility which public support provides. It is required to build the coalitions necessary for passing policy initiatives and to prevent the backlash which can arise from the assertion of prerogative. Low or declining levels of support translate into a declining probability of success for subsequent presidential initiatives. As Neustadt (1980, p. 69) observes, "a President's prestige ... may not decide the outcome in a given case but can affect the likelihoods in every case and therefore is strategically important to his power."

Thus, public support will influence what presidents are able to do and what they choose to do. Without public support, the president "may not be left helpless, but his options are reduced, his opportunities diminished, his freedom for maneuver checked in the degree that Washington conceives him unimpressive to the public" (Neustadt, 1980, p. 67). This implies that presidential support and decision making are RECIPROCALLY related. On one hand, presidential decision making will influence public support to the extent that the choices of the president successfully influence outcomes or generate drama sufficient to trigger the rally effect. On the other hand, because public support determines the probability that presidential actions will be politically successful, it will influence the choices made by presidents. President Kennedy's maxim that "there is no sense in raising hell, and then not being successful" rings true (Schlesinger, 1965, p. 651).

Applied to the case of war powers, this relationship implies that uses of force will influence public support but this decision itself depends upon the prevailing level of support. This means that the political costs of using the military are greater at low levels of support. The probability of a congressional backlash increases and, because public disapproval reduces the president's credibility, there is also a greater risk of being charged with adventuresomeness and intentional manipulation of public opinion. In such a fashion, the decision to use force is embedded in a subtle and dynamic relationship. It is not an all-purpose strategy for replenishing lost resources.

Both the value of public support and its impact on decision making is well recognized by presidents themselves. Modern presidents have, first of all, taken great pains to measure and assess public opinion. Professional pollsters are ensconced in the White House and have served the president as advisors (e.g. Louis Harris for John Kennedy, Pat Caddell for Jimmy Carter, and Richard Wirthlin for Ronald Reagan). Administration officials have also been forthcoming about the importance of public support to the president's political strategy. As Newsweek reported at the outset of the Carter term,

> There is an adversary undertone to the preparation -- that us-against-them mode in which Carter's Georgians tend to view Capitol Hill and other potential seats of organized resistance. 'The only way to keep these guys honest,' say one Carter operative, 'is to keep our popularity high and convert it into the sort of mass support a senator or congressman can ignore only at his peril.' (2 May 1977, p. 36).

Presidents also recognize the impact of their actions on public support. Near the end of his term, for example, Lyndon Johnson observed that "the Negro cost me 15 points in the polls and Vietnam cost me 20" (Wise, 1968, p. 131). Finally, presidents understand the limitations which public support places on their actions. For example, when military analysts presented President Johnson with a study showing the impressive results which could be achieved by bombing and blockading Hanoi and Haiphong, the president replied:

> I have one more problem for your computer -- will you feed into it how long it will take five hundred thousand angry Amer-

icans to climb that White House wall out there and lynch their
President if he does something like that? (Gelb and Betts, 1979,
p. 158)

Thus, presidents are well aware of the political threat posed by the connection between public support and decision making. The threat is a potentially vicious circle in which eroding public support leads to the inability to
act which, in turn, fuels further declines in support. As we will show in
the next section, the reciprocal relationship and the threat of the vicious
circle is crucial for understanding the decision to use force.

Foreign Policy Decision Making

Foreign policy is a decision making activity that takes place in a
decidedly complex environment. According to Steinbruner (1974, p. 16) a
decision is complex if (a) there are two or more values affected by the
decision which have a trade-off relationship with each other; (b) there is a
structural uncertainty so that the president does not know the range of
possible outcomes or the probabilities of getting the outcomes; and (3)
there are several actors involved in making the decision. It seems clear
that foreign policy--at least in the realm of national security affairs--is a
complex decision problem. This places the conceptualization of decision
making under complexity squarely in the center of any proposed explanation of foreign policy.

Steinbruner (1974), p. 89) notes that while "complexity should breed
indecisiveness," presidents facing major foreign policy decisions are able to
make swift decisions. Throughout the post World War II period presidents
have chosen to use military force as a major component of US foreign
policy. In many cases the situation leading up to the use of force is
highly uncertain. Despite the lack of the necessary knowledge to foretell
the consequences, presidents have repeatedly and consistently formed quick
judgments based upon strong beliefs and have repeatedly acted in a forceful
manner. In the case of Korea in 1950, Cuba in 1962, and Vietnam in 1965,
three presidents decisively resolved the attendant ambiguity and committed
the United States to a dramatic and potentially far-reaching military
actions. Furthermore, during the period from 1949-76, six presidents used
the US military 201 times in a "political" fashion (Blechman and Kaplan,
1978).

It is our contention that an understanding of the structure of decision
making is a necessary precondition for understanding the ebb and flow of
foreign policy decisions. In spite of the fact that different men have
occupied the Oval Office, Foggy Bottom, and the Pentagon, there is a
remarkable consistency to post war decision making. Thus, not only are
decisions made in a decisive fashion but the substance of the decisions
shares a fundamental commonality over time.

Decision Making: A Schematic View

The basic structure of the process of foreign policy decision making can be captured in the following simple diagram:

The diagram provides an explanation by breaking the process of foreign policy decision making into several components. At the center of the process is the president who has over time been firmly ensconced as Foreign Policy Leader.

Presidential Decision Making

The process begins when an environmental stimulus is received by the president. That stimulus, in addition to the goals and roles, will determine what information is perceived and how it is processed or interpreted. In the context of our explanation, the president is a cybernetic/cognitive decision maker (Ostrom and Simon, 1985).

The correspondence between the structure of the environment and its representation in the mind will have a decided impact on foreign policy. Hence, the interface between the environment and the mind is crucial to any understanding of human decision making. As Simon (1959, p. 272) notes: "when perception and cognition intervene between the decision maker and his objective environment, ... [w]e need a description ... that takes into account the arduous task of determining what consequences will follow on each alternative." It is important to realize that the nature of the "intervention" is far from passive. In fact, as Simon (1959, p. 272) argues: "[i]n actual fact the perceived world is fantastically different from the 'real' world. The differences involve both omissions and distortions, and arise in both perception and inference." The human decision maker makes decisions on the basis of information that may bear only the slightest resemblance to the actual state of the world.

In pursuing our characterization of the president as a cognitive-cybernetic decision maker, we address three basic issues: (1) the cognitive structure of the individual decision maker, (2) the manner in which uncertainty is resolved, and (3) the types of trade-offs between potentially conflicting values.

The three goals imposed on the president in his role as Foreign Policy Leader have created a set of beliefs that have been shared by all presidents in the postwar period. The structure of the mind has a considerable impact on the way in which the president perceives and stores incoming information. These processes insure that presidents process incoming stimuli in a consistent and structured fashion.

The tendency of cognitive decision makers to resolve uncertainty subjectively has reinforced the basic goals and placed dramatic restrictions on presidential learning. The subjective resolution of uncertainty suggests that the president will not try to figure out all of the intricacies of the environment. Instead, he imposes a definite structure which insures that only certain information will be gathered and furthermore that it will be organized in specific ways.

Of particular importance to our characterization of the president as a decision maker is value separation. In order to qualify as a complex decision problem, the decision maker must be confronted with a trade-off relationship between at least two values. A key characteristic of the cognitive process approach to this critical feature of decision making is that decision makers separate values and do not engage in any type of a trade-off. A trade-off violates the consistency principle and hence will be actively avoided. Generally speaking, national security policy making involves a very important potential trade-off between what we will call political and policy goals. By refusing to make the trade-off presidents have courted political disaster.

Policy goals refer to the desired outcomes of foreign policy. In terms of national security policy, the desired outcomes are to bring about the cessation of unrest, stop aggression, or support an existing government. In doing so it is often necessary for the US to choose from among several different means. A plausible characterization of means might focus on the following ladder of escalation. In pursuit of anti-communism and containment, a president may utilize a number of different types of action: (1) negotiation and bargaining, (2) a "show of force"; that is, to use force in a political fashion, (3) a limited use of the military (e.g., Grenada), or (4) a full-scale use of military force (e.g., Vietnam). There are different types of costs associated with each means. It is important to realize that military success may require more than a simple show of force. In order to succeed militarily it may be necessary to raise the ante and risk casualties.

Because the president is actively involved in the politics of the perpetual election, he also has political goals. In the context of the perpetual election a president is very concerned about his standing with the public. From this perspective, the president's foreign policy choices can and do have an impact on his power situation. One of the enduring legacies of the immediate post war era is that inaction on the part of the president is a very dangerous choice. Furthermore, it has become part of the conventional wisdom that uses of the military provide a short term burst to a president's public standing. It has also been demonstrated that an extended use of the military that leads to casualties may produce a steady drop in the president's standing. In sum, the public appreciates some action and success. They do not, however, react positively to large and extended uses of force or to failure.

In the context of making foreign policy, a president is faced with two distinct value structures which are often negatively related. As the level of force necessary to achieve foreign policy or military success increases, the more risky it becomes for the president's political success. Therefore, a president will be very reluctant to escalate the involvement of the level of military force to achieve policy success because to do so may lead to political failure. The limits imposed by presidents in Korea (38th parallel), Cuba (blockade), Vietnam (troop limits, 17th parallel) and Lebanon (marines to remain in a compound) are examples of the way in which political and military objectives are negatively related. From a political perspective, the president wants to act and show that the US is a credible ally. From a military perspective, certain situations may turn out to be disasters because of limits placed on the prosecution of the endeavor.

Presidents create a number of problems when they fail to make the necessary value trade-off. When presidents act forcefully in the realm of foreign policy they are operating often out of political necessity. It is also clear that there are military consequences as well. To be successful politically requires action. To be successful militarily may require an escalating level of force on the part of the US. As history has shown, such escalation without the strong backing of the American public is likely to lead to political problems for the president (e.g., Mueller, 1973). This creates a conundrum. The president is willing to commit some force but he is not willing to unleash all of the military might at his disposal. If he is not willing to use the level of force necessary, he may be unsuccessful in a military sense. In which case, he will suffer politically. By refusing to bring the two sets of values together, the president ignores the possibility of a no win situation.

The Politics of Foreign Policy

The remaining three steps in the decision making process--agenda, decision, and strategy--are undertaken in the context of three potentially conflicting forces. First, the foreign policy process is given direction when the president decides what he wants to do. As discussed earlier, foreign policy powers are shared by Congress and the president. As a consequence, the president will have to convince Congress or compromise in order to get what he wants. Congress is the second major force at work. Finally, the president will be able to bring some power and influence to bear on the final outcome to the extent that he has sufficient resources. Hence, the third major force will be determined by the depth of the president's resource reservoir. Therefore, the formulation of the agenda, the decision, and the strategy will be a resultant of what the president wants to do, when the Congress allows him to do, and the depth of his power reservoir.

The president's agenda is a short and prioritized list of issues and problems which demand the president's immediate attention. If an item is on the agenda, it is likely that the president will be interested in it and try to act upon it. We are in basic agreement with Light (1982) that the president's agenda is quite short due the limitations imposed by internal resources. As a consequence, foreign policy issues must compete with domestic, economic, and personal issues for a place on the agenda.

Insofar as the decision is concerned, our treatment of foreign and national security policy will focus on the decision to use military force. That is, the president, at any given point in time, makes a decision about the deployment of the US military. A related and interesting decision concerns the level of force that is used. The level can vary from the simple appearance or show of force to a Dominican Republic or Grenada-style invasion force to a full-scale US military presence as in Vietnam.

Once the president has made a decision concerning the use of military force, he has to decide how that decision is to be implemented. The strategy step refers to the mix of implementation styles available to the president. In the current study we are interested in three basic types. First, the president can act in a unilateral fashion through the exercise of his prerogatives. Second, by going to the nation and giving a speech, the president can engage in a symbolic act to gain support for his proposed decision. Finally, the president can turn to Congress and ask for an authorization--in the form of a resolution--supporting his actions. Note that the three strategies are not mutually exclusive. In fact, the step in the policy making process is labeled STRATEGY because we expect the president to use symbolic, congressional, or both approaches to supplement the unilateral action of committing the US military to gain some objective.

The final ingredient in the diagram is the outcome. This is important to our explanation for at least two reasons. First, the outcome will have an impact on future states of the environment. Second, it will have a direct bearing on the depth of the president's resource reservoir. This, in turn, will affect the relative strength of the three major forces discussed earlier.

All in all, the diagrammatic presentation of the foreign policy decision making process highlights the primary components of our explanation. Of major importance to our current inquiry is the role of the president as the central information processor in the context of foreign policy. The emergence of the president as Foreign Policy Leader means that he must make

109

many critical decisions. In doing so, he will gather and process information. It is important, therefore, to discuss fully the empirical implications of this characterization of the president as a decision maker.

Empirical Propositions

The preceding discussion has developed the groundwork for an explanation of foreign policy decision making relating to the use of force. The explanation can be summarized by two sets of propositions. First, there are four propositions that follow directly from the characterization of the president as a cognitive and cybernetic decision maker. The second set focuses on the remaining steps in the foreign policy decision making process: agenda setting, making the decision, and implementation. Together, the propositions illustrate that it is the intent of the president coupled with the depth of his resource base and the cooperation of Congress that determine the final outcome. The propositions apply to the postwar era and are intended to illustrate the degree to which the president, as a human decision maker, has an impact on the direction and substance of US foreign policy. The propositions along with a short discussion and some preliminary empirical evidence are presented below.

The President as a Cognitive-Cybernetic Decision Maker

Proposition 1. An opportunity for US action exists whenever there is some form of instability within a country or region that could (1) lead to an existing regime being replaced by a less favorable one, (2) threaten the safety of US citizens, or (3) otherwise threaten the basic goals of the United States.

Each president will have a preference for action in these instances given their belief structure. Each opportunity will be perceived and interpreted as an instance of communist aggression most likely financed or directed by Moscow. This proposition leads us to expect that there have been an enormous number of opportunities for the US to engage in the use of force.

To date there has been no systematic investigation of the number of opportunities. As a check on this hypothesis, we utilized a preliminary version of a data set collected by Job and Ostrom (1985). This data set was collected by locating, in Facts on File, all situations which correspond to the above definition of an opportunity. Since there was not an exact correspondence between the uses of military force compiled by Blechman and Kaplan (1978) and the set of opportunities and uses gathered by Job and Ostrom, we devised the following solution. If one assumes that each use of force identified by Blechman and Kaplan was preceded by an opportunity, it is possible to add to this total the number of Job and Ostrom opportunities that were not followed by a use of force. Table 1 presents all of the uses of force listed by Blechman and Kaplan plus all of the unanswered opportunities located by Job and Ostrom (1985). Adding these

110

two quantities in each year provides a rough idea of the number of times in which each president faced an opportunity to use force.

As can be seen from Table 1, there were at least 345 opportunities (approximately 12 times per year) for the president to use force during the 1949-1976 period. It is reasonable, therefore, to conclude that the basic beliefs in conjunction with the cognitive structure have led presidents to perceive and interpret a very large number of unstable situations as opportunities to use force.

> Proposition 2. Given an opportunity, the president is predisposed to utilize some level of force in each opportunity.

Each of the opportunities provides the president with a situation in which a decision will have to be made. The enduring goals will force the president to notice the incident and to consider the possibility of action. Consequently, it is hypothesized that all other things being equal, the president will be predisposed to use force. As a result, it is likely that the president will use force more often than not.

In their study, Blechman and Kaplan demonstrate convincingly that the use of force has been, in the postwar era, a frequently employed instrument of foreign policy. They show, for example, that between the years 1949 and 1976, the US deployed military units abroad for political purposes 201 times. Thus, in over 50% of the inferred opportunities (see Table 1), presidents have responded with some level of force.

> Proposition 3. Insofar as the level of force is concerned, a president will not be reluctant to use a major level of force.

It is likely that the president will be directly involved in those instances in which the use of force is substantial. Restricting attention only to those occasions in which major force components (ground forces larger than a battalion, naval forces involving two carriers or battleship task groups, or a wing of combat aircraft) or nuclear-capable US forces were deployed results in a catalogue of some 70 instances during the 28-year period. Put in another way, US presidents directed the major use of military force for political purposes roughly three times each year or in 20% of the inferred opportunities. It is noteworthy that in 25 of the 28 years, a major use of force was undertaken by US presidents. It seems clear that presidents have not shied away from major uses of force.

> Proposition 4. The justification for the use of force will be similar across all presidents and will include some mention of communist involvement, Soviet expansionism, and/or the domino theory.

It is not possible in the context of a short paper to capture all of the postwar rhetoric used to justify the military force by the United States. We wish to offer three representative examples which also illustrate the continuity in justifications associated with major uses of force.

In explaining America's entry into the Korean conflict, President Truman issued the following statement on June 27, 1950: "The attack upon Korea makes it plain beyond all doubt that Communism has passed beyond the use of subversion to conquer independent nations and will now use armed invasion and war" (Donovan, 1984, p. 50). Also reported was an earlier statement to an aide:

Korea is the Greece of the Far East. If we are tough enough now, if we stand up to them like we did in Greece three years ago, they won't take any next steps. But if we just stand by, they'll move into Iran and they'll take over the whole Middle East. There is no telling what they'll do, if we don't put up a fight now." (New York Times, June 26, 1950, p. 25)

President Johnson's reaction to the Gulf of Tonkin incident in the August 1964 made it clear that aggressive actions anywhere in the world would be closely scrutinized by the United States.

The challenge that we face in Southeast Asia today is the same challenge we have faced with courage and that we have met with strength in Greece and Turkey, in Berlin and Korea, in Lebanon, and in Cuba. And to any who may be tempted to support or to widen the present aggression I say this: There is no threat to any peaceful power from the United States of America. But there can be no peace by aggression and no immunity from reply. That is what is meant by the actions that we took yesterday. (Vantage Point, p. 117)

Prior to a full-scale involvement in Vietnam, President Johnson viewed and interpreted the unrest and aggression through perceptual filters which were conditioned by the basic belief structure.

Events in October of 1983 (Lebanon and Grenada) provide a vivid illustration that justifications for the use of force are still tied to anti-communism and containment of Soviet influence. President Reagan observed on October 27, 1983 that

The events in Lebanon and Grenada, though oceans apart, are closely related. Not only has Moscow assisted and encouraged the violence in both countries, it provides direct support through a network of surrogates and terrorists.

The presumption is that the problems in each of the areas are being directed and financed by the USSR. In terms of containment, President Reagan asserted

Grenada, we were told was a friendly island paradise. Well it wasn't. It was a Soviet-Cuban colony, being readied as a major military bastion to export terror and undermine democracy. We got there just in time.

112

The three basic foreign policy goals repeatedly surface as US policy makers make choices and explain those choices to the rest of the world.

The Politics of Foreign Policy

As noted earlier, the remaining steps in the foreign policy making process are the agenda, decision, and implementation strategy. What must be emphasized is that these steps are distinctly political activities. Foreign policy making is a shared activity with Congress and is affected by the president's power situation. Therefore, it is important to take the relative balance of power between the president and Congress into consideration. It is this balance of power which will determine whether the president is able to do what he wishes to do, when he wants to do it, and how he wants to do it. This is particularly true since the use of force is a presidential prerogative. As such, the president is asserting that he has the authority to use the military in the particular instance. It also means that the president can be checked by the Congress. The discussion of presidential decision making has established that presidents have a strong desire to act forcefully. The political context within which the decision is made insures that there will be considerable jockeying for control over the action of government and that a president cannot always act with impunity. The competitive atmosphere of Washington politics will have an effect on what the president is able to accomplish.

The President's Agenda. The president's agenda consists of a list of priorities focusing on what the president wants to accomplish in the near future. As Light (1982) has argued, the size of the president's agenda will be drastically limited. Due to a variety of constraints, most notably the president's own internal and political resources, the agenda is quite small. The president is not completely free to set the agenda either. There are a number of demands placed upon the president by the public, Congress, and his own campaign promises. These demands exert a potent influence on the agenda. For example, the president is expected to formulate a legislative program and usher it through Congress, strive for high employment and stable prices, and deal with any crisis situations--domestic or international--that arise.

Insofar as the political use of force is concerned, there are two considerations which affect its placement on the president's agenda. First, each opportunity provides the president with a "window" for dramatic action. Second, each opportunity must compete with other issues for a place on the agenda. It is our contention that the prominence of foreign policy actions on the agenda is connected to public concern with foreign policy issues. During those periods in which foreign policy problems dominate the public's attention, it is likely that an opportunity will be placed on the agenda. The times in which public attention focuses upon the threat of communism, the Soviet Union, or international "hot spots" (e.g. Cuba in 1962), there will be a felt need to act. The times in which domestic issues such as a bad economy, energy shortages, civil unrest, and war protests dominate the public's attention, there will be less demand for action. The president will have to devote his efforts to solving these domestic problems. The following proposition relates the president's agenda to public concerns.

Proposition 5. Each opportunity to use force must compete with other issues to gain a place on the president's agenda. Therefore, when foreign policy problems are most important, the president is more likely to engage in the use of force.

Table 2 presents the correlations between the percentage of the public identifying foreign and domestic issues as the most important problems and four measures of the use of force: number of uses of any level, percentage of opportunities in which any level of force was used, number of major uses, and the percentage of opportunities in which major force was used. As can be seen, force is much more likely to be on the agenda when foreign policy issues dominate. Concern with foreign policy is significant and positively correlated with each of the four measures of use. Concern with domestic issues, on the other hand, is not significantly correlated with three of the indicators but has a -.24 correlation with the percentage of opportunities in which major levels of force were chosen. It is anticipated, therefore, that the politics of agenda formation will have an impact on the priority of each opportunity to use force. Most importantly, a president's desire to utilize force must be tempered by a realization that foreign policy issues compete with other issues for the president's attention.

The Decision to Use Force. Once the content and priorities of the agenda have been determined, the president must decide what to do. If a foreign policy issue is on the agenda, the president must decide whether to use the military and at what level. Our discussion of decision making in the previous section implies that this choice will be routinized and therefore can be modeled as if the president and his advisors followed a simple and stable decision rule. This leads to the following:

Proposition 6. It is possible to explain major uses of force in terms of stable decision rules which connect salient features of the environment with presidential decision making.

In a previous study, Ostrom and Job (1986) have specified a presidential decision rule which ties the decision to use a major level of force to a variety of factors in the international, domestic, and personal/political contexts. These determinants include public support, economic conditions, the severity of war, the U.S.-Soviet balance of power and the level of international tension. Interestingly, it is also shown that the impact of the last two factors -- balance and tension -- depends upon the level of public concern with foreign affairs. Given the explanatory power of this model (75% of uses were correctly predicted), the Ostrom and Job results provide strong support for the assertion of a simple and stable decision rule.

114

Our next proposition is primarily an implication of the fact that modern presidents must perform the same role, satisfy the same expectations, and engage in the same struggle for personal power.

Proposition 7. Presidential idiosyncracies will have no influence on the decision to use military force.

This proposition suggests that temporal variations in the use of force are primarily determined by exogenous events and not by varying beliefs on the part of postwar presidents. The ultimate test of this proposition lies in the ability to account for the ebb and flow in the use of force over time. Table 3 offers some suggestive evidence in this regard. It displays the proportion of correct and incorrect predictions generated by the Ostrom and Job model for Presidents Truman through Ford. If the use of force were a matter of personal idiosyncracy, then we would expect to find substantial variations in the error rate across presidential administrations. Clearly, this is not the case. The rate is remarkably stable and thus casts serious doubt on the supposition that decisions to use force are a product of the unique personalities of those who serve in the office.

According to our discussion of the reciprocal relationship between power and decision making, the potential "mix" of positive and negative consequences means that a president must assess the risk associated with using the force option. Insofar as domestic politics is concerned, the negative consequences include congressional backlash, the charge of intentionally manipulating public opinion, and the reduction of the president's future power and credibility. This leads us to anticipate the following relationship:

Proposition 8. The use of force will vary directly with the level of public support. Presidents will be most likely to use force when support is "high" and least likely to choose this option when support is "low".

Table 2 provides empirical support for the proposition. All four measures of the use of force are strongly correlated with the president's approval rating. Additional support is provided by the Ostrom and Job study. Their results show that the most important determinant of the use of force is the depth of the president's resource reservoir. All other things being equal, a president is most likely to use a major level of force when his approval is greater than 60%. The use force becomes least likely when a president's approval level is less than 40%. This suggest that presidents take the level of political risk associated with the use of force into account. The ability to withstand a negative reaction operates, therefore, as a major influence on the use of force decision.

Implementation Strategies. Once the decision to use force has been made, the president must decide how to implement it. The most important features of this phase are whether the president wishes to involve Congress in the decision by asking for a resolution and/or if the president wishes to go public and give an address outlining his purposes. All other things

115

being equal, the president will want to rally the Congress and the public behind his decision. If a president decides to act unilaterally, he runs the risk of backlash. This is especially likely if the president was not able to get initial support for his actions from Congress or the public. Therefore, we expect the president to try to get support for his actions.

Presidents have often gone to Congress asking for a resolution supporting the use of military force. The congressional response is likely to be related to the president's current power situation; that is, it will be related to his level of public support.

Proposition 9. The probability that Congress will provide the president with a resolution of support is positively related to the depth of the president's resource reservoir.

While not an "exact test," the history of the modern presidency provides numerous examples which support this assertion. In particular, two types of actions by the Congress relate to the use of force. First, Congress passed a series of "hot spot" resolutions that granted the president broad authority over the use of force. On five separate occasions, the president was given, on an a priori basis, the discretion to employ "any means necessary" to defend American interests -- Formosa (1955), the Middle East (1957), Cuba (1962), Berlin (1962), and the Gulf of Tonkin (1964). Such authority included the discretion to decide whether military action was necessary, the level of force to be employed, and the timing of the action. Second, the congressional consent was required and obtained for a potentially "entangling alliance" in the volatile region of Southeast Asia. Each of these agreements contained provisions which promised, either implicitly or explicitly, military action by the United States if a member nation came under attack. In such circumstances, the credibility of the United States as an ally would be directly linked to the president's willingness to use military force.

These actions all occurred during what might be called the "golden era" of presidential power (1953-1964). During this period, the average level of public support for Presidents Eisenhower, Kennedy, and Johnson was 66.5%, a remarkable figure compared to recent times. The standard deviation in support, 7 rating points, demonstrates that these high levels were quite stable as well. In fact, during this eleven year period, public support dipped below 50% only once. Thus, these presidents enjoyed a resource level that produced congressional acquiesence to the assertion of prerogatives and provided a buffer against adverse events (e.g. the Bay of Pigs, U-2 incident).

Without the endorsement of Congress, a president who chooses to act will face the possibility of a congressional backlash. The backlash can assume a variety of forms. Congress may, particularly in the aftermath of an unsuccessful or extended use of force (e.g., Vietnam), increase its oversight of presidential behavior, refuse presidential requests for authority to act, or attempt to place restrictions on the exercise of the war making prerogative. Our consideration of presidential power and its

116

impact on competition between president and congress leads to the assertion that the likelihood of backlash will vary with the level of public support.

Proposition 10. The probability of a successful congressional backlash is inversely related to the depth of the president's resource reservoir.

Insofar as presidential power is concerned, the years after 1964 have been characterized as a period of eroding public support and "throwaway" presidents (Ostrom and Simon, 1984). This period stands in stark contrast to the "golden era". From 1965 to 1980, the average level of public support was 50.7%, nearly 16 points lower than the mean of the 1953-1964 period. In addition, the erosion of public support for Presidents Johnson through Carter was rapid and deep. Johnson dropped to a low of 35%, Nixon to 24%, Ford to 37%, and Carter to 21%. Each of these presidents also left office "involuntarily."

It comes as no surprise then that the reassertion of Congress in foreign affairs during the 1970s occurred at an historical low point in public support for the president. The actions associated with backlash were plentiful. First, Congress increased its oversight of the executive branch. This included hearings critical of presidential policy in Vietnam (e.g. the televised Fulbright hearings of 1966) and investigations of clandestine exercises of the war powers (e.g. the Church committee hearings on the CIA in 1976). There were also critical hearings held in the wake of the Mayaguez incident (1975), the Iranian rescue attempt (1980), and the bombing of the American embassy in Lebanon (1983). Second, the congress passed several pieces of legislation that restricted the president's discretion in foreign affairs (see Sundquist, 1981). The most notorious of this reform legislation was the War Powers Act passed in 1973 over President Nixon's veto. Other prominent actions included the repeal of the Tonkin Resolution (1971), the Case Act (1972), the Budget Control and Impoundment Act (1974). Finally, during this period, the Congress has been increasingly skeptical of presidential actions in the foreign arena and has refused to grant presidents the flexibility they desire in managing foreign relations. Thus, Congress imposed conditions on US policy during the Greek-Turkish conflict over Cyprus, restricted American actions in Angola, and imposed rather stringent conditions on military aid and advisors requested for Lebanon and El Salvador. It should also be noted that the treatment of the Truman Administration during the course of the Korean War was quite similar. Between the start of the war and the end of his term, President Truman's average level of public support dropped 31%. The fact that Truman did not consult with congress prior to committing American forces exacerbated the problem. As a result, Truman faced a rather severe backlash which included a congressional uproar over America's NATO policy and critical investigations surrounding the removal of General MacArthur and alleged communist infiltration of the State Department. Thus, the historical record provides numerous examples that support the relationship between backlash and public support.

Conclusion

Our discussion demonstrates that there is a strong connection between the exercise of war powers and the structure of domestic politics. We have shown that the history of the presidency in the years after World War II is a story of increasing responsibility in the foreign arena and the centralization of decision making authority in the White House. This authority flows not from the enumerated powers of the Constitution but from the results of an inherently political process involving assertions of prerogative, congressional reactions, and court decisions. We have also shown that the evolution of this modern role created widespread expectations about presidential behavior and imposed three enduring goals on the conduct of American foreign policy in general and the use of military force in particular. The result is that the choice to use military force is imbedded in a subtle and dynamic relationship between presidential power and decision making. Finally, we have shown, through the cognitive-cybernetic model, that this political structure plays a critical role in explaining decisions to use force. This model, in turn, was used to "derive" several plausible hypotheses which are, at least in a preliminary sense, supported by the historical record.

Insofar as the war powers are concerned, this analysis leads to two general conclusions. The first pertains to the continuity in use of force decisions. These choices are not a function of the different personalities and idiosyncracies of the individuals who served in the White House. Rather, the decisions are tied to a domestic political structure -- roles, goals, and the quest for power -- that weighs heavily on all presidents.

Second, the analysis illustrates that all presidents are confronted by a "vicious circle" in which declining political resources inhibit their ability to act and, therefore, their ability to satisfy the enduring goals and replenish their resources. This produces a dilemma in which the erosion of public support breeds inaction in the foreign arena. In this sense, the political structure constrains the use of force. This dilemma is not insoluble however. As we have shown elsewhere (Ostrom and Simon, 1984), the vicious circle can be reversed through an astute mix of strategies involving both policy innovation and the use of political drama. In this regard, the domestic structure provides an incentive for the use of force. Thus, the structure of domestic politics -- roles, goals, and power -- produce a decision making context which encourages and restrains the exercise of war powers.

118

Table 1

The Use of Military Force: A Summary

Year	Uses	Opportunities Unanswered	Inferred	Major Uses	Percent Major	Percent Use
1949	1	4	5	0	.00	.20
1950	5	1	6	2	.33	.83
1951	1	3	4	1	.25	.25
1952	4	5	9	0	.00	.44
1953	4	3	7	2	.28	.57
1954	7	2	9	6	.67	.78
1955	2	2	4	1	.25	.50
1956	6	7	13	3	.23	.46
1957	9	4	13	5	.38	.69
1958	9	3	12	4	.33	.75
1959	11	4	15	5	.33	.73
1960	10	7	17	1	.06	.59
1961	12	4	16	4	.25	.75
1962	11	7	18	2	.11	.61
1963	18	4	22	6	.27	.81
1964	21	6	27	7	.26	.78
1965	13	5	18	5	.28	.72
1966	3	7	10	0	.00	.30
1967	6	8	14	2	.14	.43
1968	4	5	9	2	.22	.44
1969	3	11	14	1	.07	.21
1970	6	5	11	1	.09	.55
1971	6	8	14	1	.07	.42
1972	3	6	9	2	.22	.33
1973	7	8	15	3	.20	.47
1974	4	5	9	1	.11	.44
1975	7	7	14	2	.07	.50
1976	8	3	11	1	.12	.73

Uses are drawn from Blechman and Kaplan (1978); the opportunity measure is based on Job and Ostrom (1985); inferred opportunities are the sum of "uses" and "opportunities".

119

Table 2
The Use of Force and Public Opinion: A Summary

| | | Most Important Problem | | | Presidential |
	Foreign	Economic	Social	Domestic	Approval
All Uses of Force	.25	-.08	.29	.15	.49
Percent Opportunities (All Uses)	.37	.04	-.07	-.01	.39
Major Uses of Force	.25	-.17	.18	-.01	.51
Percent Opportunities (Major Uses)	.29	-.12	-.17	-.24	.32

The table is based on annual data. The entries in the table are correlation coefficients. The most important problem measures are based on survey responses to the following Gallup question: "What do you think is the most important problem facing the country today?" Responses were grouped into the general categories presented below.

Table 3
Presidents and the Use of Force

President	Use Predicted Correctly	No Use Predicted Correctly	Use Predicted Incorrectly	No Use Predicted Incorrectly	Percent Correct
Truman	0	14	0	2	88%
Eisenhower	17	6	6	3	72%
Kennedy	7	1	3	1	67%
Johnson	8	7	3	2	75%
Nixon	2	15	0	5	77%
Ford	2	5	1	2	70%

This table is adapted from Table 3 in Ostrom and Job (1986). The analysis is based on quarterly data in which use is a dichotomous variable denoting whether a major use of force was observed in that quarter.

120

References

Blechman, B. and S. Kaplan. 1978. Force Without War. Washington, D.C.: The Brookings Institution.

Brody, R. and B. Page. 1975 "The Impact of Events on Presidential Popularity." In A. Wildavsky (Ed.). Perspectives on the Presidency. Boston: Little Brown.

Brody, R. and L. Sigelman. 1983. "Presidential Popularity and Presidential Elections: An Update and Extension." Public Opinion Quartely. Volume 47, pp. 325-328.

Cantril, A. (Ed.). 1980. Polling on the Issues. Cabin John, Md.: Seven Locks Press.

Donovan, R. 1984. Nemesis. New York: St. Martin's.

Edwards, G. 1980. Presidential Influence in Congress. San Francisco: Freeman.

Gelb, L. and R. Betts. 1979. The Irony of Vietnam. Washington, D.C.: The Brookings Institution.

Greenstein, F. 1978. "Change and Continuity in the Modern Presidency. In A. King (Ed.). The New American Political System. Washington, D.C.: American Enterprise Institute.

Hodgson, G. 1980. All Things to All Men. New York: Simon and Schuster.

Job, B and Ostrom, C. W., Jr. 1985. "The Opportunity to Use Force." Presented at the Annual Meeting of the International Political Science Association, Paris, France.

Johnson, L.B. 1971. Vantage Point. New York: Holt, Rinehart, and Winston.

Kegley, Charles and E. Wittkopf. 1982. American Foreign Policy, 2ed. New York: St. Martins.

Light, P. 1982. The President's Agenda. Baltimore: John Hopkins University Press

Muller, J. 1973. War, Presidents, and Public Opinion. New York: Wiley.

Neustadt, R. 1980. Presidential Power. New York: Wiley.

Ostrom, C. W., Jr. and B. Job. 1986. "The President and the Political Use of Force." American Political Science Review. June (80:541-66).

Ostrom, C. W., Jr. and D. Simon. 1985. "Promise and Performance: A Dynamic Model of Presidential Popularity." American Political Science Review. July.

Ostrom, C. and D. Simon. 1984. "Managing Public Support: The Presidential Dilemma," Policy Studies Journal. June.

Pious, R. 1979. The American President. New York: Basic Books.

Pyle, C. and R. Pious. 1984. The President, Congress, and the Constitution. New York: The Free Press.

Rohde, D. and D. Simon. 1985. "Presidential Vetoes and the Congressional Response." American Journal of Political Science. August.

Schlesinger, A. Jr. 1973. The Imperial Presidency. Boston: Houghton Mifflin.

Schlesinger, A. Jr. 1965. A Thousand Days. Boston: Houghton Mifflin.

Simon, H. 1959. "Theories of Decision Making in Economics." American Economic Review. Volume 49 (253-283).

Steinbruner, J. 1974. The Cybernetic Theory of Decision. Princeton, N.J.: Princeton University Press.

Sundquist, J. 1981. The Decline and Resurgence of Congress. Washington, D.C.: The Brookings Institution.

Tufte, E. 1978. Political Control of the Economy. Princeton, N.J.: Princeton University Press

Wise, D. 1968. "The Twilight of a President." New York Times Magazine. November 3.

DEFENSE POLICYMAKING UNMASKED: FOUR RECENT
CASES OF WEAPONS PROCUREMENT

by

Lauren H. Holland and Robert A. Hoover

The myth that national security policy is crafted and applied in some uniquely apolitical and distinctly rational process has died. However, the ancillary belief that defense policy, even that of procurement policy, is made in ways categorically different than domestic policy prevails. The evidence, in the form of an impressive array of case studies,[1] does point to the validity of the ancillary belief, and the attendant paradigm, the bureaucratic politics model.[2] However, in the past fifteen years, policy decisions concerning four major weapons systems were or are made in ways that dramatically deviate from the conventional wisdom: the anti-ballistic missile (ABM), the extremely low frequency communication system (ELF), the experimental missile (MX) and Midgetman. In each case, crucial assumptions of the bureaucratic politics paradigm were invalidated. The following analysis will examine the policymaking processes preceding the critical decisions on four military projects in an effort to discover whether and why they constitute deviant cases in procurement politics.

Several different models have been developed to assist in explaining the causes and consequences of governmental activity.[3] Collectively they point to (a) the impact of social, economic, and political forces; (b) the importance of various institutional arrangements and political processes; and (c) the significance of the societal consequences of public policy choices. For national security policy, one model is preeminent, the bureaucratic politics perspective. This paradigm, in emphasizing the impact of institutional factors, postulates that defense policy is always made in ways distinctive from domestic policy. In domestic policymaking, socioeconomic considerations and political interests are germane; the electoral and lobbying processes influential; and the concerns for the broader societal impacts of policy choices cogent ones. We argue that in at least four recent procurement cases, all of these forces were also operating. To demonstrate this we must show how and explain why the decision-making processes for these systems deviate from conventional wisdom. We will direct more extensive treatment to MX and midgetman which constitute cases more recent and consequential.

According to the bureaucratic politics paradigm,[4] policymaking is confined to a small group of actors within the

123

executive arena. However, these actors do not constitute an homogenous group. Rather, various individuals and organizations respond to a policy issue in differing ways depending upon their personal interests and/or those of the mission of their organizations. In other words, where you stand on an issue depends on where you sit. For this reason, procurement decisions are the resultants of bargaining and compromising that occur within the executive arena. Moreover, this conflict continues during the implementation stage, when modifications continue to be effected. Despite superior statutory and constitutional power, the president is not necessarily the most important individual in a field of actors who exercise varying power depending upon the stakes involved. Finally, domestic factors and forces are secondary to the decision-making process for weapons procurement. More precisely, Congress and the general public are deferential and supportive of executive prerogative in this policy area; and most interest groups lack the interest, experience and/or knowledge to actively lobby. If members of Congress become involved, they do so for reasons of pork barrel as opposed to strategic considerations. At most, domestic actors and forces serve to circumscribe and constrain executive power, but never to direct, determine nor substitute for it.

The core of the bureaucratic politics paradigm resides in the view that choices concerning the development and deployment of major weapons of destruction are essentially the result of organizational interests. This approach errs in failing to recognize that in at least four recent procurement cases--ABM, ELF, MX and Midgetman--the choices were also informed and influenced by other factors, namely strategic, technical, foreign policy, and domestic concerns such as the environmental, cultural, and socioeconomic trade-offs resulting from military decisions. This can be best illustrated by reviewing these four case studies.

The Anti-Ballistic Missile

The ABM procurement program, initiated in the late 1950s, grew out of the U.S. Army's desire to develop a system to defend against what was expected to be a Soviet missile threat in the 1960s.[5] It became a multimillion dollar research and development project. Controversy over the system emerged by the early 1960s, with the Office of the Secretary of Defense (OSD) and the Joint Chiefs of Staff (JCS) in conflict over whether the ABM should be deployed. By 1965 senior senators became active and forceful ABM lobbyists. Their action was an important factor in President Johnson and Secretary McNamara's decision to commit to ABM in 1967. However, McNamara proposed a "thin" system that would defend against a possible Chinese attack rather than a Soviet strike. By 1969 opposition to deployment of ABM had organized and intensified, and the Senate became a major battle ground over

124

the authorization and appropriation of ABM funds. Following the near defeat of ABM in the Senate in 1969, the Nixon administration negotiated with the Soviet Union a limitation on the deployment of ABMs (the 1972 ABM Treaty). The ABM issue was the most contentious procurement problem of the 1960s, and resulted in a major reversal for the U.S. Army and its supporters.

The Origins and Early R&D

Until the late 1960s, ABM decision making closely resembled the pattern suggested by the bureaucratic politics paradigm. The origins of the weapon system are found in the interaction between the army (the responsible armed service) and the technocrats of the laboratories of the major defense industries. The program required significant technological advancement in missile propulsion, radar detection and tracking, and rapid management of complex calculations (computer technology). The price tag on the development of that technology and the deployment of the weapon program portended one of the most expensive military items in U.S. history. As that technology developed during the 1950s and the early 1960s, the weapon system provoked little or no controversy; it was virtually invisible to individuals outside the Pentagon. Within the Pentagon, key officials split over the ABM procurement. Strategic differences between OSD and the JCS radically altered both the character of ABM decision making the its visibility in the Washington policy community. Later, other issues would widen and intensify the debate over ABM even further.

Issues that Forced Increased ABM Visibility and Saliency

During the mid-1960s, the ABM issue moved out of the narrow corridors of the Pentagon and defense industries to the Oval Office of the White House, the halls of Congress, the pages of the Washington press and onto the national evening news, and the homes of millions of U.S. citizens, especially those living near designated ABM deployment sites such as Boston. Five issues were critical in expanding the arena of conflict: technical uncertainty, strategic dissension, foreign policy problems, financial costs, and environmental/social concerns.

Strategic dissension over the role and significance of ABM was the first problem. As ABM reached the end of the design, development, research, and engineering stages (1965), important individuals outside the Pentagon, and the executive branch began to influence the deliberations. Senior southern senators were particularly active at this time. Motivated by pork barrel and strategic concerns, these legislators used their ties to the pro-military lobby and Pentagon to influence President Lyndon Johnson to commit to ABM.

125

At the same time, McNamara and others in OSD were advising Johnson against the defense system, which they viewed as wrongful for technical, strategic, fiscal, and bureaucratic reasons. For one, McNamara was not convinced that a workable ABM system could be developed; but the belief that it could provide a rationale by the Pentagon for an almost endless list of strategic weapons. Moreover, ABM was the most costly of any strategic weapon program yet conceived, and could divert huge sums of resources from other projects. Later, concerns over the price-tag would provide a target of opportunity for members of Congress seeking to cut the defense budget and transfer funds to domestic programs (Newhouse, 1972:66-102).

Third, the program had serious technical problems. It was vulnerable to surface blasts, faced serious real-time problems of locating and initiating a strike against an incoming weapon, was ineffective against the decoy problem, and perhaps was more costly as a defense than Soviet offensive counter-measures to offset ABM.

Finally, McNamara believed that ABM introduced a dangerous new round in the arms race by encouraging the Soviet Union to respond to the U.S. defense by deploying a similar system. If either side believed that their defensive system was effective, it raised the possibility that one would initiate a nuclear strike in a crisis situation where the advantage was to preempt. Thus, the race to deploy an ABM system would not necessarily produce more security.

McNamara was able to stall a commitment to ABM for several years. By 1967, however, he succumbed to pressure from President Johnson, the JCS, senior senators, and important defense specialists outside the government, and advanced the production of a "thin" ABM system to defend against the Peoples Republic of China. ABM enthusiasts geared for a battle to extend the system to protect against the Soviet Union, as well. Given the conventional pattern of procurement politics, proponents were optimistic. By 1968, however, the issue had become so politicized by the dimensions of the policy that unexpected constraints emerged. These constraints affected the nature and direction of decision-making on ABM in ways that deviate from what the conventional wisdom suggests.

More precisely, decision makers within the executive branch were confronted with opposition from local groups in the areas surrounding the designated ABM sites. Traditionally, residents have been supportive of major public works projects such as military bases that proffer jobs and an expanded tax base. Concern over the possible negative socioeconomic consequences of ABM deployment, and fears of living in a potential nuclear strike zone, precipitated lobbying against the system. New England and

126

Illinois area residents were especially effective in their opposition to the deployment of ABM in their regions.

For example, Ernest Yanarella (1977:152-153) suggests that Senator Everett Dirkson was, "Shaken by the deluge of constituent protests against building a sentinel base in suburban Libertyville, 26 miles northwest of downtown Chicago." As a result he was far more sensitive to public dissent on this issue. Senator Henry Jackson in Washington, following public pressure against the deployment of a sentinel in downtown Seattle, pursuaded the army to move the site across the Puget Sound. However, this caused Congressman Thomas Pelley from that district to become a member of the anti-ABM coalition. This type of opposition grew to be a significant factor in the 1969 and 1970 debates in the Senate and House over the future of ABM.

ABM also became a foreign policy issue following the inauguration of the Nixon administration. Senate opponents, responding both to constituent pressures and their own strategic and budgetary concerns, came within one vote of defeating ABM.

To illustrate, between 1968 and 1969 a growing number of opponents in the House and Senate initiated a concerted effort to stop the deployment of ABM. In the Senate, Albert Gore used his disarmament subcommittee of the Committee on Foreign Relations to challenge the Armed Services Committees' traditional control of procurement issues. He began a series of committee meetings on strategic policy, especially ABM deployment, that made public a stream of criticism about ABM. In addition, these senators and other members of the House began to use anti-ABM scientists to provide credibility to the anti-ABM movement in the Senate. Finally, they used the growing public concern about deployment in metropolitan areas as a way to enhance their opposition. Yanarella estimates that by mid-July 1969 the anti-ABM movement had gained sufficient strength to count support from about 47 or 48 senators (1977:157). On August 6, the Senate voted 50 to 51, with the tie-breaking vote by Vice President Spiro Agnew, to ban the safeguard system but permit other ABM research. This very narrow victory for ABM had a major impact on the Nixon administration's perception of the future of ABM deployment in the United States.

The combination of declining senate support and dissension within the administration influenced Nixon to negotiate a bilateral limit on ABM deployments with the Soviets, producing the ABM Treaty in 1972. Two years later the United States and the Soviet Union further limited deployments. By the mid-1970s, the United States had abandoned virtually the ABM weapon program.[6]

127

ABM Deviates from the Conventional Wisdom

The bureaucratic politics paradigm is applicable to the early stages of ABM decision making, particularly the R&D stages. However, the model fails to capture the full dimension of the process after 1965. After this period policymakers within the executive branch began responding directly to the concerns of congressional actors, regional groups, and non-military executive personnel. The media was instrumental in exposing the military project to residents around the proposed development sites. Coalitions began forming that brought together groups in various arenas. Finally, the motives of these groups and individuals were broader than the personal and organizational ones the bureaucratic politics paradigm views as preeminent. Rather they included strategic, technical, foreign policy, fiscal and environmental/social concerns.

ELF--Sanguine, Seafarer, Elf

During the 1960s and early 1970s, the U.S. Navy, together with the design labs of industry and government, explored the feasibility of deploying an extremely low frequency radio wave communication system (ELF), as a means to provide improved command and control capability for the SLBM fleet. The communication system, slated for installation in northern Wisconsin, was to consist of transmitters, a vast underground antenna grid, power networks, and a security system for each transmitter site (Klessig and Strite, 1980:13-14). After encountering significant resistance to the deployment of Sanguine, the navy proposed a scaled down model of ELF, Seafarer. Continued opposition led the navy to replace Seafarer with Elf, a further scaled down model that would require significantly reduced land area for deployment. Thus, the navy and successive administrations have faced opposition that has both delayed and altered the design and deployment of ELF.

The Origins of ELF R&D

Since the 1920s, the navy has utilized very low frequency (VLF) waves to communicate with U.S. submarines operating for extended periods deep under water. By the late 1950s this method of communication was no longer effective given the depths at which navy submarines were operating. The inadequacy of VLF prompted research into ELF. After nearly a decade of R&D, the navy proposed the deployment of the first ELF system, Sanguine. It would consist of "a 150 mile grid that would cover 26 counties and 20,000 square miles...[and] contain 240 transmitter sites and 6000 miles of antenna cable" (Klessig and Strite, 1980:17). Its purpose was to provide a communication capability with U.S. missile submarines to launch a retaliation attack in the event of a Soviet first-strike.

128

During the first decade of Elf decision making (1958-1967), the bureaucratic politics model does explain the nature and direction of navy R&D. As Klessig and Strite (1980:xxi) suggest

> Only the navy personnel involved and the congressional Committees on Armed Services were aware of the effort. A test cable was laid in the mountains of North Carolina and Virginia. The project was classified and there was no controversy, although there were unconfirmed reports of complaints from area residents regarding interference with telephones and television. Expenditures of $18 million were made on the project during this time.

Issues That Forced ELF Visibility and Saliency

In 1968, Congressman Alvin O'Konski announced during his reelection campaign the existence of Sanguine and its probable deployment in Wisconsin, catapulting the issue into the public arena. Most commerce and labor groups were initially attracted to the project because twenty million dollars was spent between 1968 and 1970. Thus, the initial experience of ELF, in the executive and public arenas, seemed to follow the pattern suggested by the bureaucratic politics paradigm.

However, by 1970 support for deployment of Sanguine in Wisconsin waned and opposition appeared. The potential negative environmental and social effects coupled with the fear of being a direct target of Soviet ICBMs in case of war caused Wisconsin citizens, and later residents in Michigan and Texas, to mobilize against the communication system. At one point, membership in the [Wisconsin] State Committee to Stop Sanguine reached 2500. "By the end of the year, no elected official at the state or congressional level was publicly supporting Sanguine (Klessig and Strite, 1980:xxii)." Similarly, in the 1972 elections support for ELF remained a political liability. In fact, O'Konski was later defeated by a candidate more clearly associated with opposition to Sanguine (Klessig and Strite, 1980:xxiii).

The ELF system was a hot political issue given concerns over its effects of Sanguine on public utilities, the broadcast media, local economies, and animal and human life itself. The large number of security fences was visible evidence that Sanguine would intrude in the lives of ranchers, hunters, farmers and recreationists. Importantly, the National Environmental Policy Act (NEPA) of 1969 provided the requisite statutory and legal tools for challenging the navy on this issue, in direct and unmediated ways. In fact, NEPA's mandatory environmental impact statement (EIS) process[8] with its public review options, was a threat of considerable consequence to the Pentagon. By the early 1970s, expanded political opposition in the public and congressional arenas by residents and representatives from

Wisconsin, and later Michigan and Texas when those states became likely deployment sites, led the navy to abandon the larger scope of the Sanguine project.

Although research and development of smaller ELFs (Seafarer and then Elf) continued following this reversal, to date the navy has not successfully overcome the public and congressional resistance fueled by environmental and social considerations. In fact, formidable legal problems presented by NEPA loomed even larger after the MX experience, further tempering the interest of the executive branch in deploying an ELF system. The opposition remains fearsome given the increased concern in the 1980s about nuclear war.

In addition to domestic factors, technical uncertainty has contributed to dissension within the executive branch. The rapid expansion and MIRVing Soviet ICBM force in the early 1970s raised questions about the vulnerability of even a system as massive as that envisioned by ELF. While expanding the size of ELF to increase invulnerability was viewed as a technically appropriate response, it would raise even greater environmental and social problems, thus exacerbating public concern.

ELF Deviates From the Conventional Wisdom

The pattern of ELF procurement decision making has been quite different than one would expect given the propositions of the bureaucratic politics paradigm. As with ABM, the defeat of ELF was influenced by forces and actors operating outside the executive arena. To an increasing extent after 1970, the congressional, public, and electoral arenas became battle grounds for ELF. At the state and local levels, citizens and government officials alike were mobilizing against the procurement of ELF and deployment in Wisconsin, Michigan, and Texas; activity contrary to the traditional enthusiasm that people have shown for public work projects in the past. Rather, domestic concerns became germane in a negative way, as the environmental and social dimension of ELF procurement became more visible and salient. Technical uncertainty exacerbated ELF's problems. Thus, issues beside organizational interests heavily influenced ELF decision making and drove the decision beyond the confines of the executive branch. Competing coalitions of interests were active and effective in several different arenas.

MX Or Missile Experimental

On September 8, 1979, President Carter announced the decision to build and deploy a new generation of ICBMs in a mobile, land-based mode (the multiple protective shelter or MPS system) in the Great Basin desert region of Nevada and Utah. That deceptively definitive decision followed ten years of

130

rivalry within the executive arena, and conflict between the executive and legislative branches. It also proved to be the beginning of accelerated state and public resistance to the mammoth defense project; resistance that ultimately compelled President Reagan to abandon the MPS basing mode, and Congress to several times postpone funding for the full development of the ten warhead missile itself. Although neither the Senate nor House of Representatives has ever approved terminating MX production outright, legislative opponents have succeeded in a series of actions to slow down production or link it to administrative efforts in arms control, thus retarding the deployment of the weapon system itself.

As of fall 1986 the fate of MX remains unclear. The missile system barely survived the aggressive scrutiny of the 98th and 99th Congresses. For example, Reagan's request in FY 1985 defense budget for forty new missiles was slashed by Congress to twenty-one.[10] Under a compromise negotiated before the 1984 election between Congress and the president, the $1.5 billion needed to build even those missiles was made contingent on both the Senate and House taking affirmative action twice in spring 1985 to release the money. In more recent action (FY 1986), Congress capped permanently total MX deployment at 50 missiles, striking at the logic of an earlier compromise reached between Congress and the Reagan administration following the release of the Scowcroft report (1983). Any missiles purchased in 1987 and beyond can only be used for testing purposes. The practical effect of Congress's capping action is to strike at the strategic viability of the entire MX system as currently defined; that is, deployment in retrofitted Minuteman silos. Deployment short of the 100 anticipated missiles increases the system's vulnerability. The survivability of MX still depends on how the missiles are based, defended or used.[11]

The Origins Of and Early R&D On MX

The bureaucratic politics paradigm accurately predicts that the idea for a new experimental missile would originate with air force officers and defense industry personnel seeking to develop a third generation of ICBMs as a logical follow-on to the very successful Minuteman program. As the paradigm suggests, decision making at this point was confined to those defense experts in the executive arena responsible for the operation and procurement of weapon systems. During the design and development stages, the missile and the various basing modes were influenced by intragovernmental conflicts over the character and capability of the new ICBM and by the desires of groups within the Defense Department (and their defense industry allies) to advance their organizational missions or personal interests.

131

In this period, three issues were critical in guiding the direction of MX through the organizational maze. The first concerned projections during the late 1960s and early 1970s by the Pentagon that Soviet ICBM improvements in accuracy, fractionation, and throwweight would ultimately threaten the land-based leg of the U.S. triad. The solution was a basing mode capable of making the new missile unvulnerable. From then on the weapon system developed dyadic qualities, and policymaking by necessity occurred at several levels at once.

Second, the missile was linked to the air force and OSD's commitment to develop a fully capable war-fighting strategy and capability. The MX with its greater warhead fractionation and accuracy, provided the vehicle for realizing this new military strategy.

Third, MX was viewed as being technically feasible, even in light of the sophisticated technological challenges that the system presented. In fact, engineering groups in Director, Design, Development, Research and Engineering (DDR&E) of OSD, the design labs of defense industries, especially TRW, and engineering elements in RAND Corporation portrayed MX technically as an incremental improvement of the Minuteman strategic program.

Issues that Forced MX Visibility and Saliency

Beginning in 1973, however, different forces and issues began to emerge that forced MX to emerge from the inner sanctum of the Pentagon and develop a saliency in U.S. politics seldom experienced by any procurement issue: dissension over the strategic viability of MX, technical uncertainties, financial questions, foreign policy events, and social/environmental concerns.

Since the 1970s, decisions on MX have been shaped in part by the sharp strategic differences both within and outside the bureaucratic/organizational and public/political communities.[12] MX advocates who embrace the strategic policies of assured destruction and a war-fighting capability, have sought a basing mode for the missile capable of reducing its vulnerability and preserving its hard-target capability and increased warhead fractionation. Opponents have been concerned with the fact that the missile system may be a provocation in the ongoing arms race with the Soviet Union. Many supporters became opponents during the early part the the Carter (1977) and the Reagan administrations when the war-fighting potential of MX was emphasized regardless of the invulnerability issue. Similarly, some congressional moderates have relinquished their opposition to the system in return for administrative assurances of progress on arms control. Thus, the coalitions on MX have been volatile. Moreover, the absence of a clear convergence and mutually supportive set of roles for MX has left its strategic rationale muddled.

Strategic dissension has been an important factor in the missile system's lengthy and convoluted experience, a condition exacerbated by technical uncertainty. To make MX invulnerable has been a challenging and as yet unresolved dilemma; one which centers on finding an appropriate basing mode. However, all the options, the underground trench system, the race track mode, the grid system, the superhardening of Minuteman silos, and the closely spaced basing mode, have exhibited theoretical and/or practical problems that created considerable doubts about the ability of defense labs to overcome them. Since the proposed system could not guarantee the invulnerability sought, it confronted considerable difficulties in achieving the necessary support for authorization and appropriation for MX acquisition and deployment. Most recently (FY 1986), Congress capped production of missiles at 50 pending discovery of a different basing method capable of closing the elusive window of vulnerability.

The strategic dissension and technical problems that have plagued and continue to plague the weapon system have been compounded by the enormous price-tag of MX. The projected cost of MX consistently has made it a convenient target for budget cutters both within and outside the executive branch. Heightening fiscal concerns has been skepticism over the reliability of the Pentagon's estimates of MX costs, which generally fail to factor in the additional expense of meeting possible Soviet countermeasures to offset increased U.S. invulnerability. For example, the Carter administration's projection of $40 billion for MX was considered low by a factor of two or three by many analysts. The Carter MX weapon system promised before it was significantly altered in the early 1980s to be the most expensive public works project in the history of the human race. Even now it is unlikely that MX will escape the Gramm-Rudman scalpel.

Fourth, MX was and continues to be inextricably linked to the foreign policy issue of strategic arms limitations. During the Nixon era, deployment of MX had to be consistent with the requirements of the SALT I agreement, i.e., strategic weapons could be deployed only if verifiable by independent national means. In SALT I and initially in SALT II the United States sought to negotiate a prohibition of mobile ICBM basing, imposing further constraints on basing alternatives for MX. During the Ford and Carter years the United States abandoned the limitation on deployment of mobile ICBMs, partially in recognition of the invulnerability advantage of basing mobility. Still, any basing mode, even a mobile one, must be subject to independent means of national verification. The controversial nature of the SALT

133

negotiations and U.S. negotiating positions helped to place MX onto the national agenda. Today MX continues to be embroiled in the Reagan administration's efforts to demonstrate U.S. military strength and resolve; and in the deployment of modern nuclear weapons in the West European theatre. In 1985 the Reagan administration linked success in START to further funding of MX deployment. The administration now argues that a vote against MX would undermine U.S. bargaining leverage in arms control negotiations with the Soviets. According to Congressional Quarterly Weekly Report (March 23, 1986:518) the major factor influencing the Senate votes on March 19 and 20, 1986, to approve MX production was the arms control negotiations with the Soviets. Many members who were not sympathetic to MX voted for it to avoid the appearance of interfering with the talks. MX is the classic bargaining chip for Soviet missile reductions.

Finally, MX, since its strategic viability is contingent upon a suitable basing mode, has posed environmental, social, and cultural consequences previously unimagined, consequences considerable enough to alone generate public and congressional opposition. For example, the MPS mode, in rotating 200 missiles among 4600 shelters, would have appropriated 40,000 square miles to public land supporting the interests of a variety of groups (Holland and Hoover, 1985:Chapter 5). The current plan to deploy the missile in retrofitted Minuteman silos is a temporary one at best, making the search for a basing mode still compelling.

MX Deviates from Conventional Wisdom

After 1973, the technical problems associated with MX survivability, the strategic controversy about MX, and eventually the financial costs of the weapon system, had the effect of provoking strong opposition within and later outside the executive arena: that narrow circle of interests of the air force and design labs where weapon ideas originate and evolve. Particularly active were key members of Congress, who were successful during the early 1970s (1973-76) in restricting or altering various research and development programs necessary for a new ICBM. Examples are restrictions on R&D for improvements in counterforce accuracy and warhead yield (the WS120 program), and the rejection of the Ford administration's proposal to acquire and deploy MX in Minuteman silos as an interim basing solution. The latter action was a major and almost unprecedented reversal of executive branch procurement policy by the Congress.

Foreign policy considerations have not been as crucial nor pervasive as the strategic and technical problems in MX decision making, they have had the effect of expanding the arena of conflict to include the larger national security community of the White House, the Department of State, ACDA, and additional members of Congress. For example, winning Senate ratification of the SALT II agreement was a crucial factor in the Carter decision to endorse MX MPS. It was the bait to attract conservative support for the treaty. The deployment of Pershing II and cruise missiles in Europe was a critical factor in the three acquisition decisions made by the Reagan administration between 1981 and April 1983. The Reagan administration's commitment to strategic arms reduction in START was an important factor in the president's tenuous but successful pleas for MX funding in 1983. Since 1983, the status of MX has been tied in even more direct ways to the nuclear arms policies, and therefore, national security positions of the Reagan administration.

Finally, the projected cost and environmental/social impact of MX were also salient factors in forcing MX decision making into the congressional, public, and state/local political arenas. Although Congress was involved significantly in MX R&D between 1975 and 1979, it is at the acquisition and deployment stage of procurement that we find the more direct involvement. In fact, since 1979 the fate of MX was tied to legislative activities. More precisely, members of Congress employed their appropriations powers to direct MX procurement activities in the executive arena. This pattern of activity is contrary to the thrust of bureaucratic politics paradigm. Legislative involvement with MX deviates in several other important ways: in the large scope of and variety in the participation by members of Congress, the variety of concerns motivating legislative actors, the total complex of committees and subcommittees brought into play, the scope and quantity of information generated both within and by the national legislature, and the character of executive-legislative coalition building.

There are several cogent examples of congressional involvement in the MX decision-making process during the acquisition and deployment phase (i.e., that time when the executive branch asks for acquisition and until the system is fully deployed). In May 1979, in advance of any administrative commitment, Congress initiated funding decisions that ultimately compelled President Carter to endorse the full-scale engineering development of MX in the MPS mode. Pressure from Congress and interest in securing approval of SALT II by the Senate led Carter to commit to a weapon he had previously rejected as an outrageous "Rube Goldberg" scheme. Congress then proceeded with the following steps: (1) legislate an Initial Operating Capability (IOC) of 1986 for MX; (2) circumscribe the geographic location of the missile system (P.L. 96-29); (3) reaffirm the value of full public and state scrutiny of the mammoth project (through deflecting fast-track legislation); (4) mandate the discovery of a basing mode capable of making the missile truly invulnerable; (5) require the reduction of costs and impacts on deployment areas of the MPS system in Texas and New Mexico (P.L. 96-342); (7) block funds for the development of the missile until a basing

135

mode decision was made and _accepted_ by Congress (P.L. 97-99, P.L. 97-323); (8) threaten to hold up public land withdrawal until the Draft Environmental Impact Statement (DEIS) mandated by NEPA was properly prepared (P.L. 96-436); (9) compel the air force to develop ways to mitigate and compensate for the massive environmental, socioeconomic, and cultural impacts of the military project in the selected deployment areas (P.L. 97-99); and (10) permanently cap the production of missiles to be deployed in retrofitted Minuteman silos.

Both the Ford (1976) and Reagan (1981) administrations' proposals to retrofit MX in Minuteman silos were, for all practical purposes, rejected by Congress, forcing the administration in each case back to the drawing board to discover a basing mode that was acceptable to the national legislature.[13] Congress's most recent action to cap the number of production missiles at 50, pending the discovery of a viable basing mode capable of protecting the missiles, demonstrates this. The entire strategic logic of the Peacekeeper program, as long as the ICBMs are deployed in Minuteman silos, is contingent upon the production of a minimum of 100 missiles. Congress now also expects the weapon system to pose reasonable (manageable) and feasible financial, environmental, and political consequences, as evidenced by its rejection of air-mobile, deep basing, missile defense, and dense pack. None of these alternatives met Congress's requirements for survivability and political feasibility.

The practical effect of the contention between the legislative and executive bodies over MX has been to promote bargaining and compromising in advance of congressional action. For example, the decision to deploy Peacekeeper in existing silos in Wyoming represents a carefully crafted compromise by leading figures inside both the executive and legislative branches. In that bargain (resulting from the President's Commission on Strategic Forces or the Scowcroft Commission), Congress consented to provide financial support for the deployment of the MX in Minuteman silos; and the president agreed to abandon both the concept of a window of vulnerability and much of the logic of his strategic program, and broaden his commitment to strategic arms limitation. More recently, Congress's action capping missile production followed an agreement reached with the White House, in which Weinberger both promised to abide by the 50 missile limit and not to seek additional MX funds in fiscal 1987. Ironically, by capping the number of production missiles at 50, the viability of silo basing, even as an interim measure, is in question.

Congress and the executive branch have not been the only active arenas in MX decision making. Concerns expressed by both citizens and officials about the environmental, cultural, and socioeconomic consequences of MX deployment influenced the Carter

136

and Reagan administration's decisions to abandon the MAP (multiple aim point) and MPS basing modes, respectively. Similar concerns have influenced decision making within the Reagan administration. Both interim silo-basing and dense pack reflect efforts by the administration to prevent the reoccurrance of the sort of public opposition that emerged over mobile basing; and to circumvent the more onerous and potentially obstructive provisions of key domestic legislation (e.g., the National Environmental Policy Act of 1969 and the Federal Land Policy and Management Act of 1976) that MX opponents used or proposed to use as vehicles for defeating MX.

The very existence of formal (i.e., legislatively mandated) opportunities for public and state actors to intrude upon the policymaking process for military matters illuminates a significant shortcoming in the conventional wisdom of the bureaucratic politics paradigm; that is, its failure to anticipate the devisive effects of public action. The MX MPS system was rejected by the Reagan administration in part because the project, in activating as many as thirty eight different federal laws, each with substantive and procedural conditions that, if violated, could have provided grounds for litigation, threatened to tie up the system in endless delay, at the expense of the 1986 IOC date. A delay this significant could threaten the very mission and success of the MX program, at least from the perspective of the Pentagon.[14]

The activities in the public arena have been significant, even decisive in MX decision making. Public and state groups actively involved in resisting MX ultimately compelled the Carter administration to abandon its plan to deploy the missiles in a MAP prototype in the South Platte region of Kansas, Nebraska and Colorado; and influenced the Reagan administration to abandon MX MPS and seek other alternative basing modes that would utilize less public land, command fewer budgetary dollars, and threaten less environmental and cultural dislocation than that posed by MPS basing. Despite the fact that the full deployment of MX is now in doubt, public, congressional, and state opposition has continued, fueled by concerns over Reagan's cavalier attitude towards nuclear war and the escalating nuclear arms race with the Soviet Union.

Again, there are several aspects of the MX case that demonstrate the limitations of the bureaucratic politics paradigm. First, as with ABM and ELF, the focus of decision making was not confined solely to the executive branch. Congressional, public, and non-defense executive actors have been and continue to be significant. Second, groups of actors, previously inactive on defense matters have been important. Third, proponents and opponents formed coalitions that operated in several arenas. Finally, five crucial dimensions of the MX

137

issue, two of them ancillary to national security, drove the MX debate into these other arenas and altered the normal procurement pattern.

The future of MX is really on the line in the next months. The design of the missile is complete, it has demonstrated flight worthiness, all components for the first operational missiles have been tested, and billions of dollars have already been spent. Yet, Congress knows that the MX could be either bargained away, or abandoned in lieu of a more feasible and practical ICBM, such as Midgetman. Thus, there is still no guarantee that Peacekeeper in fact will be deployed. The logic of the bureaucratic politics model suggests that such things as sunk cost and organizational mission are compelling enough to overcome technical and political shortcomings. If money is not approved to sustain the system towards its fully conceived design, contractors could begin to disband their MX-related production teams; and the costs to start-up the program again would be extraordinary (CQW, March 9, 1986:438). Thus, the fate of the system is still uncertain, defying the expectations of the bureaucratic politics paradigm.

The Midgetman Program

With the release of the recommendations of the President's Commission on Strategic Forces (Scowcroft Commission), in April, 1983, the Midgetman program was born.[15] As part of its endorsement of MX, the Commission urged the president and Congress to develop and deploy a small, mobile, single-warhead, intercontinental ballistic missile (SICM). Congress obliged, amending the 1984 defense authorization bill to require development and testing of Midgetman in advance of MX deployment in 1986. Congress also mandated that the air force complete guidance and propulsion tests for the SICM by that time, and set an upper limit of 33,000 pounds on the weight of the missile to assure its mobility and prevent MIRVing. Proponents were brought together by the belief that the small missiles would provide the requisite hard-target capability to put Soviet ICBMs at risk, while encouraging the de-MIRVing of the nuclear missile forces in each country. Opponents saw Midgetman posing technical, fiscal, social and foreign policy problems similar in nature to those of MX. The status of Midgetman is contingent upon how these latter issues are addressed.

The Origin and Early R&D on Midgetman

The Midgetman became Boeing Company's solution to the ICBM vulnerability problem, still looming as late as 1981, with the MX program in its advanced stages. The Seattle aerospace firm was instrumental in advancing the concept of a small, single-warhead missile from an idea (under discussion since the 1970s) to a

138

legitimate program with R&D funding. Boeing succeeded in addressing the three critical dimensions of the ICBM problem: technical feasibility, strategic viability, and foreign policy compatibility. Thus, Midgetman initially was embraced with enthusiasm by a variety of groups because it appeared that the system could actually be built in a way that would contribute to the creation of a truly mobile and, thus, invulnerable land-based ICBM system.[16] Moreover, it would not exacerbate the arms race with the Soviets, or violate any existing agreements or treaties. Ironically, these qualities are now the system's nemeses.

The origins of Midgetman lie in the administration's efforts to depoliticize the ICBM issue. The defeat of the Reagan administration's first two MX basing proposals (interim basing in Minuteman silos and the closely spaced basing mode), demonstrated the extent to which the president's nuclear weapons policies were mired in political conflict. After succeeding in defusing an earlier political problem with the appointment of a bipartisan committee (the fiscal integrity of social security), Reagan seized upon the same tactic. The declining strategic credibility of the administration led to the appointment of the President's Commission on Strategic Forces in January 1983.[17] While conceived by the administration as a way to provide technical and strategic justification for MX, the Commission tied its support of Peacekeeper to an administration commitment for development and deployment of Midgetman. This and another recommendation that the United States seek a strategic arms limitation agreement with the Soviets which would reduce the number of MIRVed ICBMs contributed to the Commission becoming a political vehicle for the administration. The Commission's political role was enhanced by the mandate that it coordinate the consult with members of Congress during the development of its proposals. This laid the foundation for all subsequent aspects of the decision on both MX and Midgetman which have involved compromises negotiated between members of the executive and legislative bodies as well as members of the Commission.

That the Scowcroft Commission succeeded in rescuing MX by tying it to development of a single-warhead missile and aggressive strategic arms limitation/deMIRVing efforts with the Soviets, by encouraging executive-legislative interaction and negotiation, and by salvaging the strategic policy for the Reagan administration is remarkable. Midgetman became the key to deMIRVing or as it became known, "build-down," and to increasing ICBM survivability through mobile basing.[18]

A coalition was forged between members of the administration, Congress, and key individuals from the Scowcroft Commission. This provided the impetus for the adoption of the broad outline of the proposal (Drew, 1983 and Talbott, 1985:330-42). Congress directed the Pentagon to begin the

139

development of the Midgetman concept in 1983. Following the first review of SICM released by the air force in September 1983, Lockheed Missiles and Space Company, McDonnell Douglas Astronautics, and Goodyear Aerospace were each awarded contracts to begin engineering studies on the proposed weapon system. Congress awarded additional contracts to begin studies on penetration and maneuvering reentry vehicles for the Midgetman program that would offset potential Soviet ABM developments. At the same time (1984), models of hardened mobile launchers were developed for testing. Congress continued support for research, engineering, and testing of the Midgetman concept in 1985 and 1986.

Consequently, the bureaucratic politics paradigm is only partially useful in explaining the origins of SICM R&D. Contrary to the thrust of its assumptions, Midgetman has been considerably more visible than previous weapon systems. Although the defense industry and air force were instrumental in providing the technical and strategic logic for SICM, the decisive developmental factors were political ones. A coalition directed by the Scowcroft Commission and composed of members of the executive and Congress brought about the decision for R&D on the new, small mobile missile. Since then, the program has never ceased to be a controversial political issue.

Issues that Forced Increased Midgetman Visibility and Saliency

In the summer of 1985 and in the first months of 1986, the Midgetman program moved from the halls of the Pentagon to the front pages of national journals and newspapers. The same five issues (technical uncertainty, strategic dissension, foreign policy problems, financial costs, and environmental/social concerns) that increased the visibility and saliency of ABM, ELF and MX also operated to seriously impair the possibility of Midgetman being deployed in the near future, if at all.

For strategic reasons, Congress mandated physical requirements for the missile that in turn exacerbated Midgetman's technical problems. For example, the weight limitation of 33,000 pounds complicates the ability of the missile to meet the flight requirements of the air force without significant innovations in missile casing, propellants, and exhaust nozzle technologies. As such, the missile will require a more sophisticated guidance system than is now available. Congress's expectations that the missile system be a mobile one, capable of riding on off-road terrain, complicates the development of a Hard Mobile Launcher (HML). Now, the HML must be capable of moving the ICBMs quickly on rough terrain, without jeopardizing the flight capability of the delicate missile. Further, the HML must "withstand a whole array of nuclear effects," the most demanding being survival of very high blast overpressure from a nuclear strike (Berg, 1985).

140

There are doubts about whether an HML can be developed to survive 30 lbs/sq inch overblast pressure (the recommended design characteristic) without sacrificing the mobility requirements of the missile. In fact HML may become too heavy for rapid mobility on off-road terrain as it is developed to meet the overblast requirements for survival. The Government Accounting Office's (GAO) study of Midgetman, mandated by Congress, was quite dubious about Midgetman having the necessary mobility for survivability and accuracy to meet the Pentagon's hard target requirements.

Even if a mobile HML could be designed to survive the requisite blast pressure, a barrage attack by the Soviets against a Midgetman force concentrated on a military reservation might still destroy the bulk of the missiles. Survivability of Midgetman in the face of a barrage attack is a joint function of dispersal area and vehicle hardness. However, hardening could reduce mobility, while enlarging the dispersal area could produce environmental/social problems similar to the MX program (Berg, 1985). An arms control agreement that limits the barrage potential of Soviet forces either by reductions in Soviet throwweight or warhead numbers would enhance the survivability of Midgetman without the need for greater area for dispersal or increasing the size of the HML. This complicates the issue by adding a foreign policy dimension.

Additional technical complications result from the goal of the air force for a 6,000 nautical mile range. Equipping the Midgetman with penetration aids in addition to a reentry vehicle, to foil Soviet missile defenses, would increase the missile's weight, reducing both its range and conflicting with the 33,000 pound limitation (Berg, 1985). Moreover, reductions in range could affect deployment decisions by making sites in the southwestern United States impractical. While Midgetman remains popular with Congress, support has eroded in the face of these difficult technical problems.

Strategic dissension, both within and outside the executive branch, has imposed further constraints on the ability of the Pentagon to act and the nature of its Midgetman program. For those among the civilian force of the Pentagon seeking a war-fighting capability, the value of Midgetman is uncertain. These individuals attribute the missile system's success so far to the inappropriate influence of those outside the Pentagon who are ill-equipped to decide procurement issues. Thus, there is considerable interest in either cancelling the missile or enlarging its size to give it greater hard-target kill capability.

In opposition to this group are those who embrace the SICM program as a way to render invulnerable the land-based leg of the nuclear triad through developing a truly mobile ICBM system.

Alligned with this group are those who see Midgetman as a vehicle for encouraging the de-MIRVing of the nuclear weapons forces of both the United States and the Soviet Union.

Additional constraints on procurement activity exist because of the enormous potential costs of the SICM program. The GAO report on SICM suggests that the cost of a 500 missile program would be between $43 billion and $49 billion depending on the nature of the basing mode. As Scott Berg (1985) suggests, "This translates to $86-98 million per warhead. In comparison, the MX, the most expensive ICBM to date, will cost about $25 million per warhead if based in superhardened silos." Given the technical problems and strategic concerns aired, it is difficult for some people to justify this financial commitment.

The strategic logic of Midgetman lies in its mobility, a condition that complicates its technical feasibility and renders the system enormously costly. Moreover, any mobile system poses problems of public interface. According to Berg (1985)

> For a 500 missile system, [the air force believes] at least 4,000 square miles of land will be needed for daily operations. During periods of increasing alert, that area will expand to 8,000 square miles, and if there is danger of imminent attack, the launchers would further disperse. The GAO warned that securing sufficient land for deploying a mobile system would be challenging and time consuming. In addition, it revived an important issue from the MX debate, saying, "Environmental concerns will have to be resolved before a hard-mobile ICBM can be deployed."

Having recognized this element in advance, opposition groups mobilized in many of the states viewed as likely site recipients. For example, reaction from Utahns to the military's first announcement (April 1985) identifying candidate basing areas was hostile. Governor Norman Bangerter expressed anger at not being consulted in advance of the decision identifying Utah as a possible site for Midgetman deployment. The governor immediately organized a state task force for an independent evaluation of the missile deployment and site selection process. Senator Jake Garn (ROUt) noted that he too was "angry at the shoddy treatment" Utahns were given by the air force. A Citizens Task Force on Midgetman was formed to coordinate information gathering efforts with other states. It is interesting to note that Utahns were the most active in opposing Midgetman at the state/local level; and that the air force's May 1986 decision narrowing of prospective sites eliminated only Utah from consideration.

In advance of the final deployment decision (i.e., site-selection and land acquisition), the government must complete environmental impact studies and mission conflict analyses. Eventually, a legislative environmental impact statement (EIS) must be prepared by the Defense Department. While participation of the public and governmental bodies in deciding the scope and significant issues to be addressed in the statement is not required, the military recommended public comment. Citizens in Colorado, Wyoming, and Nevada, actively involved in opposing the Midgetman are already threatening legal action against the military. Such action is made possible by the provisions of NEPA when an EIS is conducted; even a legislative one.

Midgetman became a major piece in the arms control game played with the Soviets. During the SALT II negotiations, the United States abandoned its opposition to mobile ICBM missiles on the condition that national independent means of verification of numbers could be achieved. This change in policy corresponded to the Carter administration's decision to deploy MX MPS. The Reagan administration not only once again altered the position of the United States on mobile missiles, but it also stated that it will no longer be bound by the treaty. The motivation appears to be a concern on the part of the Reagan administration over two new mobile Soviet ICBMs, the SS-25 and SS-X-24, and their potential refiring capability. The irony is that the United States is arguing against mobile missiles in negotiations with the Soviets and, thus, its own missile program. Given the central position of mobile Midgetman to earlier compromises on MX, any deviation from the original commitment by the Reagan administration could jeopardize both programs.

The five issues discussed above continue to operate to restrict the military's control of the Midgetman program. In its most recent action (June 24, 1986), the House Armed Services Committee voted to "sharply limit" the deployment of MX until "major missile components, awarding of contracts for full-scale missile development, and evidence from the Pentagon that Midgetman will be deployed by 1992 (New York Times, June 25, 1986:1). The vote reflects the concerns that some committee members have about the Pentagon's desire to see the size of the Midgetman missile enlarged to allow it eventually to be fitted with more warheads. In fact, the Defense Department has demonstrated considerable interest in developing a larger missile capable of carrying at least two warheads. Moreover, the president has ordered a study to determine the value of building a mobile 78,000 pound, multiple-warhead missile.

The House Committee's action can also be viewed as an attempt by legislators to strengthen their negotiating positions on budget issues in general, and on the SDI program in particular. In any event, the Pentagon's failure to meet the terms of the committee bill could delay the Midgetman program for up to two years, jeopardizing its IOC date and, thus, its

143

strategic logic. Perhaps not coincidentally, the administration
has indicated its plan to recommend new basing modes for MX
during December 1986, when key decisions on Midgetman are
expected to be made. The decisions may be timed to allow the
Pentagon to make their support of Midgetman conditional on
congressional approval of additional MX missiles.

Midgetman Deviates from Conventional Wisdom

Almost from its inception, the Midgetman program has
deviated from the pattern of procurement politics suggested by
the bureaucratic politics paradigm. While the impetus for the
missile came from the defense industry and Pentagon, the
decisions made by the military have been influenced, modified,
and even reversed by other actors, including congressional and
public ones. Moreover, forces other than
bureaucratic/organizational and personal administrative ones have
and continue to impinge on the decisions made concerning SICM.
The telling year is 1986. Funds for full scale development of
the system must be committed. By the end of the year decisions
will be made concerning how and where the Midgetman will be
deployed.

To date, the Midgetman has been one of the most visible and
highly politicized weapon systems in the military's history. The
fact that the conditions of the visibility and politicization of
Midgetman are similar in nature to those of ABM, ELF, and MX
allows us to speculate on the future of procurement politics.

CONCLUSIONS

The student of politics seeking to understand how and why
the United States decides to build and deploy major weapon
systems such as ABM, ELF, MX, and Midgetman will find the
bureaucratic politics perspective only partially useful. The
paradigm continues to demonstrate utility when applied to the R&D
stage of procurement politics. At the acquisition and deployment
stage, decision making sometimes deviates from the conventional
pattern. The weapon systems we selected to study, while sharing
common qualities, may together constitute a separate category of
military projects. If this is the case, then the bureaucratic
politics paradigm for procurement requires modification in order
to recognize this diversity.

What are the qualities that set apart the four military
cases examined above. How do these cases suggest modifications
in the bureaucratic politics paradigm? In each case the proposed
weapon system was promoted as a technical solution to a strategic
problem, but one that was from the start systematically
uncertain. For example, there was ambiguous evidence to support
the claims that ABM could effectively deflect a Soviet

144

first-strike, that ELF would not be destroyed prior to its use, or that MX and Midgetman could be made invulnerable. The high level of uncertainty provoked enough controversy within the executive arena to facilitate its movement outside that arena. As E.E. Schattschneider noted, "the outcome of all conflict is determined by the scope of its contagion" (1969:2). Controversy appears to contribute to the communicability of an issue.

Uncertainty is a necessary, although not a sufficient, condition for explaining the unique nature of procurement politics discussed here. Otherwise all past (e.g., Sergeant York) and future (e.g., SDI) military projects exhibiting the same technical ambiguity would have had or would be having the same experience. Another critical element is the degree to which the military project became intertwined with issues ancillary to the central strategic and technical ones; that is, foreign policy social/environmental, and fiscal ones. Again, these issues seem to have had the effect of further expanding the arena of conflict by provoking the ire of those in the congressional and public arenas.

However, this cannot explain the nature of the influence exercised by actors outside the executive branch. In important ways, the fact that the arena of conflict was broadened had an effect on policy making itself; both the process and outcomes of that process. "The number of people involved in any conflict determines what happens; every change in the number of participants, every increase or reduction in the number of participants, affects the result" (Schattschneider, 1960:2). To explain this phenomenon we need to recognize that in each of our cases those actors seeking to direct the military in its decision making had the legal means to do so in ways that compelled the Pentagon to listen, if not respond. In some cases, such as Congress's appropriations powers and the public's electora power, the means to influence procurement politics always have existed. In other cases, statutory means have been created more recently which given the public opportunities to threaten direct legal action, as evidenced by NEPA (1969). In each of the three cases decided since 1969, NEPA has been operative.

Finally, the four military systems we reviewed exhibit characteristics that set them apart; and make them more provacative. Three qualities in particular are telling: size, impact, and cost. As originally conceived, each system would be large enough to threaten to impact the social environment in disruptive ways, and be extremely costly.

Unless the United States decides to abandon the land-based leg of the nuclear triad, discovers a way to harden stationary silos to make mobility unnecessary, develops the technology to direct its nuclear missile forces in unobtrusive ways, or

145

abandons its current strategic policies, many future military projects will exhibit the same qualities as ABM, ELF, MX, and Midgetman.

1. See for example, Beard (1976), Greenwood (1975), Hammond (1963), Sapolsky (1972), Brandon (1963), and Davis (1973).

2. For a discussion of the bureaucratic politics paradigm see Huntington (1961), Allison (1969), Allison (1971), Allison and Halperin (1972), Halperin and Kanter (1973), and Halperin (1974). For a critical examination of the literature see Destler (1974), George (1980) and Caldwell (1977).

3. See for example Dey (1981).

4. For an extended discussion of the propositions of the bureaucratic politics paradigm see Holland and Hoover (1984:Chapter 2).

5. The discussion of ABM decision making is based on Halperin (1972), Newhouse (1973), Kurth (1971), and Yanarella (1977).

6. For discussion of Nixon administration's decisions about ABM, see Yanarella (1977:145-86).

7. The discussion of ELF decision making is based on Klessig and Strite (1980).

8. An EIS is required in cases where a proposed project will have a significant impact on the human environment.

9. The discussion of MX decision making is based on Holland and Hoover (1985).

10. Although, Congress did approve the production of 20 flight test missiles and 21 operational missiles.

11. The administration expects to deploy 100 MX missiles in modified silos now housing Minuteman III ICBMs. Of this, ten are expected to be deployed by December 1986, 40 by December 1987, 79 by December 1988, and the entire 100 by December 1989.

12. In fact, during April and May of 1980, several modifications in the racetrack basing scheme were accomplished, just prior to the authorization vote. Ultimately, the racetrack mode was abandoned by the Reagan administration.

13. For a thorough discussion of the twists and turns of Minuteman silo basing for MX, see Holland and Hoover (1985:Chapters 6 and 9).

14. For example, General Kelly H. Burke suggested that "Appreciable delay in any of [the procurement] steps would be detrimental to that requirement [of reaching an Initial Operating Capacity by the end of 1986]. Ultimately, because that IOC was established to meet a serious Soviet threat to the Nation's ICBMs which the Congress and President believe will exist by the mid-1980s, such a delay could significantly weaken the strategic defense posture of the country" (Farley, et al. v. U.S. Air Force, et al., 21 August 1981).

15. The Midgetman discussion that follows is based on the following sources: Baker and Wit, 1985; Gore, 1985; Berg, 1985; Herman, 1985; Talbott, 1985; and Drew, 1983.

16. An example of the Midgetman discussion making the national agenda is Kissinger, 1983.

17. For a discussion of the dynamics of the Scowcroft Commission see Drew, 1983 and Talbott, 1985.

18. See Fyre, 1983 and Gore, 1985 for a discussion of the relationship between the concept of build-down and Midgetman.

BIBLIOGRAPHY

Allison, Graham T. (1969) "Conceptual Models and the Cuban
Missile Crisis." American Political Science Review 43
(September): 689-718).

Allison, Graham T. (1971) Essence of Decision: Explaining the
Cuban Missile Crisis. Boston, Massachusetts: Little, Brown
and Company.

Allison, Graham T. and Morton Halperin. (1972) "Bureaucratic
Politics: A Paradigm and Some Policy Implications." In
Theory and Policy in International Relations edited by
Raymond Tanter and Richard H. Ullman. Princeton, New
Jersey: Princeton University Press.

Baker, John C. and Joel S. Wit. (1985) "Mobile Missiles and Arms
Control. Arms Control Today 15 (November/December):10-15.

Beard, Edmond. (1976) Developing the ICBM: A Study in
Bureaucratic Politics. New York: Columbia University
Press.

Berg, Scott L. (1985) "Midgetman: The Technical Problems."
Arms Control Today 15 (November/December):16-18.

Brandon, Henry. (1963) "Skybolt." In Readings in American
Foreign Policy: A Bureaucratic Perspective, edited by
Morton Halperin and Arnold Kanter. Boston, Massachusetts:
Little, Brown and Company.

Caldwell, Dan. (1977) "Bureaucratic Foreign Policy-Making."
American Behavioral Scientist 21 (September/October):87-110.

Davis, Vincent. (1973) "The Development of a Capability to
Deliver Nuclear Weapons by Carrier-Based Aircraft." In
Halperin and Kanter.

Destler, J. M. (1974) Presidents, Bureaucrats and Foreign
Policy. Princeton, New Jersey: Princeton University Press.

Dey, Thomas R. (1981) Understanding Public Policy. 4th Edition.
Englewood Cliffs, New Jersey: Prentice-Hall, Inc.

George, Alexander L. (1980) Presidential Decisionmaking in
Foreign Policy: The Effective Use of Information and
Advice. Boulder, Colorado: Westview Press.

Greenwood, Ted. (1975) Making the MIRV: A Study of Defense
Decision Making. Cambridge, Massachusetts: Ballinger
Publishing Company.

149

Halperin, Morton.   (1972) "The Decision to Deploy the ABM:
     Bureaucratic   and   Domestic   Politics   in   the   Johnson
     Administration." World Politics 25 (October):62-95.

Halperin, Morton.   (1974) Bureaucratic Politics and Foreign
     Policy. Washington, D.C.: The Brookings Institution.

Halperin, Morton and Arnold Kanter. (1973) Readings in American
     Foreign Policy: A Bureaucratic Perspective.   Boston,
     Massachusetts: Little, Brown and Company.

Hammond, Paul. (1963) Super Carriers and B-36 Bombers:
     Appropriations, Strategy, and Politics.   Indianapolis,
     Indiana: Bobbs-Merrill Company, Inc.

Herman, Robert G. (1985) "Midgetman and Congress." Arms Control
     Today 15 (November/December):18-20.

Holland, Lauren H. and Robert A. Hoover. (1985) The Politics of
     MX: A New Direction in U.S. Weapons Procurement? Boulder,
     Colorado: Westview Press

Huntington, Samuel P. (1961) The Common Defense. New York:
     Columbia University Press.

Kissinger, Henry. (1983) "A New Approach to Arms Control." Time
     (March 21):24-26.

Klessig, Lowell L., and Victor L. Strite. (1980) The ELF
     Odyssey: National Security Versus Environmental Protection.
     Boulder, Colorado: Westview Press.

Kurth, James (1971) "A Widening Gyre: The Logic of American
     Weapons Procurement." Public Policy 7 (Summer):373:404.

Medalia, Jonathan E. (1985) Issue Brief: MX, Midgetman,
     Minuteman, and Titan Missile Programs. Washington, D.C.:
     Foreign Affairs and National Defense Division, Congressional
     Research Service (November 25).

Newhouse, John. (1973) Cold Dawn: The Story of SALT. New York:
     Holt, Rinehart, and Winston.

President's Commission on Strategic Forces. (1983) Report of
     the President's Commission on Strategic Forces. Washington,
     D.C.: U.S. Government Printing House.

Sapolsky, Harvey M. (1972) The Polaris System Development:
     Bureaucratic and Programmatic Success in Government.
     Cambridge, Massachusetts: Harvard University Press.

150

Schattschneider, E.E. (1960) The Semisovereign People. New
  York: Holt, Rinehart and Winston.

Talbott, Strobe. (1985) Deadly Gambits. New York: Vintage
  Books.

Yanarella, Ernest J. (1977) The Missile Defense Controversy:
  Strategy, Technology, and Politics, 1955-1972. Lexington,
  Kentucky: The University of Kentucky Press.

VULNERABILITY, UNCERTAINTY, AND PRIORITIES
FOR STRATEGIC ARMS CONTROL

P. Terrence Hopmann and J. Edward Anderson

I. DETERRENCE AND MISSILE VULNERABILITY

In recent years there has been a growing debate in
the United States about the most fundamental
assumptions underlying American strategic nuclear
doctrine, weapons procurement, and priorities for
strategic arms control. Much of the debate has been
based upon assumptions about a problem that has become
known as the "window of vulnerability." This argument
suggests that U.S. Intercontinental Ballistic Missiles
(ICBM's) are becoming increasingly vulnerable to a
Soviet first-strike. Since deterrence of a Soviet
attack is assumed to depend upon an assured ability by
the United States to retaliate against such an attack,
this growing vulnerability is alleged to be undermining
U.S. strategic deterrence, thereby making a nuclear war
more likely.

Therefore, this problem of ICBM vulnerability has
caused several U.S. administrations to challenge some
of the most fundamental assumptions of postwar American
doctrine and practice about the role of strategic
nuclear weapons. Traditionally, American doctrine
emphasized the belief, enunciated in 1946 by Bernard
Brodie, that nuclear weapons were fundamentally
different from other weapons due to their extremely
destructive power. Thus their only role was to deter
the use of nuclear weapons by the Soviet Union, or any
other country, against the United States or its
allies.[1] This concept became enshrined in the 1960's
under the doctrine of "mutual assured destruction."
Mutual deterrence would be maintained by each
superpower's certainty that their society, population,
and all that they valued would be destroyed in a major
nuclear exchange.

The main assumption of the "mutual assured
destruction" (MAD) approach was that the nuclear
balance is most stable and nuclear war is hence least
likely to occur when both nuclear superpowers have
nuclear forces which are invulnerable to being
destroyed in a first-strike by the other side. In this
circumstance, neither side has an incentive to launch

152

an attack, because it knows for certain that those invulnerable forces will survive in sufficiently large numbers to wreak tremendous destruction upon the attacker. Under such conditions, there could be no "winners" in a nuclear war, only mutual losers.

By contrast if one of the superpowers' nuclear forces became vulnerable to being destroyed in a first-strike by the other, then several problems might result. First, the invulnerable nation might be tempted to launch a pre-emptive first-strike in an effort to destroy the vulnerable forces of its opponent and thus "win" a nuclear war. While this would still be extremely risky, it was feared that a vulnerable nation might be particularly tempted to consider this option in a situation of intense crisis or in an escalating conventional war.

Second, perhaps more likely and more dangerous is the possibility that the vulnerable nation, thinking it was about to be attacked, might launch a pre-emptive strike against its opponent. While it could not win in such a situation, it might try to limit damage to itself or at least have "satisfaction" in knowing that it had destroyed its opponent, rather than waiting to be destroyed itself, and then left helpless to respond. While such thinking may not appear perfectly rational, it might most likely occur in a condition of extreme tension or crisis, when nuclear war seemed likely anyway. Then a pre-emptive strike might seem like the less bad of two undesirable choices. For this reason, such a situation is generally considered to be highly unstable in crises.

A third danger of asymmetrical vulnerability is that the vulnerable nation will place its forced on a "hair trigger" alert, perhaps launching them upon receiving a warning of an attack. While an invulnerable nation can wait to be absolutely certain that an attack is under way, knowing that its invulnerable forces can ride out the attack, a vulnerable nation cannot afford to wait. Any forces that are not fired before the opposing missiles arrive are in danger of being lost. But since warning times will usually be no greater than 30 minutes, a policy of launching retaliatory forces upon receipt of a warning places decision-makers under great time pressure to make momentous decisions. Under these stressful circumstances the probability that they might launch their forces accidentally as a result of a false alert or of a miscalculation of their opponent's behavior increases substantially. Thus the probability of inadvertent nuclear war is also greater when one of the nuclear superpowers is vulnerable than when both are invulnerable.

Finally, both superpowers could have forces that are vulnerable to being destroyed in a first-strike. Under these conditions, great advantage goes to the nation that strikes first, so such a condition would be extremely unstable, especially in a crisis. Mutual vulnerability increases the likelihood of nuclear war by premeditation, pre-emption, and inadvertently.

This theory of mutual deterrence also challenged several traditional assumptions of conventional warfare. First, it reduced substantially the importance of the number of weapons. No longer was there an advantage to be obtained just from numerical superiority. Rather the survivability of forces, a qualitative factor, became far more important. A smaller number of survivable forces was thus to be preferred to a larger number of vulnerable ones. Second, the advantages of superiority also largely evaporated. There was little to be gained from being invulnerable if the opponent was highly vulnerable. If, in an asymmetrical condition, the vulnerable state initiated a nuclear war either pre-emptively or accidentally, the invulnerable state would still find its population and economic base destroyed, even if some of its missiles survived. Thus the stability of the nuclear balance depended upon both nuclear superpowers remaining invulnerable, so that neither side had an incentive to initiate a nuclear first-strike.

This stability of mutual deterrence was further strengthened by the much more demanding technical requirements for launching a disarming first-strike versus a retaliatory second-strike. In order to retaliate against so-called "countervalue" targets such as cities and industrial centers, one only needed weapons capable of reaching the general proximity of their target with some reasonable probability. These targets are inherently highly vulnerable and impossible to protect, so pinpoint accuracy was hardly essential. Furthermore, since these targets cannot be emptied rapidly like a missile silo, the precise timing of an attack is not essential. Numerous shots can be fired at the same target at lengthy intervals to insure its destruction.

By contrast, a so-called "counterforce" first-strike is very demanding technically. One must hit and destroy small targets that are either dispersed and in hardened shelters or highly mobile. Timing is essential, because, unless all forces are destroyed simultaneously, the initial attack will signal any forces that survive it to retaliate. Therefore, any subsequent salvos may well be directed at empty weapon sites. In short, the technologies of the 1960's and 70's tended to reinforce mutual deterrence, because both sides clearly had a capability to carry out the less demanding mission of countervalue retaliation in a second-strike, while neither side had the capability to meet the far more demanding requirements of a counterforce first-strike.

In order to maintain this traditional mutual deterrence posture, the United States concentrated in the decade of the 1960's on the deployment of invulnerable strategic retaliatory forces, capable of being used in a second-strike if the U.S. or its allies were attacked by Soviet nuclear weapons. Arms control was also actively pursued in order to stabilize the balance of mutual deterrence through preserving the mutual invulnerability of American and Soviet retaliatory forces. Especially the SALT I Treaty and, to a lesser degree, the SALT II accord, sought to maintain mutual deterrence through preserving secure, second-strike forces on each side. Technologies such as Anti-Ballistic Missiles (ABM's) that might make a first-strike strategy more plausible were severely limited.

The recent trend in American policy, introduced by the Nixon/Ford administration, expanded under the Carter administration, and brought into full bloom by the Reagan administration, has challenged and overturned some of these most fundamental assumptions of postwar American doctrine and practice concerning the role of nuclear weapons. Numerous officials have argued that the increased accuracy of Soviet missile warheads, combined with the proliferation of missiles with multiple warheads (MIRV's), has made a large percentage of the American strategic forces vulnerable to a first-strike from the Soviet Union. This has become a principal justification since the early 1970's for the development and deployment of new strategic weapons such as the B-1 bomber and the MX missile. But more significantly it has introduced some profound changes in strategic doctrine.

155

Especially since 1980 a number of theorists, some of whom are close to or are members of the Reagan administration, have argued that the United States must itself possess first-strike strategic weapons, capable not only of retaliating against Soviet cities, economic targets, and societal infrastructure, but also capable of striking Soviet strategic forces on the ground. Thus the United States has moved from a position of trying to deter the Soviets through threats of unacceptable punishment in second-strike retaliation to being in a position where the U.S. "must prevail and be able to force the Soviet Union to seek earliest termination of hostilities on terms favorable to the United States."[2] Although administration interpretation of these phrases has been quite vague and ambiguous, it is clear that they seek to exploit the growing vulnerability of Soviet ICBMs by obtaining a U.S. ability to target these weapons with American strategic nuclear forces.

This has also had a profound effect upon the U.S. approach to strategic arms control negotiations. Indeed, these negotiations were renamed the STrategic Arms Reduction Talks (START) to signal a change of emphasis towards purely quantitative reductions. All U.S. proposals at the strategic arms control negotiations in Geneva since 1981 have thus been based upon various formulas for reductions of launchers and especially warheads, while permitting or even encouraging qualitative improvements to continue. Much of this approach seems to be based upon the assumption that the days of deterrence through mutual invulnerability are past. Indeed, since 1983 the Strategic Defense Initiative (SDI or "Star Wars" in more popular parlance) has emphasized a goal of significant strategic arms reductions along with the eventual construction of a large-scale population defense, presumably eventually by both superpowers. Yet such a defense, if it is to have any hope of working (and a clearcut majority of informed scientists tend to believe that it has virtually no hope of working as planned), requires significant reductions in offensive nuclear forces in order to make the job of the strategic defense less difficult. Yet much of this reorientation of policy by the Reagan administration, and the acceptance of the extraordinary political and economic costs required by such a shift in policy, seems to be based on the assumption that traditional deterrence through mutual invulnerability has been or will soon be outmoded by the "window of vulnerability." Even those who are more skeptical about SDI as a

156

population defense often support the program because of its more modest, but more realistic, role as a point defense of allegedly vulnerable ICBM sites. In this sense, the vulnerability problem is a critical stimulus to a large number of current defense programs and arms control priorities.

In short, this assumption about the growing vulnerability of land-based ICBMs has become the justification for a series of weapons procurement decisions and the foundation for a reassessment of both strategic doctrine and arms control philosophies. This assumption has thus become the basis for a complete turnabout in U.S. strategic weapons policy. Therefore, in considering the most basic choices about future directions for American strategic policy, it is essential that the underlying assumption itself be examined carefully and critically. Such an assessment is essential in order to determine whether the changes emanating from the alleged "window of vulnerability" are in fact justified.

Contrary to the prevailing arguments of recent administrations, we contend that the problem of ICBM vulnerability has been grossly exaggerated. Furthermore, the policy conclusions that have been derived from this inaccurate assessment of the vulnerability problem are not only unnecessary, but blatantly dangerous. These new deployments, doctrinal changes, and the resultant uncontrolled technological arms race can significantly decrease the stability of mutual nuclear deterrence and thereby dramatically increase the likelihood of nuclear war.

II. HOW VULNERABLE ARE U.S. ICBM'S?

A crucial assumption underlying most U.S. defense and arms control positions in recent years thus concerns the alleged "window of vulnerability." According to proponents of this theory, a large percentage, usually around 90%, of U.S. land-based ICBMs are vulnerable to being destroyed in a Soviet first-strike. Since the United States now has deployed 1030 ICBMs, that would leave only a little over 100 surviving to retaliate.

The main component of this force, 1000 Minuteman missiles, is deployed in underground silos hardened to withstand approximately 2000 pounds per square inch (p.s.i.) of overpressure from a nuclear shock-wave. A one-half megaton nuclear warhead, such as those carried

157

on the most accurate Soviet ICBM's, would thus have to land within about 300 meters of the silo in order to destroy the missile and to prevent it from being fired. The argument then assumes that Soviet missiles such as certain models of the SS-18 and SS-19 will hit within 250 meters of their targets about 50% of the time. This would give each warhead a theoretical capability to destroy its target about 63% of the time. The argument further suggests that with two independent warheads targeted at each ICBM, the probability of destruction would increase to about 86%. Thus with multiple warheads on current missiles, some 2100 warheads could destroy about 86% of the 1052 ICBMs in the U.S. force.[3]

The argument goes on to suggest a scenario in which the Soviets launch such an attack and largely cripple the U.S. ICBM force. Proponents of this scenario further assume that civilian casualties would be limited to between 10 and 20 million people due to the relatively sparse population concentration near American ICBM bases. Of course, any possible long-term consequences such as a "nuclear winter" has been completely overlooked in such a scenario. So they then assume that the Soviets might present the United States with an ultimatum either to surrender or to face a second salvo launched against American cities and industrial centers by the less accurate Soviet missiles that remained. Of course, since these targets are not hardened and cover large areas, the same level of accuracy is not necessary to destroy them, so they are inherently vulnerable targets. Such an ultimatum might then present the United States with two unacceptable choices: to surrender to the Soviet Union or to engage in a massive retaliatory response against Soviet cities and industrial/economic targets, which would in turn provoke an all-out Soviet strike against similar targets in the United States, destroying both countries.

When presented in these terms, this sounds like a frightening scenario that any prudent defense planner would want to avoid at all cost. The scenario has been widely introduced into the political arena and has been cited in various versions frequently by President Reagan, Secretary of Defense Weinberger, and many others. But is this scenario sufficiently likely to justify making it the central focus for much of American national security and arms control policy? It is our contention that it is not a realistic or feasible scenario, partly because it is based on

158

questionable assumptions about the accuracy and reliability of Soviet ballistic missiles in operational use against American ICBM's and partly because the scenario itself is not very logical.

Indeed, the term "window of vulnerability" is somewhat misleading, because it implies a dichotomous distinction between missiles that are vulnerable to being destroyed in a first-strike versus those that are invulnerable and thus capable of surviving a first-strike. Yet in fact these represent ends of a continuum, that can be expressed in probabilistic and percentage terms. Vulnerability increases as the probability of the Soviets destroying a high percentage of U.S. retaliatory forces increases. Vulnerability becomes a serious problem for defense planners only at the point on this continuum when the attacker might believe that he can be sufficiently confident of a high enough probability of destroying a large enough percentage of the retaliatory force to offset the tremendous risks involved. Thus the precise threshold of vulnerability is a highly subjective concept.

The estimate of a threshold of vulnerability, therefore, depends upon estimates of the reliability and accuracy of an attacker's forces. The reliability refers to the probability of an operationally successful strike, and the accuracy affects the probability that a successful attack will actually destroy the intended targets. Accuracy, in turn, depends on the radius of the area destroyed by the missile's warhead and the precision of its guidance system. American estimates of Soviet reliabilities and precision are based upon observations of test firings of their missiles under experimental conditions that bear little resemblance to their likely performance under wartime conditions. The basis for these estimates of Soviet missile reliability and precision is shrouded in official secrecy, and some U.S. Defense Department officials have contended that classified information confirms unambiguously their estimates about the high accuracies of Soviet missiles. In this view, access to such information would settle the question about ICBM vulnerability once and for all.[4]

On the other hand, the basic technology of missile guidance is well known from public sources, and in any event the performance of ballistic missiles is subject to the laws of physics, probability, and logic. Therefore, in spite of official secrecy, there is enough information available to demonstrate that the

159

operational reliability and precision of ballistic missiles is subject to many potential problems not taken into account in most official pronouncements about the vulnerability issue. These problems would create a great deal of uncertainty for a Soviet decision-maker who was contemplating using his ballistic missiles in a coordinated first-strike against all 1052 U.S. ICBM's.

The deterrent effects depend upon how this situation is evaluated by Soviet decision-makers. Given the terrible consequences for them of a miscalculation, they are unlikely to launch the kind of attack envisioned in these scenarios unless they can be extremely confident of success. Thus any doubts or uncertainties about success will serve as a significant deterrent. As we shall indicate, Soviet leaders contemplating such an attack would be faced with numerous sources of uncertainty.

In contemplating a first-strike Soviet leaders would have to estimate the probability of destroying U.S. missiles as well as the consequences of various rates of success. The kill probability, in turn, depends on: 1) the reliability of the missiles, 2) the problem of fratricide, 3) the kill radius of the warhead, 4) problems of fusing, 5) the precision of guidance, and 6) incorrectable systematic or bias errors. We consider each of these problems one at a time.[5]

First, problems of reliability concern the likelihood that missiles will perform without malfunction. A multistage ICBM like the SS-18 contains many components that can fail: rocket motors, gimballed thrust-direction controllers, stage-separation mechanisms, electronic circuits, computers, guidance systems, mechanisms for separating re-entry vehicles from the parent rocket or "bus," and fusing systems, just to mention the basic components. A failure of any one of these components on any of the several stages may cause a major departure from the planned trajectory. Because of the expense of testing, the amount of data available is much too small to estimate accurately the operational reliability of a fleet of ICBM's of the size required for a first-strike. Furthermore, although an effort is made to make tests resemble operational launches as much as possible, all such tests in peacetime are quite different from the conditions that would prevail in a time of nuclear war.

160

The reliability of a group of ICBM's can honestly be given only in terms of a broad range of numbers, such as between 50% and 90%. The probability of kill can be augmented by increasing the number of missiles fired at each target. For example, if the single shot reliability is 50%, the double-shot reliability is 75%, the triple-shot is 87.5%, and the quadruple shot is 93.75%. In other words, if it is conservatively estimated that 50% of the re-entry vehicles (RVs) would perform completely as expected, then it would take at least four warheads to have a better than 90% chance of destroying a silo.

These multiple-shot reliabilities are derived under the assumption that the performance of the second, third, and fourth RV's is not influenced by the performance of the first one. The assumption is not valid if all RVs come from the same MIRV'd missile; for example, if the booster were to fail, all of its RV's would be destroyed. Therefore, "cross targeting" is used so that each RV aimed at a given target comes from a different missile.

Reliability is not only a matter of technical performance but of timing. In a surprise attack, the Soviets would have to launch all of their attacking missiles at the same time from various locations throughout their country without giving any advance warning to the U.S. Any delayed launches would give the U.S. missiles that had been targeted an opportunity to be fired before the attacking warheads arrived. Such a coordinated attack against U.S. ICBM's would be an extremely complex operation involving many technical systems and many people. The individual components of the attacking missiles, their ground support equipment, communications equipment, and so forth will all perform differently when used operationally as an integrated system than they did when tested individually. There is simply no way to know what will happen in a first-strike without testing the entire system, which can never be done. Furthermore, to obtain statistically significant estimates of kill probabilities, the whole system must be tested many times. Since that is impossible, only a wide range of kill probabilities can be assigned, thus forcing any potential attacker to operate with a great deal of uncertainty about the reliability of the attacking missiles.

161

A second problem is often called fratricide, in which an attacking warhead which arrives first at a target destroys subsequent "brother" warheads which arrive even seconds later before they can explode. Indeed, all scenarios that predict a Soviet capability of destroying 90% or more of U.S. ICBM's assume that the Soviets are firing at least two to four warheads at each ICBM silo. These warheads will arrive at their targets in waves. If the first warhead arrives near its target but not close enough to destroy it, it will still produce a nuclear explosion and subsequent "mushroom" cloud in the vicinity of the target. Ironically, this will tend to shelter the target from attacking warheads that arrive afterwards.

If the second warhead follows too close behind the first, it is likely to be destroyed by the strong X-ray flux produced by the first nuclear explosion. Even if it is further behind, it may be destroyed by the enormously hot gases that are produced from the aerodynamic shock-wave caused by the explosion of the first warhead. After full expansion of the shock wave, there is a momentary pause, after which the atmosphere rushes in to fill the vacuum created by the expanding gases. This inflow will raise enormous quantities of dirt and rocks with vertical winds up to 500 MPH plus turbulence and extreme temperatures. If the incoming RV's are set to explode at or near the ground in order to maximize the effectiveness of the attack, they may be destroyed by this rising debris. Eventually this debris rises to create an atomic cloud which may be lethal to subsequent warheads over an area about seven kilometers in diameter for a one megaton explosion. If an ICBM field has been attacked, the clouds from numerous such explosions may join together and blanket the entire field with a protective shroud. Even if subsequent warheads are able to arrive within the few seconds necessary to fit through the momentary pause, they must still pass through very hot gases before they detonate. Since they are already very hot from the air friction generated by speeds in excess of 7000 meters per second (16,000 MPH) with which they re-enter the earth's atmosphere, the extra heat load may destroy them.

The precise effects of fratricide have never been determined with certainty. The Partial Nuclear Test Ban Treaty of 1963 prohibits the testing of live warheads in the atmosphere. Therefore, a nuclear warhead has <u>never</u> been exploded after atmospheric re-entry, so that any estimate of hitting the "window"

162

provided by the momentary pause is purely theoretical. To be sure that subsequent warheads will be effective it is better to wait until the nuclear cloud has settled, which may take up to half an hour. Since the cloud is more lethal to a freefalling re-entry vehicle than to a missile launch, the nation under attack could probably fire its surviving ICBM's through this cloud before the second wave arrived. In this case, the subsequent attacking missiles would fall on empty holes, and the attacker would already be receiving a major retaliatory counterstrike. Given the uncertainties associated with the problem of fratricide, it would be extremely risky for an attacker to count on his ability to overcome this problem. And if he failed to overcome it, the probable consequence would be the large-scale destruction of his own country.

A third problem concerns the reduced kill radius of lower yield warheads against hardened targets. The kill radius of the warhead depends on two factors. First is the explosive yield of the warhead, usually measured in equivalent megatons (one million tons) of TNT. Second, the kill radius depends on how well the concrete silo is shock mounted against the ground shock produced by a surface explosion and on how high an overpressure from the shock-wave the silo can withstand without causing the missile inside to malfunction during launch. As noted previously, U.S. Minuteman ICBM's are deployed in silos hardened to withstand up to about 2000 pounds per square inch of overpressure. This dynamic load has the equivalent effect of a static load on a ten-foot-diameter silo cover plate of almost 23,000 tons.

One of the consequences of the introduction of multiple re-entry vehicles (MIRV's) on a single missile is that the explosive yield of warheads has been reduced. While early Soviet missiles carried largely multimegaton warheads, the yield of the multiple warheads on the more modern and accurate SS-19 is about .5 megatons. The kill radius of a warhead increases as the cube root of the yield against an identical target. This means that a potential attacker must recognize that a smaller yield warhead will produce a lower kill radius. Furthermore, the kill probability falls off very rapidly as the kill radius decreases because of the exponential relationship between these quantities. Typically a reduction in the kill radius by a factor of two increases the miss probability (one minus the kill probability) by a factor of more than six. Thus recent

163

increases in warhead precision may be partially offset by reductions in the kill radius due to the widespread use of lower yield warheads.

Fourth, there are serious problems in fusing nuclear warheads to detonate at precisely the right instant necessary to destroy the target. The detonation problem would be most serious if the Soviet Union were to use air bursts of their warheads in a first-strike. Ground bursts of several thousand warheads necessary to destroy the 1052 ICBM silos will produce enormous quantities of radioactive dust that, depending on weather conditions, will fall and kill within 30 days up to ten percent of the population of the United States. Furthermore, ground bursts will produce more atmospheric dust that will cool the earth and make more likely the "nuclear winter" effect, doing great damage to the Soviet Union as well as to the United States. Therefore, the high "collateral" civilian casualties would make it virtually impossible to interpret even such a limited strike as a purely counterforce attack, enhancing the likelihood of an immediate American response with surviving nuclear forces. All of these factors might persuade the Soviets to use air bursts if they were to launch such a "surgical" first-strike. Yet this enhances the uncertainties of warhead detonation.

The preferred altitude of an airburst is at about 300 meters. Above this altitude, the kill radius of an air burst declines rapidly. Below this level the explosion will generate successively greater quantities of radioactive debris. Because of the re-entry speed of 7000 meters per second, pressure fusing at this altitude is not practical. A radar altimeter is subject to radio blackout because of the hot gases surrounding the missile and may be jammed. A timer activated at launch is the remaining option. While time can be measured very accurately, the flight time from launch to detonation must be known to at least 1/50th of a second (through which time the RV moves 140 meters). The time involved in correcting for an error of only 1.5 seconds of arc in the launch angle, a not uncommon degree of error, changes the flight time by at least this amount. Thus it is very difficult to time an explosion with sufficient precision. Even if one chose to use a ground burst by impact fusing to overcome these problems, severe difficulties would remain. The nuclear explosion is triggered by a TNT explosion. At the high impact speed, the RV may travel several feet after the TNT explosion is triggered, possibly crushing the warhead before the nuclear explosion occurs. In a nuclear war, therefore, there may be many duds.

The fusing uncertainties are compounded by the fact that ICBM's have never been tested with live nuclear warheads, since this would constitute an atmospheric explosion prohibited by the Partial Nuclear Test Ban Treaty. Therefore, whether or not any warhead will detonate is a largely theoretical argument, based on underground tests of warheads and separate tests of the RV's without live warheads. No ICBM has ever been tested by the United States or the Soviet Union as a complete system including warhead detonation. Therefore, measures of precision should not be equated with the probability of destroying the target. This will be affected by additional uncertainties about the probability of warhead detonation at precisely the right time and place, if at all.

A fifth issue concerns the precision of guidance in modern ballistic missiles. Precision is normally measured in terms of the circle of equal probability (CEP). This is the radius of a circle of observed impact points, which is centered at the centroid of a large number of impacts and contains half of the points. Accuracy is a measure of the mean distance from the centroid to the target, i.e., the bias. A one megaton bomb airburst at 300 meters or less would have to occur within about 180 meters of a missile silo hardened to withstand 2000 pounds per square inch of overpressure. A missile which has a CEP of 180 meters and zero bias thus has a 50% chance of destroying the target. In order to have a 90% chance of destroying such a target, one would need to have a missile with a CEP of less than 100 meters and zero bias. This exceeds even the best reported CEP's of presently deployed Soviet missiles. It must be emphasized how small such targets are. A CEP of 100 meters at a range of one quarter of the earth's circumference would correspond on a rifle range of 500 meters to placing one half of a large number of shots within a circle one centimeter in diameter.

Present intercontinental range missiles are all ballistic missiles. This means that the missile is launched with a given velocity and direction towards its target by the main rocket. This main rocket then separates and a postboost vehicle or "bus" makes final changes in the trajectory to aim the RV's towards their target. Once the RV's are released, their course to

their target cannot be modified. Essentially they are
in free fall, propelled by their velocity and direction
at the moment of release, and affected by external
factors such as gravity and friction as they re-enter
the earth's atmosphere. Therefore, the missile's
guidance system must make very precise calculations
during the boost and postboost phases, because during
free flight and re-entry no further changes can be made
in the RV's course.

ICBM's use an inertial guidance system, in which
position and velocity information are obtained from
integration of the signals from three mutually
perpendicular accelerometers aligned very precisely by
means of gyroscopes with respect to a navigational
reference frame aligned with respect to the local
vertical at launch and the spin axis of the earth. To
obtain a miss distance in the order of magnitude of 100
meters, the initial alignment must be accurate to about
0.6 seconds of arc, the initial velocity of the RV
release point in space (considering the motion of the
earth) must be known to about two centimeters per
second, and other errors due to instrumentation, thrust
cutoff timing, and so forth must be known to comparable
levels of accuracy. The precision of this initial
angular alignment may be illustrated by imagining a
searchlight shining on a building one mile away. If
the searchlight is rotated through an angle of 0.6
seconds of arc, the spot of light will move less than
five millimeters.

The initial alignment must be determined and
maintained by optical transfer of data from
observations of stars through telescopes and mirrors
into the guidance system. The slightest change in
temperature or humidity or the slightest earth shock or
vibration can shift the alignment. While it is
maintained automatically within the guidance mechanism,
it is dependent on the rigidity of the component
linkages, which may be affected by the shock and
vibration from the rocket blastoff.

Precision may also be affected adversely by the
re-entry atmosphere. If there is a slight imbalance in
the location of the center of mass of the RV with
respect to its center of pressure (determined by the
shape of the external surface of the RV, which can be
changed by even the slightest scratch on its surface),
the very high re-entry velocity of 20 times the speed
of sound creates a very strong imbalance in aerodynamic
forces. This causes the RV to depart markedly from the

planned trajectory. This problem can be reduced by spin stabilization, but that produces its own set of problems.

In short, the precision requirements for a counterforce first-strike mission against the 1000 U.S. Minuteman missiles is analogous to asking 1000 marksmen to fire at 1000 targets from 500 meters distance and to expect them to place half of their shots within a circle one centimeter in diameter. Their success would depend on training all 1000 marksmen to fire with this precision. They must wait 24 hours a day, 365 days a year, for many years to fire their one shot. And if they fall short of their expectation, they, their families, and most of their society will be destroyed. There is one additional problem, namely that the marksmen are not able to correct their rifles for windage. This is analogous to systematic or bias error in missile guidance, the sixth problem to be considered.

Bias errors may systematically affect all of the missiles fired, not just some random portion of them as is the case in many of the problems discussed previously. On an ICBM trajectory one of the major sources of bias results from lack of precise knowledge of the earth's gravitational field. Anomalies in the gravitational field can substantially affect the course of the RV during its free fall. Furthermore, the accelerometers in the inertial guidance system cannot tell the difference between acceleration and gravity. Therefore, the gravity field must be mapped in advance and stored into each guidance computer to an accuracy of about six decimal places. The U.S. Defense Department contends that they have mapped the earth's gravitational field to approximately this level of accuracy based on satellite observations. But these satellite observations are affected at low levels by atmospheric drag on the satellites. In addition, anomalies in the earth's gravitational field are greatest near the ground, so that an accurate model must be based on ground observations; satellite observations are likely to produce biased estimates of these gravitational fields near the earth's surface, which affect the RV as it approaches its target.

Only tests of missiles over the polar trajectories that would be employed in an actual attack can produce the necessary accuracies in estimating gravitational anomalies. The Soviets test their ICBM's over a range of about 6500 kilometers from West to East. Frequent flights over the same range make it possible to correct

167

for systematic bias over that range, producing deceptively small miss distances. However, bias corrections obtained from such test flights bear no relationship to the corrections required for many different polar trajectories with ranges of as much as 10,000 kilometers required for an actual attack on U.S. ICBM's. Tests along actual polar ranges would obviously be indistinguishable for the potential victim from a real attack, making them clearly impossible.

Thus it would be extremely unfortunate if political leaders in either superpower were to place too much confidence in the accuracy of maps produced by their scientists of the earth's gravitational fields over the entire range of an operational flight path. Since the kill probability decreases very rapidly as the bias error increases, these errors can significantly reduce the accuracy of missiles fired in real counterforce missions. If the bias error is as great as the kill radius, the kill probability is less than 50% regardless of the theoretical CEP.

Indeed, all six factors discussed above may significantly decrease the kill probability, making the percentage of missiles destroyed in an actual first-strike significantly smaller than might theoretically be predicted. Indeed, any potential attacker will invariably be very uncertain about the kill probability, which cannot be predicted with any confidence.

There is no statistical basis for determining precise probabilities such as the 90% figure so frequently cited in nightmare scenarios. Statistical theory at best can enable one to calculate a range of probability values, called confidence limits, based on test data. One is necessarily limited, therefore, to statements like the following: "In 90 out of 100 first-strikes at 1000 targets one can expect to destroy between 580 and 930 targets." In any particular firing, statistical theory gives one no basis for determining whether he could destroy 930, 580, any number in between, or conceivably any other number from 0 to 1000. Furthermore, any such inferences must make the assumption that test conditions and operational conditions are identical. Since we have already suggested that they are not the same, statistical theory has no basis for providing valid answers about kill probabilities.

168

There is one final and all important problem in addition to the technical issues mentioned above, namely human problems. Firing thousands of missiles at one time from various locations throughout the Soviet Union in a single coordinated attack against U.S. ICBM's without giving any advance warning would be an extremely complex operation. Individuals would have to communicate and act in a manner perfectly coordinated with the various technical systems in order to achieve success. And the price of failure, again, is the probable destruction of their entire country.

In summary, each of the problems mentioned above complicates calculations that would be necessary to undertake a disarming first-strike attack against U.S. ICBM's. Even if no one of them alone were significant, the compounded effects of all would be very great. Under no conceivable conditions could national leaders have any confidence in their ability to launch a successful first-strike against ICBM's. Given these uncertainties, it is extremely unlikely that any sane person would risk the consequences of failure in such an attack. As a result, it seems to us that the problem of the "window of vulnerability" has been largely exaggerated by many U.S. political and military leaders.

This does not necessarily mean that there can never be a "window of vulnerability." The forward progress of technology may always make systems that are now relatively invulnerable become more vulnerable in the future. Indeed, there is no question that the deployment of MIRV's and improvement in guidance precision in the decade of the 1970's did reduce ICBM invulnerability. As we have already argued these problems are not so serious as long as we are dealing with purely ballistic missiles. The major uncertainties already noted frequently are due to the fact that ballistic missile accuracy depends essentially upon inertial guidance systems that cannot be corrected at mid-course or at the terminal end of the trajectory. Once the initial course of a missile has been programmed by the inertial guidance system during the boost phase, the RV follows a free-fall trajectory to the target. There is nothing to reprogram during the free-fall trajectory to compensate for any errors, such as bias errors, in the initial trajectory.

Innovations in satellites such as the NAVSTAR Global Positioning System may improve missile accuracy.

169

Of even greater concern theoretically is the possible development of Precision Guided Re-entry Vehicles or MARV's (Maneuverable Re-entry Vehicles). These systems are designed to provide terminal guidance of the warhead as it approaches its target. A similar system called Correlatron, a radar based terminal guidance system, has been used on the Pershing II missile. This intermediate-range missile (with a range of about 1800 kms.) has recently been deployed in West Germany, with a claimed CEP of about 40 meters. This system would not function on a full intercontinental range missile, however, because such missiles travel at higher speeds and enter the atmosphere at shallower angles, thereby setting up an ionized shock layer that would block radar signals. However, research and development is underway for similar systems on longer range missiles, including the D-5 missile scheduled to be deployed on the Trident II submarine at the end of the decade of the 1980's and the so-called Midgetman Intercontinental missile tentatively scheduled for deployment sometime in the 1990's.

The technical problems facing these new systems are quite severe, perhaps delaying or preventing their actual deployment. First, satellites such as NAVSTAR are extremely vulnerable to being destroyed by anti-satellite weapons that may soon be available. Second, communications signals sent to a missile to change its course are subject to interference by the defender, which could seriously distort the course of the attacking missile. Third, precision guidance systems contained within the warhead itself may avoid this problem, but they are extremely difficult to design. An ICBM re-enters the atmosphere at a angle of about 22.5 degrees and at a speed of about 16,000 MPH. At about 100,000 feet of altitude the atmosphere through which it passes becomes thick enough to create a shock layer around the RV. This layer is ionized, so that no electromagnetic device such as radar or infrared optics can see through it. Therefore, so far terminal guidance for ICBM's can only mean inertial guidance to correct the trajectory for atmospheric effects by slightly shifting the center of mass of the warhead. Finally, any system for mid-course correction or terminal guidance adds complexity to already complicated systems, contributing still another source of performance uncertainty.

If these and other serious technological problems were to be overcome so that missile guidance was no longer solely dependent on inertial guidance systems,

170

then significant improvements in accuracy might be achieved. Although these improvements would still be subject to considerable uncertainty, they would move states targeted by these weapons closer to the vulnerable end of the continuum. Due to the tremendous technical problems still to be overcome, these destabilizing improvements are not likely to be realized without an extensive program of missile testing. If testing, development, and eventual deployment of these technologies proceeds unabated, it is quite possible that the two superpowers could find themselves in the future in a position of much greater mutual vulnerability than at present. That is also likely to increase the chances of war by premeditated surprise attack, by pre-emption due to low crisis stability, or inadvertently due to greater reliance on policies of "launch on warning."

III.   IMPLICATIONS FOR DETERRENCE

The preceding analysis suggests that much of the recent shift in defense policy in the United States has been based upon a fallacious set of assumptions. Movement away from the doctrine of mutual assured destruction, the major buildup of new strategic weapons, the pursuit of the Strategic Defense Initiative (SDI), and an emphasis on purely quantitative reductions in arms control all reflect the extent to which this misleading analysis of the "window of vulnerability" has driven defense and arms control policy in recent years. The foregoing analysis should thus suggest that a further re-examination of these policy choices is essential before further destabilizing developments occur.

First, the theory of deterrence must be re-evaluated in the light of the preceding arguments. Deterrence in the future must be based upon a combined uncertainty regarding first-strike attacks and a virtual certainty of a surviving capacity to carry out second-strike retaliation. Deterrence must be viewed in large measure from the perspective of a hypothetical Soviet leader contemplating a first-strike. The basic logic behind the analysis that such a leader would have to make may be summarized in terms of an "aggressor's risk calculus."[6]

According to this simple cost-benefit model, anyone contemplating a premeditated nuclear attack

171

would have to take into account the following considerations:

1) the expected benefits of an attack, i.e., the value of victory times the probability of winning;

2) the expected costs, i.e., the value of punishment received in retaliation times the probability that such punishment will be delivered.

These two values may then be compared. Only if the expected benefits exceed the costs by a wide margin would a decision to launch a first-strike be plausible. Deterrence is achieved then when the expected benefits are not sufficient to justify the risks involved. This is essentially a psychological conception of deterrence, not one that can be operationalized in fully objective terms by referring to "exchange ratios," "counter military potential," or other similar measures of the strategic balance. The psychological component is highlighted by the essentially subjective nature of the estimates of various probabilities, which are characterized by considerable uncertainty. The leader's decision will also be influenced by his tolerance for taking risks. As long as there is sufficient risk of very substantial destruction, an aggressor may be deterred by the uncertain likelihood of achieving sufficient benefits from an attack to justify the risks involved and the overwhelming consequences of miscalculation. Thus uncertainty with respect to first-strike counterforce capabilities will generally enhance deterrence.

On the other hand, deterrence is also strengthened by a potential aggressor's knowledge that his own country will receive overwhelming destruction in retaliation. This could come in the form of a retaliatory, second-strike launched by the victim or even from the long-term physical effects of his own attack. For example, the "nuclear winter" effect predicted by Carl Sagan and his associates would imply that an attacker could suffer enormous damage even if no retaliation ensued.[7] Yet survivable forces that can meet the much less demanding requirements of second-strike retaliation are likely to enhance deterrence at least for the near future. Thus, paradoxically, deterrence is maximized by greater uncertainty regarding the performance of first-strike forces and by greater certainty concerning the survivability of second-strike forces.

172

This model, therefore, is substantially different from the traditional conception of "mutual assured destruction." MAD places most of its emphasis upon the cost component of the cost-benefit model, emphasizing both that the punishment would be severe (i.e., complete destruction) and that its probability would be virtually certain (i.e., assured). Our model also considers the benefits side of this equation as well. Not only does it emphasize the uncertainty of winning by a first-strike, but it also takes account of the benefits that might result even if one did succeed in a first-strike. It is not clear that the Soviets would gain overwhelmingly from such an attack. Although the opportunity to gain a victory over an ideological opponent might have some appeal to Soviet leaders, they also have demonstrated considerable concern throughout the last several decades for practical considerations, foremost of which is their national survival.

A first-strike, even if "limited," would wreak considerable damage upon the United States. As mentioned previously the radioactive fallout produced by such an attack would probably kill at least ten percent of the U.S. population. The Soviets, at a minimum, would cut themselves off from a major source of grain, and their political relations with the entire noncommunist world would be totally destroyed. Even if they were successful in destroying most U.S. ICBM's in a first-strike, they might then find that the U.S. was still not willing to surrender outright. In such a case, they would have to launch a second salvo against population and economic targets. This would leave their victim virtually destroyed, with few "spoils" for the victor. The only fruit of such a strategy, even if successful, would be the elimination of their strategic rival. While this is not an unimportant goal, it must be weighed against the risks involved. In particular, such a massive countervalue attack would be very likely to generate the "nuclear winter" effect which would conceivably destroy them in return.

Alternatively, even if the U.S. did surrender, then the Soviet Union would have to occupy one of the world's largest and most populous countries. Given their recent troubles in small countries on their own borders, such as Poland and Afghanistan, it is unlikely that they would relish the opportunity to take on the burdens of occupying a far larger country, with an extremely hostile population in the aftermath of a nuclear attack, especially one so far from their own country. In short, while the Soviets might hope to gain some benefits from an attack on the United States, these gains are by no means as clearly and unambiguously attractive as some would contend.

Our model of deterrence also suggests that expected benefits must always be evaluated in comparison with expected costs. Thus the Soviets would have to take into account the probability of various possible responses by the United States to a Soviet attack against ICBM's. Broadly speaking, there are four possible responses that an American president might make to such a Soviet first-strike, even if it were successful in destroying a large percentage of ICBM's.

First, the U.S. president could use all remaining forces to retaliate massively against the Soviet Union in a countervalue attack. Such an attack could include the surviving ICBM's (about 100 with about 215 warheads in the most scary scenarios), 592 SLBM's with 5344 warheads, and 297 long-range bombers with 3296 bombs and warheads on Air-Launched Cruise Missiles carried by these bombers (1985 data). Although retaliation of this magnitude might seem to be out of proportion to the provocation, a Soviet planner could not rule out such a response altogether. A retaliatory response involving as many as 8855 warheads would clearly wreak overwhelming destruction on the USSR, regardless of any protective measures such as civil defense that they might undertake.

Second, the U.S. president could launch American ICBM's against Soviet ICBM silos, including those with unfired missiles, upon receiving a warning that an attack was underway. Indeed, some analysts have proposed that the president should strike when an "assessment" was made that Soviet leaders were preparing to launch a first-strike.[8] While American leaders have reasonably been reluctant to adopt such policies publicly because of their potential destabilizing consequences, a Soviet leader would have to recognize that there is some possibility that an American president might choose this option. In such a case, since approximately 74% of Soviet warheads are based on ICBM's, they might find that they had virtually disarmed themselves by such an attack while leaving the United States with its SLBM's and strategic bomber forces still in tact.[9]

Third, an American president might launch a "limited" nuclear response using surviving weapons

174

against selected economic and industrial targets in the Soviet Union. This retaliation could be undertaken with a relatively small percentage of surviving U.S. forces, and it could inflict upon the Soviet Union damage approximately equivalent to the "collateral damage" to the American population and economic resources resulting from the Soviet attack on U.S. ICBM's. This could be accompanied by diplomatic efforts to halt the conflict at that level. Sufficient invulnerable American forces could be kept in reserve to deter the Soviets from responding with a second salvo directed at American population and economic targets. In other words, options do exist between "massive retaliation" and "surrender" which do not necessarily require American possession of weapons capable of engaging in counterforce attacks. A flexible targeting policy thus does not inherently require a counterforce capability.

Fourth, an American president might elect to do nothing, an unlikely option since about ten percent of the population would probably die from the effects of even a "limited" strike against ICBM silos. Only in this unlikely situation could a Soviet leader expect to initiate a surprise attack and escape without receiving any retaliatory punishment. The low probability of such an American response would not seem to justify the risks that the Soviets would have to run or the amount of punishment that they would receive if the United States adopted any of the first three responses.

All of these options exist even if ICBM's were completely vulnerable, so long as the other two legs of the strategic triad, the nuclear submarine fleet and the strategic bombers, remain relatively invulnerable. Some have argued that the problem of ICBM vulnerability must be corrected immediately as a hedge against potential vulnerability of the other two legs of the triad. However, even if improvements are made in anti-submarine warfare techniques and in better defenses against the manned bombers, these too are likely to still be highly uncertain in their effectiveness. Furthermore, since the ICBM's cannot be safely assumed to be totally vulnerable, a potential Soviet attacker would always have to consider that a substantial number of ICBM's might survive an initial strike and be fired against the Soviet Union before they could be attacked by later Soviet salvos.

Moreover, the United States would have a great incentive to fire any ICBM's that survived a first wave attack rapidly before they could be attacked by the second wave. This makes it very likely that at least all surviving ICBM's would be fired in retaliation, and only 100 ICBM's with about 215 warheads could deliver approximately 135 megatons on the Soviet Union, almost 4000 times the destructive power of the bombs dropped on Nagasaki and Hiroshima at the end of World War II. This alone would clearly constitute very substantial punishment. When this is combined with the possible use of the other two legs of the strategic triad and/or the adoption of a policy of "launch on warning" for U.S. ICBM's, Soviet leaders would clearly be confronting overwhelming risks if they contemplated a first-strike against present U.S. strategic forces. In this light, arguments about the alleged weakness of U.S. strategic forces appear to be largely mythical.

In short, the many uncertainties concerning the reliability and accuracy of present ICBM's for launching counterforce attacks should deter any national leader from contemplating a first-strike. At the same time, an attacker would be confronted with the virtual certainty that, even after a first-strike, enough of the victim's forces would survive, including residual ICBM's, strategic bombers, and SLBM's, to inflict substantial punishment on the aggressor. Thus there would be a relatively low probability of achieving questionable benefits, compared with a very high probability of receiving overwhelming punishment in return. In this respect, deterrence can remain stable so long as counterforce strikes continue to be characterized by substantial uncertainty, while the capability to engage in second-strike countervalue retaliation remains a virtual certainty.

More modest claims have been advanced by some analysts who acknowledge that a Soviet first-strike is not a likely event, but who contend that their possession of such a capability would enable them to threaten such an attack. In political bargaining over many global issues such as Eastern Europe, the Middle East, "liberation struggles" in the third world, the Soviets might exploit this capability to their advantage. Other things being equal, it is true that an advantage may go to the party in a bargaining relationship that can threaten the more severe punishment if their opponent does not yield. Yet it is doubtful that the Soviets currently have or are likely to obtain in the near future such a clear-cut military advantage.

176

On the contrary, the ICBM vulnerability problem, insofar as it is significant, is a much more serious problem for the Soviets than for the United States. The MK 12A warhead recently deployed on 220 U.S. Minuteman III missiles is alleged to have a CEP of 220 meters, slightly better than the 300 meters of the best Soviet warheads, the SS-18 Mod 4 and the SS-19 Mod 2 and 3.[10] Furthermore, improvements in precision have been made at about the same rate by the two superpowers.[11] Thus Soviet missiles continue to be slightly less precise than their American counterparts. Furthermore, the Soviet strategic forces rely far more heavily upon land-based ICBM's, the most vulnerable component of strategic forces, than does the U.S. Insofar as there is an ICBM vulnerability problem, it affects 67% of Soviet strategic warheads in contrast to only 20% of U.S. warheads. Moreover, when one accounts for the fact that lower percentages of Soviet submarines and bombers are maintained on station at any one time than is the case for the U.S., the imbalance is even greater.

Therefore, insofar as the vulnerability of strategic forces is a factor in political bargaining between the superpowers, the effects would seem to be overwhelmingly in favor of the United States. If the United States suffers any political damage from the alleged vulnerability problem, it is only from a self-fulfilling prophecy in which public exaggeration of this problem for domestic political purposes creates an illusion of American impotence. As the London-based International Institute of Strategic Studies summarizes the issue:

> Therefore, if the Soviet Union were able to make political gains during the period of the "window of opportunity," this would not be because of any objective strategic balance in her favor, but rather because the limited perspectives of the American strategic debate had led to an underestimation of the conditions of nuclear deterrence and U.S. capabilities.[12]

IV. IMPLICATIONS FOR ARMS DEVELOPMENT, PROCUREMENT, AND DEPLOYMENT

The alleged vulnerability of the Minuteman and Titan missiles has provided an important justification for major new programs to strengthen American strategic forces. After assuming office in 1981, President Reagan announced an extensive stepup in the U.S. strategic weapons program, including the following:

1) Deployment of 100 MX missiles in "superhardened" silos previously holding Titan and Minuteman missiles.

2) Production of 100 B-1 bombers capable of avoiding radar detection by flying at low altitudes.

3) Stepped up development of the "Stealth" bomber equipped with highly secret systems designed to avoid radar detection altogether.

4) Deployment of the D-5 missile in the Trident II submarine by 1989.

5) Deployment of several hundred Sea-Launched Cruise missiles (SLCM's) on general purpose submarines.

6) Development of a new generation, highly accurate, single warhead missile usually called the Midgetman for deployment in the 1990's.

7) Upgrading the systems for communications, command, control, and intelligence (C3I) so that they could survive a first-strike.

In addition, in his so-called "Star Wars" speech in 1983, President Reagan proposed the development of a multi-layered ballistic missile defense system, including laser and particle beam weapons based in space. Such a program would initially provide added protection for more vulnerable ICBM's and would eventually be intended to provide a full-scale population defense as well.

There was considerable surprise that the Reagan administration eventually decided to deploy the MX missile in Minuteman and Titan silos, since they had long contended that these silos were highly vulnerable. Yet many other basing modes were considered and rejected, and the eventual decision amounted to a tacit acknowledgement that the ICBM vulnerability problem was not so serious after all. The additional hardening will make only marginal reductions in the kill probability for an attacking missile, and such measures could have been applied to protect the older Minuteman missiles. Originally, the MX deployment was justified largely on the basis of the need to respond to the problem of Minuteman vulnerability. Yet the eventual deployment does little to make the MX more invulnerable than the Minuteman. Therefore, the only real advantage that has been claimed for the MX is that its warhead is more accurate than the Minutemen it will be replacing, with more warheads per launcher. Indeed, the White House background statement justified the MX deployment primarily because it was a "much stronger and more accurate missile than Minuteman...."[13] The practical consequence is thus to increase U.S. "nuclear war fighting" potential rather than enhancing invulnerability.

Indeed, the MX will be equipped with an Advanced Inertial Reference System (AIRS) guidance that is estimated to have a CEP as low as 30 meters on test ranges. Our previous analysis would suggest that even such theoretical precision would not be sufficient for an American president to consider launching a first-strike against Soviet ICBM's due to the many uncertainties that would be involved. Hopefully, Soviet leaders would be aware of these constraints. Nevertheless, by any measure, the MX represents a substantial increase in the precision of American missiles. One hundred MX missiles with 1000 warheads would certainly not be enough alone for the U.S. to launch a first-strike against the Soviet Union, even if it were as reliable and precise as claimed. Yet additional American deployments may be even more accurate and precise, if the fundamental and serious problems confronting terminal guidance can be overcome. Already 108 intermediate-range Pershing II missiles have been deployed in West Germany with a terminal guidance system that gives it counterforce accuracy against Soviet silos and C3I within its 1800 kilometer range. The D-5 SLBM and the Midgetman are anticipated to possess even greater precision when they are to be deployed at the end of the decade of the 1980's and into the 1990's. The D-5 may convert the submarine, heretofore considered an element of stability in deterrence due to its invulnerability and its lack of a counterforce capability, into a weapon capable of launching a counterforce strike. Although the Midgetman represents a desirable trend away from multiple warheads, which give an edge to the offense over defense, the improved precision of its warheads will also enhance American counterforce potential. Finally, U.S. improvements in ballistic missile defense (BMD) may give the U.S. a perceived, though probably illusory, capability to protect its cities against

Soviet retaliation from a limited number of surviving strategic forces.

Therefore, it is extremely likely that Soviet political leaders and defense officials regard the new United States defense program as threatening to the stability of mutual deterrence by making the Soviet Union potentially vulnerable to an American first-strike, perhaps as early as the beginning of the 1990's. Just as the trend of growing numbers of more precise Soviet missiles have caused alarm in the United States in recent years, there is every reason to believe that the new directions in American strategic policy will create grave fears for the Soviets. In short, the planned U.S. deployments, taken in their entirety, are extremely provocative to the Soviet Union if they use a similar logic to the one employed by American officials concerning the "window of vulnerability." In their totality, all of these systems are claimed to give the United States a capability to pursue a "nuclear warfighting" strategic doctrine such as that advocated by analysts like Gray and Payne, who contend that the U.S. should seek "the ability to wage a nuclear war at any level of violence with a reasonable prospect of defeating the Soviet Union...."[14] The present degree of strategic uncertainty will be reduced, and with it deterrence will become more unstable, and the outbreak of nuclear war may well become significantly more likely. Therefore, it is extremely likely that these new weapons, if deployed, will make the United States considerably less, not more, secure.

V. IMPLICATIONS FOR ARMS CONTROL: THE ROLE OF A TEST BAN

Not only do our arguments about ICBM vulnerability have important implications for the deployment of new strategic weapons, but they also have great significance for the future of arms control. The arms control philosophy ever since SALT I was signed in 1972 has been to emphasize limitations on the quantitative arms race. The main thrust of SALT II was to place ceilings on the number of strategic launchers and indirectly on warheads. This emphasis was reinforced by the Reagan administration. Throughout the strategic arms negotiations the Reagan administration has opposed qualitative arms control measures, such as a comprehensive nuclear test ban, while emphasizing proposals for reductions such as the "build down" proposal introduced in 1983. This proposal called for the number of weapons to be reduced as new delivery vehicles were deployed. For example, for one new ICBM unit deployed, two old ones would have to be dismantled, and for every two new SLBM units deployed, three old ones would have to be retired. Yet this proposal contained no limits on the qualitative improvements that would have been permissable on the newly deployed weapons, including improvements in accuracy; indeed, such improvements would have been encouraged under this proposal. This general emphasis upon large-scale quantitative reductions, while permitting qualitative improvements, was continued as well in the round of strategic arms negotiations that opened in 1985.

Throughout this period the United States seems to have been motivated by an approach which would enable it to exploit its technological lead over the Soviet Union. It is not surprising that Soviet analysts generally perceived this as an effort for the United States to improve the accuracy of its missile forces, while reducing the number of targets that would have to be attacked in a disarming strike, thereby moving the United States towards a capability perhaps by the 1990's of actually being able to launch such a first strike. Indeed, many U.S. officials had advocated American procurement of such a capability prior to entering office. Typical of these was a statement by Richard Burt, at first Assistant Secretary of State and later U.S. Ambassador to the Federal Republic of Germany, who opposed limits on the testing of new weapons such as anti-satellite weapons on the grounds that it is undesirable to restrain "an area of clear American technological superiority."[16]

Our arguments would seem to suggest, on the contrary, that the priority for strategic arms control ought to be on preventing the development of emerging technologies that might upset the stability of the strategic balance, rather than on quantitative reductions in existing forces. Although the present strategic balance is not fully safe, our arguments certainly suggest that it is founded upon a sufficiently stable balance of mutual invulnerability to make a nuclear first-strike an extremely risky and costly enterprise that no sane national leader could seriously contemplate undertaking. However, some of the technological improvements in guidance systems and ballistic missile defenses referred to earlier could, if successful, be extremely destabilizing. The

181

development and deployment of these new technologies could create a "window of vulnerability" for whichever superpower failed to obtain them first. If both superpowers obtained them simultaneously, they could create the most unstable situation of all, in which both were vulnerable to nuclear first-strikes from each other.

However, there is still time to head off or at least slow down significantly the advent of these new destabilizing technologies before it is too late. As indicated previously, such new devices and terminal guidance systems on intercontinental range missiles or space-based ballistic missile defenses will require very extensive testing before they are ready to deploy. Neither of these systems has yet been tested by either superpower, so the most effective means of prevention is likely to be a ban on their testing. This has the dual advantage of being easier to verify than bans on production or even deployment of new weapons, while heading off new technologies before the political pressure builds to deploy them simply because the technology already exists.

The development of new, more precise guidance systems can be best handled by a ban or strict limitation on missile testing. Such a ban could take several forms. The first and most desirable from an arms control perspective would be a complete ban on all ICBM and SLBM flight testing. Among the foremost advantages of such a ban is the relative ease with which it could be verified. Ceteris paribus, the more complete the ban, the easier it is to verify. This is particularly true with the testing of intercontinental range missiles which cannot be hidden from the many national technical means of verification, especially satellites, available to the U.S. and the U.S.S.R. In addition, a complete missile test ban would make it virtually impossible to improve guidance technologies except in the laboratory; however, no national leader could ever rely on such a technically complex system that had never been tested operationally, especially when any failure might mean the destruction of his own nation.

While some might argue that such a ban could be evaded through taking satellites out of orbit and testing them as re-entry vehicles, this would not seem to pose insuperable problems. The testing of sufficient satellites in this form to develop new guidance systems would itself create considerable

182

suspicion, and provisions against this form of evasion might well be incorporated into an agreement. In particular rules could be developed to distinguish between such tests and the return of photo reconnaissance capsules which would be permitted for purposes of verification. For example, angles of re-entry might be established for such capsules that would be quite different from the trajectory of attacking warheads.

Furthermore, even if new guidance systems were to be tested in this fashion, it would be done independently of testing the re-entry vehicles when carried by intercontinental range missiles. It is unlikely that a national leader would risk using a weapon that had only been tested in its individual components and not as a complete system. Therefore, such a ban should significantly retard or prevent altogether the development of reliable new guidance systems. Furthermore, a complete missile test ban would have the added consequence that the two superpowers' existing missiles would also slowly become more obsolete and their operation would become even more uncertain for first-strike purposes. As such it might contribute even more to the stability of mutual deterrence.

However, some opposition to such a ban may arise from those who fear that missiles might also become obsolete in their role as second-strike, retaliatory weapons. If one side believed that its missiles might become obsolete more rapidly than those of its opponents, which it could never determine with certainty due to the absence of testing, then it might oppose such a complete ban. If this concern creates an insurmountable obstacle to a comprehensive missile test ban, two other less restrictive forms of a missile test limitation might be considered.

The first such alternative would be to limit the number of annual tests of intercontinental-range missiles of the U.S. and the U.S.S.R. to some relatively small number per year. For example, the Carter administration proposed during the SALT II negotiations a limit on flight tests of ICBM's and SLBM's to six per year each. Most or all of these tests would be used to determine the reliability of missiles that had already been deployed. With a low number of annual tests neither side could gain sufficient confidence in the reliability of new guidance systems except over a very long period of testing. This proposal was set aside during the negotiations, apparently for two major reasons. First, it was rather strongly opposed by the Soviet Union. Second, Defense Department officials evidently convinced President Carter that the Soviets had already achieved the level of missile accuracy that this limitation was designed to head off, so that it was already too late to prevent Soviet attainment of first-strike, counterforce accuracy.[16]

Our previous arguments certainly challenge this second assessment due to the many uncertainties affecting the performance of Soviet missiles in wartime operations. Since any major advances in guidance are likely to come in a transition from inertial guidance to missiles with mid-course correction and Maneuverable Re-entry Vehicles (MARV's), and since such systems have not yet been developed and tested, then the proposal of the Carter administration would still seem to be as valid in the late 1980's as it was in the late 1970's. However, the knowledge that the United States is working on such new technologies may give the Soviets greater incentive to consider such a limitation more seriously a decade after they initially rejected it. Certainly little would be lost and much might be gained by reintroducing it into strategic arms control negotiations.

A numerical limit on the number of flight tests per year is also an easily verifiable provision, since the number of flight tests can readily be observed and counted. The only major disadvantage of this second option is that it might permit some gradual improvements in guidance systems if some or all of these test flights were used to test new guidance technologies rather than the reliability of existing missiles.

A third option would be intended to overcome this problem by making specific prohibitions on the testing of re-entry vehicles employing either mid-course corrections or terminal guidance. This proposal would permit unlimited testing of existing missiles if that were thought to be desirable. At the same time the testing of those specific technologies that are of greatest concern for the mid-term future would be prohibited. The most significant disadvantage of this option is that verification would be far more difficult than in the first two options. It would not only be necessary to determine whether a missile test had taken place, but also whether or not the test had involved

184

any alterations in the inertial guidance. If changes in trajectory were observed, it would be difficult to determine if they were due to some of the possible unintended problems identified previously or if they were due to deliberate course changes. Since similar verification problems have led to intense disputes about alleged Soviet violations at SALT II, such a limitation would require access by both sides to open telemetry from the missile tests of a less ambiguous variety than provided for in the SALT II Treaty.[17]

Not only is the development of advanced guidance systems a threat to stable deterrence, but so also are sophisticated systems of ballistic missile defenses, such as space-based lasers, proposed for the Strategic Defense Initiative (SDI). However, many scientists are extremely skeptical about the technical feasibility of these systems.[18] Even proponents of these systems acknowledge that many problems must still be overcome through a lengthy program of research, development, and testing, which may take a decade or more. Therefore, a limitation on the testing of these weapons would go a long way towards preventing them from ever becoming a military reality. In the case of SDI a complete ban is both simpler and easier than for missile flight tests, since, unlike intercontinental-range missiles, such BMD systems do not now exist at all.

If a test ban prevented a reliable and effective system of ballistic missile defense from ever being deployed, then doctrines of "nuclear warfighting" could never truly be implemented. Nuclear war would still involve very high risks of substantial or total destruction to the attacker as well as to the victim. Thus the prevention of such weapons from ever being tested would help to stabilize nuclear deterrence well into the next century.

Hopefully by that time sufficient political change can occur in the international system, and in the domestic politics of the superpowers, so that an alternative can be found to dependence on nuclear deterrence as a mechanism for maintaining peace. But in order for any political evolution to take place, time must be bought and deterrence must be stabilized. Obviously technological progress cannot be stopped altogether, but it is certainly within our power to halt the development and testing of those military technologies which provide the greatest threats to stable deterrence in the next few decades.

VI. CONCLUSION

The clear-cut balance of scientific evidence would seem to suggest that the vulnerability of fixed-based, hardened ICBM's is not as serious as claimed by many critics, including officials of several U.S. administrations. There is a significant difference between the accuracy of Soviet missiles obtained along test ranges versus what one would expect in an operational first-strike against 1052 ICBM's in a coordinated Soviet attack. Many potential uncertainties exist about the reliability of attacking missiles and the precision of their inertial guidance systems, and this should be sufficient to deter any rational leader from launching such a first-strike attack. This technical uncertainty would be further compounded by a Soviet leader's uncertainty concerning how American leaders might respond to such an attack. And if either the first-strike failed to destroy the vast majority of American ICBM's or if the United States decided to retaliate with surviving bombers and SLBM's, the Soviet Union would assuredly be destroyed as a functioning society in retaliation. The primary deterrent in the present strategic environment is this uncertainty with respect to first-strike or counterforce capabilities, backed up by a certain capacity to destroy the aggressor through retaliation with invulnerable forces that could survive a first-strike.

Insofar as deterrence of first-strikes depends upon this uncertainty, then a primary goal of national security policy ought to be to preserve and enhance this uncertainty rather than to reduce it. Since present deterrent forces are sufficiently invulnerable to make a Soviet leader have substantial doubts about the success of a first-strike attack, it is not necessary to replace them with expensive and potentially destabilizing weapons such as the MX, Trident D-5, and ballistic missile defense. Since these new weapons may be equipped with advanced guidance systems capable of making mid-course or terminal corrections to correct for departures from planned trajectories, they would undoubtedly make the Soviet Union feel vulnerable to an American first-strike.

On the contrary, a preferable policy option is to move to the forefront of the arms control agenda negotiations which seek to maintain present levels of uncertainty about the reliability and precision of missile guidance. This can best be achieved through a ban or stringent limitation on the testing of all intercontinental range missiles. While present missiles are clearly sufficiently accurate for retaliatory second-strike missions, a test ban would prevent them from becoming sufficiently reliable and precise to engage in first-strike attacks with any degree of confidence. Thus a limitation would slow down or prevent the development of a new generation of missile guidance systems which might someday make it possible for one or both superpowers to contemplate launching a disarming first-strike.

Furthermore, additional arms control measures designed to assure mutual invulnerability of retaliatory forces are essential. High priority must thus be given to heading off new and threatening developments in areas such as anti-submarine warfare, anti-satellite warfare, and extensive ballistic missile defenses. If such arms control measures are negotiated in the near future, it may be possible to preserve the essential features of mutual invulnerability. On the other hand, just as was the case in the 1940's with atomic weapons and in the 1970's with MIRV's, if the new technologies are developed, tested, and deployed, it will be far more difficult to put the "genie back in the bottle" once it is out. Therefore, the best time to ban testing is before it has begun. Delay could mean that a significant opportunity to bring the strategic arms race under control might be lost forever.

FOOTNOTES

[1] Bernard Brodie, The Absolute Weapon (New York: Harcourt, Brace, 1946).

[2] "Fiscal 1984-1988 Defense Guidance," quoted in The New York Times, June 4, 1982, p. A10.

[3] These arguments are summarized by Matthew Bunn and Kosta Tsipis, "The Uncertainties of a Preemptive Nuclear Attack," Scientific American, Vol. 249, No. 5 (November 1983), p. 40.

[4] Eliot Marshall, "The Question of Missile Accuracy," Science, Vol. 213, No. 4513 (September 11, 1981), p. 1231.

[5] More detail may be found in J. Edward Anderson, "First Strike: Myth or Reality?" The Bulletin Of Atomic Scientists (November 1981), pp. 6-11, including its references and technical papers available from the author.

[6] Glenn H. Snyder, Deterrence And Defense: Towards A Theory Of National Security (Princeton, N.J.: Princeton University Press, 1961), p. 12.

[7] Carl Sagan, R.P. Turco, P.B. Toon, T.P. Ackerman, J.B. Pollack, "Nuclear Winter: Global Consequences of Multiple Nuclear Explosions," Science, Vol. 222 (December 23, 1983), pp. 1283-1292.

[8] See, for example, Blair Stewart, "MX and the Counterforce Problem: A Case for Silo Deployment," Strategic Review, Vol. 9, No. 3 (Summer 1981), pp. 23-25.

[9] The argument that a Soviet first-strike against U.S. ICBM's might result in the virtual disarming of the USSR has been made by John P. Steinbruner and Thomas M. Garwin, "Strategic Vulnerability: The Balance Between Prudence and Paranoia," International Security, Vol. 1, No. 1 (Summer 1976), pp. 138-181.

[10] International Institute of Strategic Studies, The Military Balance, 1982-83 (London: International Institute of Strategic Studies, 1982), pp. 112-113.

[11] Farooq Hussain, The Impact of Weapons Test Restrictions (London: International Institute of Strategic Studies, Adelphi Paper 165, 1981), p. 25.

[12] International Institute of Strategic Studies, Strategic Survey, 1980-81 (London: International Institute of Strategic Studies, 1981), p. 13.

[13] The New York Times, October 3, 1981, p. 8.

[14] Colin Gray and Keith Payne, "Victory is Possible," Foreign Policy, No. 39 (Summer 1980), p. 19.

[15] Richard Burt, "Arms Control and Western Security: A Question of Growing Irrelevance," in Lawrence S. Hagen (ed.), The Crisis In Western Security (New York: St. Martin's Press, 1982), p. 73.

[16] Strobe Talbot, Endgame: The Inside Story Of SALT II (New York: Harper and Row, 1979), p. 157.

[17] See Farooq Hussain, op. cit., pp. 39-48, for a further elaboration of the difficulties of verifying such a ban.

[18] For confirmation of these doubts by the physicist who received the Nobel Prize for his role in the invention of the laser, see Charles Townes, who observes that laser and particle beam weapons are "technologically very difficult and hence can be classified for the time being as imaginary weapons. But even these still imaginary weapons increase competetive tension and probably waste money." Charles Townes, "Discussion," in Roman Kolkowicz and Neil Joeck (eds.), Arms Control And International Security (Boulder, Colorado: Westview Press, 1984), p. 83.

189

MAINTAINING STRATEGIC NUCLEAR STABILITY

Earl C. Ravenal

THE SCOPE OF THE PROBLEM

In an age that threatens intense and widespread nuclear devastation, and yet an age in which nations feel they must keep the arsenals that could inflict this devastation, a premium must be placed on preventing escalation to nuclear war. In other words, nations must aim at stability--more precisely, "crisis stability"--in the design of their nuclear postures and doctrines, and even in their larger national strategies and their foreign policies (whom they protect, up to what point, how far forward, and with what mix of denial and threatened reprisal, as well as arms control and disarmament measures with adversaries and among allies).

Another approach, strategic defense, is seen here not as a radical substitute for retaliatory deterrence or preemptive nuclear attack, but rather as an adjunct to these, and as a condition for preserving our extended deterrence over European allies. Indeed, strategic defense, even if it can be technically devised, economically developed, and practically installed, will not obviate the desideratum of stability. One of the criteria for judging strategic defense is whether it conduces to or derogates from stability, particularly crisis stability.

Strategic stability presumes, but also transcends, the correct design of nuclear forces and doctrines. Insofar as it involves the broader objective of war-avoidance and the possibility of compartmentalizing conflicts among nations, it invokes the structure of the international system, in two directions: (1) The kind of international system affects the prospects for arms control and a stable nuclear balance; and (2) the degree of strategic stability and the distribution of nuclear arms affect--and in a sense define--the kind of international system. The achievement of elemental safety for a nation, particularly a present alliance guarantor, may require the renunciation of its function of extended deterrence. In turn, if an essential member of the international system were to change this central relationship to allies and antagonists, the system would necessarily change. Unless another single

190

nation immediately picked up the pieces of power, the international system would become looser and more unaligned.

PROBLEMS OF PEACE

The "peace movement," though it has provided needed stimulus and criticism to national security bureaucracies, has not been consistently useful to the discussion of arms acquisition and arms control. The German military historian Clausewitz remarked on the "fog of war," which obscures and frustrates the best calculations of strategists. There is also such a thing as the fog of peace. We have been seeing it in the cloud of proposals to reduce the threat of nuclear war and curtail the buildup of nuclear weapons. But to be "concerned" about war is not necessarily to be serious about peace.

Typically, peace groups and polemicists propagate several false, simplistic, or self-contradictory notions that involve nuclear dispositions as well as our role in the international system. The first is the emphasis on numbers: that the more nuclear weapons there are, the worse. It matters less what kind they are, where they are, or even who has them. No less than, in their own way, the extreme hawks, the doves believe that numbers themselves can lead to nuclear war. Every other day, it seems, one gets a piece of second-class mail from these Cassandras of "overkill" saying: "...The Pentagon now has the equivalent of 600,000 Hiroshima bombs....We have enough missiles to destroy Russia forty-four times....20 percent more nuclear weapons [are] deployed than are necessary to destroy the entire human race...." etc., etc. The irony, and the perversity, is that the doves can talk about overkill precisely because their preferred strategic response is counter-city retaliation, as pure and horrifying as John Foster Dulles ever threatened. All we "need" to execute this kind of strike is a handful of megatons somewhere in our force structure; the rest, by definition, is overkill. There may be some limited sense in the emphasis on numbers, if one is hung up on the fear of a nuclear accident that might trigger a general holocaust. But the most likely case, (insofar as any case is really likely) is deliberate-- though, of course, contingent--escalation to nuclear weapons by the leaders of one country against the territory and forces of another. If one is attentive to this relative probability, one will be less

191

concerned about numbers and more concerned about incentives--particularly the incentives that are built into the concrete dispositions and characteristics of the nuclear forces and doctrines of contestants.

Second, most peace proposals simply stress trust and good will, as if those were the primary, or the only, missing factors. Those who fervently desire peace often become disillusioned with the arid complexities of the contemporary arms debate. They look for some Gordian knot to cut with an immediate and comprehensible stroke of exhortation. But trust and good will are not enough. Trust must be founded on the technical and logical conditions of strategic stability. Just as lack of understanding can impede efforts to control arms, strategic instability can raise suspicions and undermine political confidence. Third, having misplaced the problem, many advocates of peace equally misconceive the answer. They are quick to cry "pathology."

But that does not fully explain the behavior of national leaderships. Though they have often traduced the real security and the real interests of their constituents in the name of "national security" or "the national interest," generally leaders and policy-makers are, in a recognizable sense of the word, prudent and rational. Some day, no doubt, the present accumulation and use of arms will be regarded as madness. But it is madness of a special kind. It has to do with the convoluted, but genuine, quest for safety. It is the madness of responsible people, or responsible organizations. Therefore, curing individuals, even if this were possible, would not be an effective remedy.

Finally, many who criticize our possession and use of arms nonetheless advocate an active American protective role in the world, both in extending nuclear deterrence and in intervening with conventional force in situations where valued societies or political principles are threatened or suppressed. Theirs is the familiar assertion that "there is no peace without justice"--an aphorism that is either blind or tautological. Often the claims of peace and justice-- not to mention order--are antithetical. Our unreciprocated reduction of arms may be worthwhile, on balance, but it will not bring all good things in its train. The United States might lose its influence on the behavior of other nations and have to accept the results of some arbitrary and forcible interventions

192

and the persistence of some ugly and destructive regimes.

THE LOGIC OF INCENTIVES

To assure nuclear peace for ourselves, strategic stability is the minimum necessary condition, but it is also probably the minimum sufficient condition. In any event, stability may be the most that we can achieve.

Strategic stability can be defined in terms of the pattern of incentives, for both sides, to initiate or not to initiate nuclear war under a variety of circumstances. And the circumstances that are of most interest are not the placed moments in international relations, but the crisis situations--those rare and rather improbable confrontations that are, nonetheless, as contemplated by the powers of the world, at the foundation of the arms race.

The logic of incentives comprehends numbers, both aggregate among the nuclear adversaries and, more importantly, comparative between them; but it transcends these numbers. Simply put: To have a nuclear war, someone must start it. Thus, the key question is: Why would either side want to strike first? What would have to be the scenario, the antecedent moves, the impending situation? We can dispose of the notion that a nuclear war would start "out of the blue" because one of the contestants, the moment it reached some critical ratio of "superiority," either initially or after projecting the result of a hypothetical nuclear exchange, would have an incentive to attack--to cash in its paper advantage, to convert it into the harder coinage of military victory by waging a sudden first strike against the nuclear forces, or even the society, of the other. That is not how it works. A future nuclear war might grow out of some festering, escalating crisis--say, a confrontation in the Middle East or the Persian Gulf, or a series of political and social upheavals and ambiguous moves in Central Europe--where conflict had already been joined and each side had developed reasons to be nervous about the other's resort to nuclear weapons. Then, in this game theorists's nightmare, an edgy or desperate enemy might be inspired to unleash a nuclear strike, if he had the ability to destroy a large portion of his adversary's nuclear forces, while reserving enough weapons to hold the adversary's society hostage.

193

Thus, the capability of each side's nuclear forces in a counterforce mode, and the vulnerability of each side's forces to a counterforce strike, are critical elements in the logic of incentives. Capability and vulnerability are interrelated. "They" are capable to the extent that their nuclear force has accuracy and large numbers of warheads. "We" are vulnerable to the extent that our forces are fixed in known places ("sitting ducks") and not well protected (not in effectively hardened shelters or not guarded by antiballistic missiles). A simpler way of summarizing the relationship is this: If they can't disarm us, they aren't going to hit us.

THE RATIONALE OF COUNTERFORCE

The competition in counterforce is driving the current stage of the arms race. Counterforce represents the dedication of some portion of one's nuclear arsenal to attacking enemy military installations, logistical complexes and nets, military-related industries, command facilities, nuclear storage sites, nuclear forces in general, and—specifically— "time-urgent" nuclear weapons such as missiles in silos. To the extent that one believes that the United States is not simply addicted to aggressive force expansion or gratuitous coercive pressure, one must explain its current inclination to a counterforce nuclear strategy.

I reckon that America's drift to counterforce is neither perverse nor accidental. To grasp the rationale of counterforce, it is necessary to understand the logic of extended deterrence. For ultimately it is adherence to alliance commitments that skews our strategy toward counterforce weapons and targeting and warps our doctrines of response toward the first use of nuclear weapons, prejudicing crisis stability and increasing the likelihood of escalation to nuclear war. Few realize how intertwined our weapons and strategies are with our commitments. And few understand how integral to our entire foreign policy stance has been the strategic paradigm of deterrence and alliance that we have maintained for almost four decades—and therefore, how much would have to change, if we set about to achieve an alternative, more stable, nuclear stance, that might provide greater safety for Americans in an age of pervasive nuclear danger.

194

Counterforce, since it involves "hard-target kill capability," is an extremely demanding requirement for our nuclear force. To cover some 2,000 silos and nuclear weapons storage sites in the Soviet Union, and some 700 leadership centers, requires at least two independent nuclear weapons each, 5,400 out of the 9,400 needed for the entire target system. And since our hard-target kill weapons would themselves be the prime targets of a Soviet preemptive strike, more than the usual redundancy is needed in these categories. Thus, hard-target kill is responsible for the major part of the current "ideal" deployment of 15,000 to 20,000 reentry vehicles in our strategic nuclear force. (These are in addition to the cruise missiles, short-range attack missiles, and bombs carried by bombers.[1]

Why would the United States have opted for this demanding strategy? We can bypass the stated rationales of merely "neutralizing" the Soviets' hard-target kill capability or symmetrically matching their nuclear force. There must be more to counterforce than that. A more interesting rationale is to induce crisis stability. In this explanation, our counterforce deployment would threaten Soviet fixed land-based missiles and thus force the Soviets to redeploy those missiles to sea or, second-best, to land-mobile basing, thus eventually leading to the mutual invulnerability of both sides' nuclear forces and so ensuring crisis stability. But even this more attractive rationale for counterforce is tenuous. For this more stable state of affairs would exist only at the end of a long process that must pass through a phase of acute _instability_. Since no basing mode for our land-based counterforce missiles would credibly confer invulnerability, our attainment of hard-target kill capability would be correctly construed as a first-strike posture. The Soviets might initially react by planning to launch their threatened missiles on warning, or even preemptively.

In fact, there is a more compelling motive: damage limitation--that is, limiting the damage to the United States in a nuclear war. Part of that intent would be to destroy Soviet missiles in their silos. Such a damage-limiting attack, to have its intended effect, must be preemptive. By exploring the logic of the preemptive strike, I do not accuse anyone of plotting a preventive war--the definition of which is a war, _ex nihilo_, to destroy an adversary before he reaches the point, allegedly, of waging a war to destroy one's own country. In distinction, a

195

preemptive strike is contingent and occurs only in an already developing confrontation. But the logic remains: Counterforce and first nuclear strike are mutually dependent. A first strike implies counterforce targeting, since the only initial attack that makes sense is a damage-limiting strike, the destruction of as much of the enemy's nuclear force as possible. And counterforce targeting, in return, implies a first strike, a preemptive attack, because a second strike against the enemy's missiles is useless to the extent that one's missiles would hit empty holes.

Thus we come to the matter of extended deterrence. American alliances, particularly NATO, have always depended on the threat of our first use of nuclear weapons, and our promise of continuous escalation from battlefield nuclear weapons, to more potent theater types, to the final use of our intercontinental strategic force. Any American strategic policy will try to protect certain values that are at the core of our national identity and sovereignty. These values include our political integrity and autonomy and the safety and domestic property of our people. These are the proper--and largely feasible--objects of our defense or deterrence. It is when we attempt to protect more than these objects with our strategic nuclear force that we court the peculiar problems of extended deterrence. Then the calculus of credibility that we make with regard to strict central deterrence does not hold. The assumptions of deterrence apply to peripheral areas and less-than-vital interests with much less strength and validity. American protection of Western Europe, in particular, requires both initial conventional defense and credible extended deterrence. One cannot be substituted for the other. Extended deterrence, in turn, requires the practical invulnerability of our society to Soviet attack. (This is not to be confused with the invulnerability of our nuclear weapons.) I say practical invulnerability, since absolute invulnerability is beyond America's, or anyone's, reach. Rather, what is necessary is the ability to limit damage to "tolerable" levels of casualties and destruction. This is so an American president can persuade others that he would risk an attack on our homeland, or that he could face down a threat to attack our homeland, in spreading our protective mantle over Western Europe and other parts of the world.

The United States would have to attain societal invulnerability through both its defensive and its offensive strategic system. But could this be done? First, we would have to achieve a strategic defense. This would require measures such as area anti-ballistic missiles (ABM) and laser or particle beam weapons in space, air defense against Soviet bombers and cruise missiles, and anti-submarine warfare against Soviet submarines, and a vast program of shelters and evacuation. These measures are very expensive; they might cost, conservatively, hundreds of billions of dollars to even a trillion dollars, over a decade. And they probably would not work sufficiently well; or, more meaningfully, we could not assume that they would work well enough to engage in nuclear escalation and entrust our further safety to strategic defense. As a second condition of societal invulnerability, American would have to hold in reserve, after any of the earlier stages of a protracted nuclear exchange, enough destructive power to threaten counter-city strikes, so the enemy would never with relative impunity threaten to attack our cities and exact a political price that might include our surrender. Finally, an indirect but most significant requisite of societal invulnerability is the acquisition of nuclear counterforce capability, specifically hard-target kill. Counterforce contributes to damage limitation in several related and mutually reinforcing ways, both indirect and direct. High accuracy in our missiles, great destructive power in our warheads, and large numbers of independently targeted reentry vehicles (MIRVs) would enable us to execute a damage-limiting strike against the Soviets' "time-urgent" nuclear forces, primarily their missiles in silos. Thus--indirectly damage-limiting--our counterforce capability would erode the enemy's ability to attack our nuclear forces; in turn, our nuclear forces would survive in larger numbers, the better to deter the enemy's eventual attack on our cities by holding his own cities hostage. And--directly damage-limiting--our counterforce capability would erode the enemy's ability to attack our cities in his earliest nuclear strike, if that were, irrationally, to be his move.

We see that counterforce "makes sense," as an attempt to fulfill some of the necessary conditions of extended deterrence--but, it is fair to say, only as such. Our willingness to protect our allies rises or falls with the prospective viability of counterforce and, more generally, with our ability to protect our own society from nuclear attack. If there is any explicit doubt--technical, economic, political--that we will achieve that invulnerability, then there is implicit doubt that our extensive commitments, especially to Western Europe, can survive.

THE ROLE OF STRATEGIC DEFENSE

Strategic defense is the only novel strategic thrust of the Reagan administration (that is, innovation beyond the designs of the late Carter administration). It comprises two related, but conceptually distinct, subjects: (1) the "strategic defense initiative" (SDI) as such--that is, the defense of American society or American intercontinental strategic nuclear forces (or both) against ballistic missiles launched by the Soviet Union; and (2) anti-satellite weapons, to destroy or blind Soviet space satellites that might support, in various functional ways, a Soviet nuclear attack on the United States.

Both strategic defense and counterforce, insofar as they are adjuncts to societal invulnerability, are designed to enhance the ability of the United States to deter threats to objects beyond our normal "sphere of credibility"--that is, to give the United States more freedom of strategic action, a wider scope of foreign policy. Of course, strategic defense also has the more limited intermediate mission of directly shielding our deterrent itself. But this mission, too, does not differ much, in function, from a preemptive counterforce attack. Thus, strategic defense competes with deterrence, in the usual conception, but enhances it, in another important way. Three sets of questions arise with respect to strategic defense. The most obvious relates to our arms control stance: the impact of, and use of, strategic defense and anti-satellite weapons in the current strategic arms bargaining. Are strategic weapons to be bargaining chips or "crown jewels"? The latter means technology that is so unique, unchallengeable and unmatchable by the Soviet Union, inherently useful and cost-effective, and technically feasible--in a word, so "sweet"--that the United States must hold onto it and continue to develop it, no matter what the Soviets might offer in exchange; in other words, not negotiable at all.

The second question is how the American tilt toward strategic defense might affect the integrity of deterrence. Does the prospect of even a relatively impermeable societal defense against incoming nuclear

198

weapons, or of the effective defense of our offensive weapons against a Soviet first strike, make deterrence of nuclear war more certain, by denying entirely or just lowering the confidence of a Soviet countervalue retaliation, in one case, or a preemptive counterforce strike, in the other? Or, on the contrary, does it make the strategic balance more precarious; does it derogate from crisis stability by creating the presumption of a now unanswerable American first strike and forcing our adversary to consider, and offset in various ways, our own preemptive counterforce strike?

And third, is strategic defense even feasible, technologically and fiscally? There is a wide divergence of assessments of the feasibility of this proposed system, in meeting various levels and weights of stress. And estimates of the overall cost of putting in place some sort of strategic ballistic missile defense have ranged from about $50 or 60 billion (General Daniel O. Graham; and Max Kampelman, Zbigniew Brzezinski, and Robert Jastrow in The New York Times, January 26, 1985) to $1 trillion over a decade or two (James Schlesinger).

My own view is as follows: (1) Strategic defense, insofar as it may be reasonably hoped, eventually, to substitute partially for strategic offense, and as it may serve as an adjunct, not as a barrier, to some form of arms control, is a morally worthy and strategically interesting concept. (2) It is not absolutely foreclosed that strategic defense, including some form of boost-phase interception, is technically inaccessible, or beyond the fiscal capability or the political will of our society, under some circumstances; but the odds, in those two categories, are against it. (3) American programs for research and development in strategic defense have been responsible, in significant measure, for bringing the Soviet Union back to the negotiating table,and may elicit more substantive and satisfactory Soviet proposals to constrain their heavy, counterforce, potentially first-strike missiles (SS-18s and 19s and successors). (4) Finally, a sensible American bargaining strategy must attempt the precise and difficult (because apparently contradictory) feat of keeping strategic defense alive, in order that it remain a bargaining chip, and seeming to be forthcoming at some point and at some responsible price, in trading it away for the proper Soviet concessions, in order that it be a bargaining chip and not a fixed feature in the American strategic firmament.

199

AN ALTERNATIVE STRATEGY

Our present nuclear strategy is costly and demanding, because of the target system it addresses, the types and numbers of weapons needed, the protection those weapons require, and the urge to acquire societal defense. Moreover, it is crisis-unstable and makes nuclear war more likely.

But it cannot be easily and directly fixed. A real alternative prescription for our nuclear strategy would diverge more radically from the present strategy than most critics of that strategy realize. A nuclear policy cannot be a strong of self-contained prescriptions for quantities or qualities of forces. It must implement some national strategy and in turn express some foreign policy design. That is why relevant nuclear strategies will come in wide step-functions, not an infinite gradation of nuanced options. In this case, there can be no middle positions, certainly none that merely borrow and cobble together the attractive features of several other proposals. We must either satisfy the requisites of extended deterrence or move to a nuclear stance compatible with a disengaged position.

Thus, an alternative nuclear policy will serve a different national strategy: Instead of the paradigm of deterrence and alliance, which is synthesized in extended deterrence, it will support and implement a policy of non-intervention, consisting of war-avoidance and self-reliance. War-avoidance and self-reliance indicate the compartmentalization of conflict. Our security would depend on abstention from regional quarrels. This strategy implies the delegation of defensive tasks to our regional allies and the acceptance of the results of this, win or lose. We would, over time, accommodate the dissolution of defensive commitments that oblige us to overseas intervention. In doing so, we would be concerned to decouple conflict in another region of the world from our ultimate resort to strategic nuclear weapons.

In the strategic nuclear dimension, a policy of war-avoidance and self-reliance would be implemented by what I would call "finite essential deterrence." In a nuclear age, crisis stability is the key to central peace and relative safety. To achieve safety for ourselves (though not necessarily for others), our strategy should enhance crisis stability.

A nuclear strategy consists of posture and doctrine. We can strengthen crisis stability by designing our posture and our doctrines of targeting and precedence of use--or, more generally, occasion or context of response (to what kinds of situations, involving threats to or attacks on what objects?)--to discourage either side's first use of nuclear weapons. First, we can dissuade the other side from starting a nuclear war. Since an enemy's first strike must logically be a damage-limiting attack on our nuclear forces, we can change our posture to eliminate our fixed land-based systems. These systems are inevitably vulnerable, despite the efforts of a succession of administrations to put them in multiple or closely-spaced shelters (as with the MX), or to acquire a redundant and dispersed force (as with the prospective "Midgetman" single-warhead missiles).

The abandonment of land-based missiles would move our nuclear posture from the present triad of forces to a diad consisting of submarine-launched missiles and bombers armed with medium-range cruise missiles. We would make this move only as we developed the technology to insure sufficiently accurate coverage of the required targets with undersea weapons systems. Among other things, we would need to solve the command-and-control problem, sending reliable orders and receiving timely information from submarines on station. The 1981 Reagan decision to accelerate the development and deployment of the longer-range Trident II (or D-5) missile and the Trident (Ohio-class) submarines is not unconstructive, though expensive and premature. And we are installing medium-range cruise missiles in our existing B-52 bombers. There is no need to have revived the penetrating bomber (the B-1B--and, for that matter, the "Stealth"), although it is, at worst, expensive, not provocative or destabilizing.

With respect to the doctrine of targeting, we would not aim at enemy missiles in their silos. To do so might provoke the Soviets, in a crisis, to launch preemptively. Rather, we would develop a list of some 3,000 military targets[2]--such as naval and air bases, concentrations of conventional forces, military industrial complexes and arms industry--that are relatively far from large civilian population centers. (We would also not deliberately target Soviet cities. This doctrine is derived from both moral and strategic

201

reasons: If we avoid the enemy's cities, we give him no incentive to strike our cities. Of course, if our cities came under an enemy's nuclear attack, it would be excruciatingly difficult, politically and psychologically, for a president to restrict our counter-attack to military targets. Yet even in that extremity, striking "enemy" populations would make no more strategic sense than it ever did, and no moral sense at all.)

With respect to the doctrine of precedence and occasion of use, we should also seal off the temptation ourselves to start a nuclear war. (That is why we should not design our forces to execute a preemptive strike.) Such a first use of nuclear weapons could hardly occur unless we were to escalate in the midst of a conventional war. Thus, war-avoidance would be most comprehensively implemented by dissolving our defensive commitments. To reinforce that, or even short of that, we can express our overriding interest in avoiding the spread of nuclear war to our homeland by imposing upon ourselves a stringent doctrine of no first use. Such a policy, joined with the targeting restrictions on our retaliatory strike, creates a triply restrained doctrine: We would not use nuclear weapons except (1) in response to a nuclear attack (2) on our homeland; and our riposte would be (3) confined to military objectives of a non-silo nature.

NO FIRST USE

The doctrine of no first use requires further explanation, particularly in its appropriate context, extended deterrence over Western Europe.

Nuclear war can occur only if someone starts it. Therefore, the most important move toward a stable nuclear balance is for nations to adopt, and to build into their defensive plans and postures, an intention not to use nuclear weapons first.

The international legal mechanics of no first use are less important than embodying the intention and expectation of no first use in the tangible weapons systems and actual doctrines of nations. It is also less important to achieve reciprocity in a pledge of no first use, or formal acceptance of the principle in a binding treaty, than it is to begin and expand, even through independent moves, the adoption by individual nations of the stance of no first use. We should try

202

to negotiate such an agreement among nations, particularly between the United States and the Soviet Union; but we should not shrink from adopting no first use independently. We do not gain by requiring reciprocity as a necessary condition for our moving to a no first use doctrine.

But some recent arguments for no first use (such as that of McGeorge Bundy, George F. Kennan, Robert S. McNamara,and Gerard Smith[3]) fall short of logical closure in that they insist on maintaining the integrity of our extended deterrence for Europe. If one is committed both to defend Europe and to avoid the extension of conflict to our own homeland, one must try to reconcile these awkward objectives. What conditions would be necessary to effect this reconciliation?

Important in the Bundy-Kennan-McNamara-Smith proposal is that the apparent renunciation of the first use of nuclear weapons is conditional on the attainment of adequate conventional defense. But those who opt reflexively for conventional defense cannot mean just any conventional effort. They must mean the high confidence defense of Europe with conventional arms. And they have the further burden of not just prescribing or exhorting that the United States and its allies "must" do more to guarantee the integrity of Western Europe, but predicting that this will happen.

In order to determine the feasibility--and so the predictive probability--of conventional defense, we must have a bill of costs. But nowhere in the Bundy article is that bill set forth. In fact, our present share of the conventional defense of Europe--and this is not even designed to be a self-contained conventional defense--is about $133 billion for 1987. This is 42-1/2 percent of the $312 billion requested for defense by the Reagan administration. Given a reasonable projection of current cost growth, over the next ten years Europe will cost us $1.8 trillion. Will even those resources be forthcoming, let alone the greater ones required for self-sufficient conventional defense?

Moreover, it is the very fear of inevitable extension of a nuclear conflict to American territory that constitutes the essential element in the coupling of our strategic nuclear arsenal to the local defense of our allies. For extended deterrence to work, the escalatory chain--from conventional war to theater nuclear weapons to the use of America's ultimate

strategic weapon--must seem to be unbroken. Yet Bundy
et al. propose to introduce a "firebreak" at the
earliest point of nuclear war. Since firebreaks and
coupling are antithetical, we cannot have both.

A consistent stance of no first use of nuclear
weapons by the United States implies the dissolution of
the Atlantic alliance. Those who opt for no first use
without considering its impact on NATO are implicitly
opting for the disengagement of the United States from
the defense of Europe. The only practical difference
between their position and mine is that I accept the
consequence of mine, while they do not admit, or even
seem to understand, the consequence of theirs.[4]

There are problems with my war-avoiding nuclear
strategy. By limiting the occasion of our response, we
would explicitly terminate extended deterrence, and so
increase the odds of a war in some region that is under
pressure. Even by limiting just the weight of our
response, we would perhaps also weaken deterrence of
direct threats to the United States (though there is a
good chance that our counter-military response would be
sufficient; certainly its credibility would be a of a
high order, since we would be threatening retaliation
for a direct nuclear attack on our own homeland). Thus
we encounter the ultimate contradiction between crisis
stability and deterrent stability.

There is no way to escape this contradiction. It
is not a peculiar weakness of my case. It is simply a
fact of life. There is an essential tension, not an
easy complementarity, between achieving safety for
ourselves through crisis stability and achieving safety
for the objects of our protection in the world through
deterrent stability. But we can lessen the incidence
of this tension by diminishing our obligations to
extend nuclear protection. Crisis stability more
closely coincides with deterrent stability as we shed
external commitments and concentrate on our own
defense.

THE FUNCTION OF ARMS CONTROL

In an independent American strategy of
disengagement and conflict avoidance, arms control has
an important, but ancillary, role. All aspects of arms
control are not designed to enhance stability; some
serve the additional purposes of reducing the cost
burden of preparing for war and the contingent
destruction of war, and in other ways conduce to a more

204

benign international system and a more moral exercise of foreign policy. These other virtuous purposes should not excessively be traded-off against stability.

In fact, a strategy of finite essential deterrence, because it need not maintain an arms-heavy counterforce stance to support alliance commitments, and because the occasions for war are reduced in number and probability, unlocks arms control and allows more scope for substantive disarmament. But in the past, proposals of arms limitation assumed that progress would come only through multilateral or bilateral bargaining and formal agreements among nations. Draftsmanship and legalism were emphasized. This ignored the potential of independent, national, informal moves to disarm, selectively and prudently, and otherwise to defuse the potential of war. Indeed, in some important areas, the only effective moves might be independent.

Formal arms control implies specific conditions: an explicit and semi-public bargaining forum; agreements that carry the expectation of effective inspection and even policing; and, above all, reciprocity. It also gives rise to posturing, stone-walling, constructing bargaining chips, and playing games of "chicken." It is these conditions that have made it hard to achieve progress in mitigating arms competition, and, even where agreements have been reached, have given rise to recriminations and accusations of cheating.

This disappointing record does not mean that we should oppose partial measures of arms limitation or denigrate entirely the use of the formal bargaining context and the effort to involve our global competitors in binding treaties and cooperative undertakings. Arms control can play a significant role in creating a world that is safer for ourselves, and perhaps for other nations. Some of the postures and doctrines that we would adopt in any case could be codified and reciprocated through explicit agreements.

Such agreements should be sought across a wide range of situations and functions: significant reductions in the levels of strategic arms; and explicit and mutual pledge of no first use of nuclear weapons; a moratorium on the introduction of destabilizing new weapons systems; a ban on the testing of nuclear warheads in any environment and the testing of new delivery vehicles; treaties to regulate the development of strategic defense technologies and to ban anti-satellite weapons; the establishment of nuclear-free geographical zones; efforts to control the proliferation of nuclear arms, materials, and weapons technologies; the outlawing of chemical and biological weapons; limitations on conventional forces; restrictions on arms transfers; curtailment of foreign military bases and deployments; cuts in overall military budgets; mechanisms for peace-keeping and mediation; confidence-building measures; and legal codes that discourage war initiation and war crimes.

To attempt these measures, the formal bargaining process must be supplemented and backstopped by initiatives in other forums, including non-governmental transnational measures and independent actions carried out by and within individual nations. There has to be room for initiatives, taken by nations for their own prudent purposes, to reduce the risks and burdens of military postures and doctrines. Genuine unilateral moves must make strategic sense in themselves, so they can be sustained whether or not they are reciprocated by the other nuclear superpower. The independent moves (such as eliminating fixed land-based missiles, no first use of nuclear weapons, large cuts in conventional forces, attenuation of military alliances) should be accommodated in a comprehensive framework and methodology, along with the more formal bilateral or multilateral arms control or disarmament negotiations. There should be provision for verification of these independent moves by the other side. Independent initiatives would function to create momentum for the arms control or disarmament process and break deadlocks at critical points; to indicate the scope of possibilities; and to generate public and even elite support, transforming the climate in which arms control and disarmament might proceed. The insistence on independent moves within a framework of comprehensive arms control and disarmament is not a contradiction, but a frank recognition of reality and actually an unconditional commitment to progress in arms reduction and war avoidance.

Also, arms "control" must be transcended; substantive and extensive arms reductions must be reinstated. Arms control and disarmament are not incompatible, if they are held in a proper mutual perspective. Arms control should be viewed as a series of staged and partial steps toward more comprehensive disarmament--resting points, each of which offers a chance to establish stability, political acceptance, and mutual confidence before moving to the next stage. More comprehensive disarmament should be seen as a goal; but not only that--it must also be seen as a reason for accomplishing the steps of arms control, and a standard against which one can measure each interim arms control move, to see whether, even if valid in itself, it also leads to the greatest practicable disarmament.

All this makes it imperative to redefine comprehensive disarmament to make it compatible with the fragmented world that will persist for the next century--a world of nation-states, autonomous centers of political and strategic initiative, occupied with their own self-defense, commanding considerable elements of force,and not reliant on a safety net in the form of an authoritative and potent world organization with effective police powers, or in the form of the protection of big alliance guarantors. It will also be a world still characterized by competitive nationalism and a measure of strategic distrust.

In these probable circumstances, disarmament should be pursued down to forces that cannot feasibly conduct aggressive war against other nations, but that will allow nations to conduct the defense of citizens and their property against external attack. These forces--which would be conventional military forces-- would be higher than the residual level envisaged in the U.S.-Soviet drafts of 1961-62.[5] A practical regime of disarmament would also have to allow for some uneven implementation by the parties, a lack of meticulous reciprocity on some points, and some failures of detailed verification.

The system of disarmament I am describing would be unenforced. This should not be taken on its face as unrealistic. Though it requires an act of imagination, it is simply an expression of the kind of world that can be predicted for the next hundred years. It might be tempting to "solve" this problem by designing structures of world government and mechanisms of supranational enforcement. But that would be simply to substitute one kind of imagination for another. That is precisely what has been wrong with previous proposals of disarmament. Moreover, it is hard to see how ingenious novel measures (such as the forfeiture of performance bonds) the more traditional kinds of sanctions (communications disruption, economic embargo) would be any more feasible than global police forces. All suffer from the probable lack of an unarguable central agency to dictate and implement enforcement. One conceivable partial recourse, since we are not thinking of enforcement by a centralized coercive authority, would be to non-governmental groups--some of them even transnational organizations, which would operate, however, through the legal systems of each country (even if such operation would be uneven across the spectrum of states). Such organizations would reinforce the extension of international law within nation-states; they could formulate new laws, monitor the compliance of leaders, expose violations, and bring actions in national courts against statesmen.

So whatever degree of comprehensive disarmament is achieved will fall short of the ultimate and pure vision of a quarter of a century ago, though it should it be much broader than the "arms control" mechanisms we have relied on since then. But disarmament exercises should not be occasions for peace organizations to outbid each other in asserting perfect worlds and sweeping international regimes, fielding ingenious gimmicks, and displaying eloquent draftsmanship. The point is to introduce ends that are sustainable, a sequence that makes sense, a process that leads to more but can be stopped at any point with mutual profit and general stability. Thus disarmament could command the practical respect and the real allegiance of elites as well as bodies of citizens.

A DIFFERENT INTERNATIONAL SYSTEM

With the purpose of enhancing strategic stability, and also, if possible, achieving reductions in the burden of arms and the contingent destruction of war, we have reviewed a panoply of measures. Independent national actions, in the design of forces and in the implementation of selected measures of restraint and reduction, supplement initiatives in more formal arms limitation. Such measures are intended to minimize the chance of nuclear conflict, as consistently as we can with other objectives, such as the discouragement of all kinds of aggression and the adoption of strategies that are as moral as possible among the grim choices available to us.

The attainment--even the consistent pursuit--of these objectives by a nation entails a fundamental change in its foreign policy and national strategy, to disengagement from defensive commitments and to a much lower propensity to intervene in conflict. A nation

208

that adopted such a strategy would tend not to pursue "milieu goals"--the shape and character of the international system, balance, in general or with a particular antagonist, and even the more abstract notion of order in the system. These generic milieu goals would be distinguished from more palpable security interests. The term "vital" would be reserved for those truly supreme interests that derive so strictly from the identity of the nation that they could not credibly be alienated.

In turn, such a fundamental change in the foreign policy of a nation such as the United States, an essential participant in the international system, would entail a concomitant change in the structure of the system. Lacking a large portion of the extended deterrence it had enjoyed, the system would be marked by the further disintegration of alliances and the advent of general unalignment. A dozen or two of the nations that are now coopted or subordinated by the present superpowers could exercise, or even flaunt, a good deal of autonomous political and military initiative, particularly in their own regions, and would have great (though not always sufficient) incentives to acquire more potent arms.

Thus, it is not to be imagined that the achievement of strategic nuclear stability by a pair of superpowers in their own global relationship would necessarily dampen regional conflict, either in its incidence or its scale. In some cases (perhaps even in Europe), a policy of war-avoidance and self-reliance by the United States could lead to cooperative regional initiatives across the present East-West political boundary. But, conversely (especially in other regions), it could lead to a competitive and in some cases uneven scramble by individual nations to compensate for the loss of immediate defensive resources and assurances. Ironically, the restraint of nuclear weapons by some nations (particularly the principal guarantor nations) might encourage the proliferation of nuclear arms throughout the international system. Abolition of the alliance system might lead to a "Gaullist world." This is not to say that widespread and rapid proliferation would be inevitable. Each nation, in contemplating its concrete moves, would be faced with a host of practical impediments and inhibitions: the cost, the exposure to other nations' countermeasures, the alienation of regional friends, some sanctions by the larger nuclear powers. And some moves could be taken in international agencies and cooperative circles to slow or impede the process of nuclear diffusion. But it should be realized that, in theory and in aggregate reality, extended deterrence and proliferation run in opposite directions.

Perhaps the best that can be said, on the international systemic plane, for an American policy of nuclear restraint and military non-intervention is that such conduct would meet a "Kantian" test: First, the adoption by each nation of a policy of self-restraint and conflict-avoidance would be entirely appropriate to an international system of autonomous nation-states, each lacking the ability to control the behavior of others or the course of the entire system. But then, though we cannot control the behavior of others, we can behave as we will others to behave. Admittedly, this is not a self-executing policy. but, at least in moral theory, it could be a self-fulfilling prophecy.

1.   An elaboration of this and related arguments appears in Earl C. Ravenal, "Counterforce and Alliance: The Ultimate Connection," _International Security_, Spring 1982, and in the Report of Panel Three, "Rethinking Essential Equivalence," in _Rethinking US Security Policy for the 1980's_ (Washington, D.C.: National Defense University, the Seventh Annual National Security Affairs Conference, July 21-23, 1980).

2.   Or somewhat fewer, if we determine that the consequences of this scale of destruction would include a global, or northern hemispheric, "nuclear winter."

3.   "Nuclear Weapons and the Atlantic Alliance," _Foreign Affairs_, Spring 1982.

4.   But American disengagement from Europe--which, in any case, would be accomplished only over a ten-year period--is not tantamount to the "loss" of Europe to Soviet aggression.   Western Europe, even without American protection, would not be automatically overrun by Soviet forces, or intimidated into political subservience to the Soviet Union.   The countries of Western Europe, even if not formally united in a new military alliance, have the economic, demographic, and military resources, and the advantage of natural and man-made barriers, to defeat or crucially penalize a Soviet attack.   See the more ample treatment of this point in Earl C. Ravenal, _NATO: The Tides of Discontent_ (Berkeley, Cal.: University of California, Institute of International Studies, 1985).

5.   See the September 1961 McCloy-Zorin "Joint Statement of Agreed Principles" and the 1962 draft treaties by the United States and the Soviet Union, presented to the Eighteen-Nation Committee on Disarmament.   These represent the high-water mark of the movement toward "general and complete" disarmament.

References

Earl C. Ravenal. "Counterforce and Alliance: The Ultimate Connection," _International Security_, Spring 1982.

_____. "Rethinking Essential Equivalence," _Rethinking US Security Policy for the 1980s_ (Washington, D.C.: National Defense University, the Seventh Annual National Security Affairs Conference, July 21-23, 1980).

_____. _NATO: The Tides of Discontent_ (Berkeley, CA: University of California, Institute of International Studies, 1985).

McGeorge Bundy, George F. Kennan, Robert S. McNamara, and Gerard Smith, "Nuclear Weapons and the Atlantic Alliance," _Foreign Affairs_, Spring 1982.

SENSIBLE DETERRENCE AS ARMS CONTROL

Bruce Russett

Deterrence Defined

Deterrence forms the centerpiece of security policy. We depend on it to preserve our way of life, our liberties—and our lives. But for all its importance, the concept of deterrence is full of ambiguities, questionable assumptions, and untestable conclusions. Errors in our reasoning about deterrence, and in the policies based upon it, could cost us our lives. It bears careful logical and empirical analysis. A sensible deterrence policy has the same aims, and can achieve many of the same goals, as can a sensible policy of arms control negotiation. To understand this we must begin by understanding deterrence itself.

A fairly standard definition of deterrence reads like this: "Dissuasion of a potential adversary from initiating an attack or conflict, often by the threat of unacceptable retaliatory damage." (Kincade and Porro, 1979) Several aspects of this definition deserve comment.

First, its application here is to military conflict, rather than to the much wider spheres of action (such as international economic conflict, criminal justice, or even rather ordinary interpersonal relations) where we may commonly speak of trying to deter another party. Nevertheless, its application to military affairs is rooted in, and draws conclusions from, theory and experience of these wider spheres.

Second, it refers to dissuading an adversary from initiating an attack or conflict. In other words, deterrence is an effort to prevent another party from doing something he or she has not yet done, rather than to persuade the party to cease pursuing a course of action already begun. Thus in the very early years of the Vietnam War the United States hoped to deter the North Vietnamese from giving large-scale military support to the Viet Cong guerrillas; in later phases of the war, after deterrence had failed, the American task became one of trying to persuade the North Vietnamese to stop their action and to change their behavior. Thomas Schelling (1966, p. 79) has distinguished the latter by the term "compellence."

Compellence is almost always more difficult than deterrence. Individuals commit themselves emotionally, physically, and financially to a course of action in which they are engaged. Large "national security" bureaucracies commit the interests and careers of thousands of people to the success of a policy, and become very

213

reluctant to abandon it. With efforts at compellence, however, we often have a pretty good sense of whether we have succeeded. Our antagonist either does what we wish, or does not. It is possible that he does what we wish for reasons unrelated to our compellence (doing what we wish would benefit him anyway, and our threats are irrelevant), but in most instances we can usually attribute some significant role to our compellent threats.

With deterrence, however, the result often is much less clear-cut. Deterrence refers to the use of military means to achieve a necessarily uncertain psychological effect. NATO deterrence of a Soviet military invasion of Western Europe well illustrates the difficulty. Very possibly the Soviet Union would long ago have occupied Western Europe, were it not for NATO military strength. But very possibly it would not have done so even in the absence of significant Western military power. Perhaps the Soviets never had any serious interest in occupying such a large, populous territory where they are so unpopular; the daunting prospects of trying to govern such an over-extended empire might alone have been enough to "deter" an invasion. Or perhaps not. As it is, we can confidently say only that NATO military deterrence has not yet failed: the Soviets have not invaded. Whether military deterrence has succeeded or been irrelevant, or whether it could have succeeded with a much lower level of military deterrent threat, we cannot know. Without access to the full archives, and minds, of the Kremlin, we can only have opinions. It becomes an article of faith, not subject to empirical confirmation. The result is not merely an academic point in logic-chopping. It cuts to the heart of military and political issues of deterrence.

Third, note the reference to the threat of "unacceptable" damage. How much is enough, or excessive? For successful deterrence, must we have "the clear and present ability to destroy the attacker as a viable 20th century nation?" (McNamara, 1968, p. 47)[1] Or would some much lower level of nuclear capability suffice? Former national security advisor McGeorge Bundy (1969, p. 10) asserted that the explosion "of even one hydrogen bomb on one city of one's own country would be recognized in advance as a catastrophic blunder." Or if some military deterrence is necessary, might not conventional (non-nuclear) means alone be enough? Continuing policy debates—what constitutes "overkill"; can NATO defend Western Europe without the threat of "first use" of nuclear weapons—stem from the impossibility of confident, concrete answers to the question, "how much is enough?" In doubt, a temptation exists to err, if at all, on the side of excessive deterrence. It may seem safer to have too much than too little. A consequence of having too much, however, is the possibility of enormous, throughly disproportionate, damage if for any reason deterrence fails. (Should we really blow up the world if the Russians invade Austria?)

214

An often neglected point is that what is enough to constitute "unacceptable" damage varies substantially. Presumably it would take a stronger threat to prevent an enemy from occupying an economically and strategically important area than from seizing a piece of useless desert. More subtly, deterrence of the <u>same act</u> may require a stronger threat under <u>different circumstances</u>. In "normal" peacetime almost all countries have a great deal to gain from continuing peace, and from the prosperity that peacetime growth and international trade can provide. A Soviet attack "out of the blue" seems to offer costs to the Soviet Union entirely disproportionate to the economic and physical damage that country would suffer from even a blunted Western retaliation. In times of severe military and political crisis, however, the equation changes greatly.

Suppose, for example, the situation is not "normal" peacetime, but a military confrontation, somewhat like the Cuban missile crisis of 1962, where each side fears the other may attack. Each might prefer continued peace. But if my nuclear retaliatory forces are vulnerable to an attack and I think that attack is imminent, I may feel it necessary to launch them in a "preemptive" strike: the "use it or lose it" situation. The temptation to launch a preemptive" strike is even greater if my opponent's forces are also vulnerable to a first strike. That is, each side is more tempted to strike first if by doing so it can significantly diminish the other side's capacity to retaliate. If both sides' forces are vulnerable the temptation to shoot first in a crisis may become almost irresistible. That is precisely the reason so many analysts fear the destabilizing effects of vulnerable but highly accurate land-based missiles.

Suppose further that the political situation is one of widespread revolts in Eastern Europe, aided by "volunteer" forces from Western Europe. Even very substantial NATO nuclear forces might not be enough to deter a Soviet attack on Western Europe if the Soviet alternative seemed to be the loss of its Eastern European empire. Both military and political conditions, which can change drastically within short time periods, affect a determination of what is "unacceptable retaliatory damage." Each side has an interest in seeing that peace remains tolerable, even attractive, to the other.

Fourth, the reference to broader economic and political conditions of peacetime should alert us to limitations of the purely military terms of the definition. The threat of direct military retaliation is surely <u>one</u> way to deter attack. Others may include the threat of an escalated arms race (American rearmament was one clear consequence of the North Korean attack on South Korea in 1950), and the prospective loss of markets and goods in peacetime international trade. Economic sanctions are not a notably successful instrument for compellence, as we have seen recently vis-a-vis Afghanistan and Poland, but the prospect of a near-complete shutdown of trade may deter some military adventures. Henry Kissinger tried to enmesh the Soviet Union in a web of interdependence with the West as a means of giving the Soviets something substantial to lose if they strayed too far from detente. Many of the most effective instruments of deterrence in international politics involve the subtle, and even unconscious, manipulation of a broad range of non-military punishments--and rewards--for continuing good behavior.

Extended Deterrence

Our definition of deterrence was vague on the matter of what (other than "an attack or conflict") is to be deterred. In fact, the question of how much is enough depends critically on just what action we are trying to deter. Nuclear powers surely do develop and build nuclear weapons to deter other states from attacking them with nuclear weapons. But the history of nuclear deterrence shows that this is not the most common purpose for having nuclear weapons. The United States, for example, built atomic bombs and intercontinental bombers during the years 1945-49, before the Soviets had even a single atom bomb. Israel is thought to be capable of deploying nuclear weapons in very short order (a matter of days), even though none of Israel's neighbors is remotely close to having operational nuclear weapons. In both cases, the purpose of nuclear weapons is to prevent large-scale conventional war or invasion rather than nuclear attack. And in the case of the United States in the 1940s (and even now) the perceived threat was not plausibly of a Soviet invasion of American home territory. Rather, nuclear weapons were intended to deter a Soviet invasion of our allies, most importantly those in Western Europe.

Nuclear weapons therefore may address a variety of deterrent purposes: deterring a nuclear or conventional attack on oneself, or deterring a nuclear or conventional attack on allies, client states, or friendly neutrals. Deterrence of attack on states other than oneself has become known as "extended deterrence." It is a central and explicit part of both superpowers' logic.

What determines the success of extended deterrence? Certainly it is not just a matter of weighing the strategic military balance on both sides. If it were, the Soviet Union would never have been prevented from invading Hungary in 1956, at a time when American nuclear superiority was very great and well-recognized by knowledgeable people. Comparative case studies of deterrence during the past century (Huth and Russett, 1984; Huth and Russett, 1986; Blechman and Kaplan, 1978) have failed to uncover any systematic relationship between strategic or long-term military superiority and successful deterrence, though local superiority, in the immediate area of conflict, does help. One reason the Soviets were not deterred in 1956 was that the United States never made any explicit threats, no warning of retaliation

216

for an invasion. That in turn was partly due to the balance of conventional forces in Central Europe, which was by no means favorable to the United States. NATO military forces in Europe were at best on a par with those of the Soviet Union and its allies; at worst they were somewhat inferior. Because of the geography of the area it is impossible for Western forces to reach Hungary without first going through a neutral country like Austria or through a Soviet-allied country. Clearly the Western position for a conventional war in Hungary was as bad as its nuclear strategic position may have been favorable.

The local military balance matters because a state may seize an opportunity for a quick victory, a fait accompli, and think its major power adversary will not take on the costs of a long war. But if the opportunity for a quick victory is not presented, it is the rare aggressor who willingly embarks on a long war of attrition. The costs, even in winning such a long war, are not worth it as a basis for deliberate aggression. Thus even if the long-term or strategic balance seems to favor the attacker, he is likely to be dissuaded if he has no immediate, local advantage. The nuclear balance loses relevance for the same reason: the prospect of fighting a nuclear war is like that of a long war of attrition, only all at once. The costs, even in "winning," are too high against an opponent with a credible if not necessarily fully equal nuclear capability.

For both superpowers, but especially for the United States, nuclear weapons have increasingly come to provide the military "muscle" behind efforts at deterrence. Nuclear weapons are, relative to large-scale conventional forces, rather cheap. In the words of Secretary of Defense Charles Wilson in the 1950s, they give "more bang for the buck." They have seemed to promise, to a technologically superior West, an economically tolerable means of holding off numerically superior forces of the "Eastern hordes." The policy became official with Secretary of State John Foster Dulles' exposition of "massive retaliation" ("in a manner and at a place of our choosing") in 1954. It was refined with the United States deployment of tactical nuclear weapons in Europe during the 1950s under the doctrine of, if necessary, fighting a tactical nuclear war to repulse a conventional Soviet attack. The policy seemed somewhat more attractive during the short period before the Soviet Union deployed its own tactical nuclear weapons in Eastern Europe. Even so, NATO maintains an official policy of "flexible response:" to reply, at whatever level of violence seems necessary, to any Soviet incursion. This means, explicitly, the threat to use nuclear weapons whether or not the Soviet Union's attacking forces have yet used them. The United States has also used the explicit or implicit threat of nuclear first use to deter war in various other parts of the world, such as Korea and, most recently, the perceived threat of Soviet invasion of Iran during the last year of the Carter Administration. Much of the debate about nuclear deterrence turns on the question of whether the threat of nuclear weapons is being employed too widely and cavalierly, or whether alternative (conventional) means of deterrence are really beyond the ability or willingness of the Western alliance. The evidence above suggests the need to give more attention to conventional means.

Deterrence is much more than a military matter; it is also a matter of psychology and politics. The patterns of military and political escalation matter very much. In the bargaining and negotiating process that occurs during a deterrence crisis, the defender can be appeasing (giving in to diplomatic demands), be bullying (making no concessions, and many demands), or follow "firm-but-fair" tactics of essentially matching, but not exceeding, the attacker's threats and concessions. Similarly, in the process of military alert, deployment, and use, one can be very restrained, very threatening, or follow tactics of "tit-for-tat," being neither supine nor provocative. In studies of successful deterrence and war-avoidance in this kind of situation, it is clear that tactics of moderation--firm-but-fair, and tit-for-tat--are the ones that work most consistently. The others, against an opponent of more or less equal capability, are dangerous. One related aspect: if there was a previous deterrence crisis between the two states, it matters now how they behaved then. If the defending state appeased and effectively surrendered, that is likely to encourage the attacker the next time. (British and French appeasement over Czechoslovakia in 1938 merely emboldened Hitler for is 1939 move against Poland.) On the other hand, a clear-cut victory for the defender, humiliating the attacker, is likely to make the attacker much more intransigent the next time. Successful deterrence is much more than a matter of standing tough; it requires moderation and knowing when to concede. Otherwise, as with the deployment of destabilizing weapons systems, an act intended as a deterrent can instead be seen as provocative. A defender must be able to threaten credibly, but also to reassure that his aims and intentions are limited. (Huth and Russett, 1986; Huth, 1986; Leng, 1983)

Extended deterrence also depends on the stake the deterring power is perceived to have in the country or area at question. Partly that derives from the area's intrinsic importance: a large population, a strategic location, wealth, industry, or natural resources like oil. Also important is the extent and nature of various military, political, and economic ties between the deterrer and the country to be protected. A written military alliance between the two can provide an indicator of the deterring power's resolve, and can give the deterrer something important to lose if it fails to honor its pledge ("If we don't fight to defend this country, both our allies and our enemies will see us as weak and irresolute in the next crisis.") Also relevant are various less formal ties between the two countries, such as a significant program of military assistance from deterrer to the armed forces of the smaller ally, or foreign trade between the two states. Trade

both gives individuals and groups within the would-be deterring
state something material to lose (markets, supplies of commodities)
if the smaller state is conquered by the opponent, and helps to
expand the image of self interest held by citizens of the deterring
state. (Huth and Russett, 1986)

Counterforce and Counterpopulation Targeting

Even when the instruments of deterrence are nuclear weapons,
there often is equal ambiguity about just what are the means of
deterrence: the threat of strikes against what kinds of targets,
by what kinds of nuclear weapons.

In the early days of the nuclear era only atomic bombs
existed, and not many of them. They were to be delivered by long-
range bombers to targets in the Soviet homeland. They had to be
targeted in a way that would have maximum effect on Soviet war-
making capabilities. In the first conception--an extension of
American success against Nazi Germany--that was thought to be
against the Soviet petroleum industry, creating a severe bottleneck
in industry, transportation, and military operations. Soon,
however, Air Force planners gave more attention to the larger
industrial and population damage ("bonus" effects) that would
result from using atom bombs against targets in urban area.
Consideration of different kinds of damage melded the two, and in
some plans, as in the first Strategic Air Command (SAC) operational
plan, the aim points were "selected with the primary objective of
the annihilation of population, with industrial targets
incidental." (Quoted in Rosenberg, 1983, p. 15) The target list
of a war plan charmingly known as BROILER called for 34 bombs on 24
cities. The list was rapidly expanded as more bombs became
available, with a combination of industrial and population damage
being intended.

As the nuclear and later thermonuclear (hydrogen bomb)
stockpiles of both the superpowers grew, so did the number and kind
of targets. Some strategists continued to emphasize the primary
importance of crippling immediate Soviet war-making capability:
military targets per se, transportation, petroleum and electrical
generation facilities, and war-related industry. Others, like
General Curtis LeMay, urged that "we should concentrate on industry
itself which is located in urban areas" so that even if a bomb
missed its target, "a bonus will be derived from the use of the
bomb." (Quoted in Rosenberg, 1983, p. 18) "Bonus" in this
instance clearly included the death of Soviet civilians.

In discussing nuclear deterrence policy we must distinguish
between declaratory policy and operational policy, between what a
government says it will do with weapons, and what it in fact plans
to do with those weapons in actual military operations.

219

American declaratory policy has, until very recently, been deliberately ambiguous about just what would be struck. In his famous 1962 statement at Ann Arbor, Michigan, Defense Secretary Robert McNamara said the principal military objective should be "the destruction of the enemy forces, not of his population." He later retreated from this public declaration, and in the same statement cited earlier about destroying the attacker "as a viable 20th century nation" defined that as the ability to destroy one-fifth to one-fourth of the enemy's population and one-half of its industrial capacity. (McNamara, 1968, p. 48) This public characterization certainly was not unique to McNamara; similar words were expressed by many other officials before and after him.

Whether the effect of civilian casualties is deliberately sought as a deterrent, accepted as an unintended but welcome "bonus," or reluctantly accepted as a relatively unavoidable consequence has varied with different strategists and different times. In 1973, Defense Secretary Elliot Richardson testified, "We do not in our strategic planning target civilian population per se any longer." This kind of statement has been repeated frequently and publicly by the current administration. Declaratory deterrent policy is no longer one of deliberate counter-population strikes.

We cannot be so sure of what operational policy might become during the course of a nuclear war. But the expansion of the set of targets associated even with a purely "counterforce" deterrent strategy has been enormous, a thousandfold from operation BROILER. By the end of the 1950s SAC had identified over 20,000 targets in the Soviet Union, and by 1980 40,000. (Rosenberg, 1983, p. 50) They included "military significant" industry, transportation and communication facilities, command centers, tactical military forces and support complexes, and of course Soviet submarine pens, airfields, and missile silos. The list of targets has regularly outpaced--and driven upward--the number of strategic bombs and warheads available to hit them. (For example, the current inventory is more than 10,000 warheads and bombs on long-range delivery systems.) Attempts to be selective have been overwhelmed by the number of targets. For instance, the 1979 SIOP (Single Integrated Operational Plan) identified 60 "military" targets within the city of Moscow alone. (Zuckerman, 1982)

In the evolution of nuclear strategy, American planners had to confront a growing unpleasant fact. Whereas in the first years targeting could be directed at Soviet war-making capability in general, it soon became necessary for American strategists to think specifically about limiting the ability of the Soviet Union to hit the United States with nuclear weapons (the problem of "damage limitation"). But a capability of hitting Soviet nuclear forces inevitably threatens to degrade Soviet retaliatory capacity. As we noted, stable deterrence depends on the confidence each side has in its ability to survive a first strike from its opponent with enough

220

of its own retaliatory forces intact to insure "unacceptable" damage to the attacker.

In the bomber age this was not a serious problem, especially once both sides had good air defense and radar systems in place. An attacking bomber force could be spotted long before it reached targets in either the Soviet Union or the United States. Intercontinental missiles, however, shortened the time between launching an attack and the impact of incoming warheads to only about 30 minutes. American Pershing II missiles in Europe, and Soviet submarines near the coast of North America, have now shortened potential warning time to no more than 5 or 10 minutes. If used in a "decapitating" attack against the national command authority, they could bring the real decision time--the period covering adequate confirmation of the attack and the actual launch of retaliatory forces before the "use-them-or-lose-them" point is reached--to nothing at all. (Blair, 1985; Wallace, Crissey, and Sennot, 1986) This could mean, in effect, a policy of launch on warning. With the advent of highly accurate missiles (accurate within about .12 miles) and MIRVs (multiple independently-targeted re-entry vehicles) whereby one MIRVed missile can, with 10 warheads, perhaps destroy five or even ten enemy missiles on the ground, land-based missiles have become highly vulnerable to attack. Attempts to "harden" missile silos with steel and concrete to resist blast have essentially been overwhelmed. Missile silos cannot effectively be concealed from information-gathering satellites, and proposals to make land-based missiles mobile, to evade precise targeting, meet objections on grounds of cost. Counterforce targeting, in the broad sense of a wide variety of military and military-industrial targets, need not endanger retaliatory capability. But these new technological developments, coupled with deliberate targeting of an opponent's land-based missile silos, could do so and become profoundly destabilizing. Increasingly, therefore, assurance of retaliatory capability has come to rest on bombers (which might be launched, and if necessary recalled, in the fact of impending attack), smaller more mobile cruise missiles, and especially sea-based missiles launched from submarines which can be kept moving and whose location can be kept secret.

Many people are troubled by the ethics and morality of counterpopulation warfare--deliberate strikes to kill civilians who are in most respects innocent of whatever crimes their leaders may commit. These people, therefore, may welcome the apparent shift in American declaratory policy toward counterforce. Some strategists--especially, but not only, members of the current administration--have justified the latest round of improvements in strategic weaponry as a movement in the direction of greater moral acceptability. They say that improvements in accuracy, coupled with elimination of the very large warheads placed on older missiles like the Titan, will have the effect of limiting collateral damage. The number of (supposedly greatly reduced) civilian casualties sustained when military targets are hit could, therefore, be judged appropriate to some aims of war or deterrence. Modernization of the strategic arsenal, with more accurate weapons like the MX, is, therefore, morally permissible and even required! Similar claims are made for "small" battlefield tactical nuclear weapons. Those dovish critics of administration "limited war" policies who rely on extreme versions of MAD (Mutually Assured Destruction) counterpopulation strategies have no good answer to the question of what to do if deterrence fails.[2]

But the problems with a limited nuclear war policy are immense. When the Pentagon talks about "controlled" nuclear war it envisages a range of acts "from a low-level exchange through a massive homeland-to-homeland exchange followed by a protracted series of lesser-intensity strikes." One problem, therefore, is that any large-scale nuclear exchange, even of "discriminating" weapons, would inevitably produce millions or tens of millions of civilian casualties. Numerous studies, drawing on private and government material, reach this conclusion. The combination of immediate casualties from blast and radiation, with longer-term casualties from fall-out, disruption of the medical, sanitation, transportation and communication systems, ecological devastation, climatic effects, and so forth, would be very, very great--even from attacks that were "limited" to such "strictly military" targets as the 1018 American and 1398 Soviet land-based ICBMs. (Russett, 1983, ch. 3; Adams and Cullen, eds., 1981; Chivian, ed., 1981; Riordan, ed., 1982; Erlich, et al., 1984) Actually, the Defense Department's list of military and militarily related industrial targets (remember, 40,000 of them) includes industry and utilities essential to the economic recuperation of the Soviet Union.[3] If the Soviet (American) economy is destroyed, more tens of millions of Soviet (American) citizens will die of hunger and disease.

The Risks of Escalation

The other problem is with the expectation that nuclear war could be fought in some precise fashion of strike and counter-strike, that in any substantial nuclear exchange the war could be restricted to a limited number of strictly military targets. There are people who imagine it could be done, with acceptable consequences. The majority of analysts, however, consider the likelihood of such limitation, under wartime conditions of anger, fear, confusion, ignorance, and loss of control, to be extremely small. No one can definitively rule out the possibility, but neither should anyone bet the future of civilization on it. One of the most knowledgeable experts on this matter is John Steinbruner, director of foreign policy studies at the Brookings Institution. In his words, "If national commanders seriously attempted to implement this strategy (controlled response) in a war with existing and currently projected U.S. forces, the result would not

222

be a finely controlled strategic campaign. The more likely result would be the collapse of U.S. forces into isolated units undertaking retaliation on their own initiative against a wide variety of targets at unpredictable moments." (Steinbruner, 1981/82; Steinbruner, 1985; Ball, 1981)

This statement identifies a fundamental dilemma of command and control: If it is diffused and delegated, there is the risk of unauthorized use, against unintended targets, in the "fog of war" or even high-level political crisis. An opponent, fearing such diffusion, might see an incentive to strike first before his own capabilities came under fire. But if it is kept centralized, in the hands of the commander-in-chief, there is the risk of decapitation—that no response would be possible. If the opponent knew decapitation was feasible, that too could lead to a failure of deterrence. No truly satisfactory balance, assuring adequate control for reliably "limited" warfighting, seems likely.

Thus to many people talk about "winning" or "prevailing" in nuclear war seems only a dangerous fantasy, as would any notion of "sovereignty and continued viability of the United States and of the Western democracies as free societies" after such a war.[4] Belief in the probability of "acceptable" limited nuclear war would play into the hands of those who think that in nuclear war "victory is possible." It would encourage the continued reliance on a threat of first use of nuclear weapons to deter a wide range of acts in Europe, the Middle East, and elsewhere, at the expense of building up alternative, non-nuclear means of defnding ourselves and our allies.

Another approach is what some analysts call "manipulating the shared risk of war." (Schelling, 1966, p. 99) A would-be deterrer might well threaten to do something that, in the event deterrence failed, he would not in fact want to carry out. The United States might threaten to go to all-out nuclear war if the Soviet Union occupies West Germany. In the event the Soviet Union did occupy West Germany, the United States government might not want, for practical reasons, to execute its threat. In fact, a government fully in control of its military forces probably would not want to initiate all-out nuclear war. One way to deal with this situation would be to build some variant of a "doomsday machine": commit oneself irrevocably and automatically to an act of mutual destruction that one would not want to carry out if one retained a choice at the time. Almost everyone rejects the "doomsday machine" solution as grossly imprudent and disproprotionate.

But a less drastic solution is building into the situation an element of unpredictability and uncontrollability. In practice, a Soviet invasion of West Germany might very well trigger an all-out nuclear war whether or not the American government wished it to do so. American nuclear weapons would be widely dispersed. Low-level commanders would have operational control over the weapons if, as is quite possible, the PAL (Permissive Action Link) codes that prevent unauthorized use in peacetime should be released to low-level commanders in a time of high crisis in Europe. One of those commanders, in the "fog of war" with his troops under siege, might very well use the weapons. (Bracken, 1983) Or the Soviet Union, fearing they would be used, might stage a preemptive attack on them. Use of a few tactical or theater nuclear weapons would be very likely to escalate into a strategic exchange between the American and Soviet homelands. The threat of unintended use of nuclear weapons in the event of a conventional war or even a high-level crisis in Europe thus provides a powerful deterrent to deliberate initiation of war of any kind in the center of that continent. No rational Soviet leader would deliberately run such a risk.

If we believe that political crises (unlike military events) are always fully controllable, then perhaps such a deterrent seems prudent. But if we believe that political crises are not always controllable or avoidable (1914 again, or a revolt in East Germany that attracts support from West Germany, or a political breakdown in Yugoslavia that draws in regular or volunteer fighters from East and West), it does not seem prudent. In the apt words of the distinguished British military historian, Michael Howard (1982/83), military forces must serve two purposes: they must deter enemies, and they must reassure enemies, as well as friends, that war will not be initiated recklessly. Nuclear "deterrent" systems that depend on their uncontrollability are not reassuring to anyone.

Forms of Restraint

A key and increasingly recognized element of any acceptable resolution of dissatisfaction with both counterpopulation deterrence and many elements of counterforce deterrence rests in a "no first use" of nuclear weapons posture. This would require that non-nuclear attacks be resisted by other than nuclear means. It would be part of a policy of deterrence by planning to resist attack at approximately the same level of force (conventional or nuclear) as initiated by the attacker, without beginning an escalatory process that could very well lead rapidly to all-out war.

A policy of first use of nuclear weapons is not the same as a policy of first strike. The first implies some (usually at first limited and controlled) use of nuclear weapons in response to the opponent's initiation of conventional warfare. It is thus an escalation of existing military hostilities, but not typically large-scale strategic war. First strike does imply large-scale strategic use of nuclear weapons, perhaps before conventional war has even begun, in an effort to "disarm" the opponent or at least to blunt seriously his retaliatory capacity. Analytically they should not be confused. But in practice they blur together.

Without a credible first strike capability--and such a capability is, in my view, nothing but a mirage--a policy of first use cannot be sustained. It must inevitably fall from its contradictions. One risk is that it will increasingly be seen as not credible: deliberate initiation of nuclear war too readily invites escalation to one's own destruction. The other is that it will have to depend on uncontrollability: the likelihood that nuclear weapons will be used without deliberate authorization by responsible authorities. The latter would leave us hostage to the whims of fate.

Abandonment of a threat of first use would, in addition to restoring greater potential controllability and avoiding provocation, have major and beneficial implications for broader strategic planning and procurement. There would be no need for the particularly dangerous kind of counterforce weapons like the MX and Pershing II missiles--extremely accurate, short time from launch to impact, themselves vulnerable to attack--that would most endanger crisis stability.[5] The risks of escalation are high under the best of circumstances. If our opponent should begin nuclear war, <u>some</u> of those risks would already have been taken. To deter that act, and to bring the war to a negotiated halt as soon as possible, it makes sense to prepare certain very restricted and perhaps slow-acting forms of nuclear retaliation. That retaliation could include a variety and limited number of military targets--largely tactical ones, including Soviet forces devoted to internal security, maintaining control over Eastern Europe, and containing China. The prospective loss of these capabilities would threaten the heart of Soviet power, yet the ability to strike them would not require the United States to have "prompt hard-target kill" weapons that imply a first-strike threat.[6] Possession of limited forces for such restricted retaliation would be compatible with full recognition--on both sides--that the risks entailed in any first use of nuclear weapons are too high to justify setting the process in motion.

Strengthening conventional defense would be a reasonable price to pay if it would reduce the probability of nuclear war. Development of adequate non-nuclear defense will take time. Military experts differ as to whether non-nuclear defense in Western Europe is really possible, but there are many cogent and informed arguments for its feasibility.[7] General Bernard Rogers, the NATO Commander, has reservations about whether a full no-first-use policy is feasible, but he has campaigned vigorously for the conventional forces that would at least provide a credible no-early-use posture. The same position has been adopted in several expert reports. The hurdles in the way are political rather than economic or military, and the lack of current political will, in America and in Europe, need not be taken as a given for all eternity. Furthermore, there are other ways to protect Western Europe than only by nuclear <u>or</u> non-nuclear forces. A general lowering of international political tensions would help, as would a structure of rewards implicit in the extension of East-West economic interdependence.

While the need for military deterrence cannot be evaded in a conflicting world of nation-states, relatively lower levels of threat may be adequate. Lower but adequate levels of threat mean no "city-busting" and no first-strike capability, that extended deterrence of conventional attack avoid significant reliance on nuclear threats, and that rewards, as well as punishments, play a key role in deterrent posture. A shift to lower levels is required because of the ever-present and never fully controllable chance that deterrence may fail, bringing our threats to reality. Deterrence will remain dangerous, especially when crises erupt. Deterrence probably works best when you don't need it ("normal" peacetime) and is most problematic in the confrontations when you need it most.

Much of the message of this essay is that devising and implementing a sound, restrained deterrence policy is itself a form of arms control. Given the long string of recent failures of arms control negotiations, and the lessened willingness of either superpower to pursue agreement seriously, the role of unilateral restraint becomes ever more important. Some policies—like not acquiring first-strike weapons, or relinquishing the threat of first use—make sense whether or not the other side adopts them. The Strategic Defense Initiative (SDI) also poses risk of upsetting strategic stability. If an effective defense of American cities should be possible (most informed observers think that very unlikely; e.g., Brown, 1985), it would be even more effective against the "ragged" Soviet retaliation that might follow an American first strike than against a Soviet first strike. The result would be to upset the reassurance provided by MAD and possibly provoke a Soviet first strike in crisis. It represents another instance where sensible policy would refrain from pushing apparent technological advantages to the limit.

The hope that we can force concessions from the other side by adopting weapons or policies that endanger us both—an especially pernicious form of "bargaining chip" psychology—has repeatedly brought us trouble in the past. MIRV, Pershing II, and the MX were all justified as "bargaining chips" that could be relinquished in return for appropriate concessions in arms control negotiations. The expected negotiations have not occurred, and we are left in a more dangerous world than we would have if those weapons did not exist. Arguably, even, we are left in a more dangerous world than if only the Russians had such weapons. (I believe that one-sided Soviet possession of MIRVs in any number would be intolerable. But I also believe that a world with hundreds of Pershings and SS-20s is more dangerous than the world we might have had from the 1982 "walk in the woods" proposal for a few tens of SS-20s, no Pershings, and the Western deterrent for Europe relying solely on cruise missiles and American long-range weapons.)

Sensible nuclear deterrence is not a game of simply matching the adversary weapon for weapon or policy for policy. Some policies threaten ourselves as much as they threaten our adversary, and it is in our interest to move away from these policies. It would be best if the adversary would do the same, and very possibly our adoption of sensible policies will encourage him to do so as well. But the second best--where we alone restrain ourselves in some respects--should not be discarded if the best is unattainable. Self-restraint of this sort is not "unilateral disarmament;" it is just street-wise good sense.

Footnotes:

1. Secretary McNamara's words on this occasion were not peculiar to him, but rather were typical of much of American deterrent rhetoric. In practice McNamara almost certainly thought this level of damage to be greater than necessary, or prudent.
2. See the exchange between Theodore Draper and Defense Secretary Caspar Weinberger (New York Review of Books, 1982/1983).
3. Counterforce stragegies have, in the past, repeatedly had the effect of enlarging the list of targets. (Rosenberg, 1983, p. 50) That is therefore a trap inherent in contemporary counterforce policies.
4. The phrase is Secretary Weinberger's. See New York Review of Books (1982/1983).
5. In March 1982 a speech by General Secretary Brezhnev offered an agreement to keep submarines away from each other's coastlines, but there was no American response and it was overtaken by the moves and countermoves of Pershing II deployment.
6. I have discussed this, a type of "countercombatant" strategy, at some length, most recently in Russett (1983), ch. 7.
7. Participants in this debate include Bundy, Kennan, McNamara, and Smith (1982); Kaiser, Leber, Mertes, and Shultze (1982); Blackaby, Goldblat, and Lodgaard, eds. (1984); McNamara (1983), Mearsheimer (1983); Steinbruner and Sigal, eds. (1983); Gottfried, Kendall and Lee (1985); Rogers (1982); and European Security Study (1983). "No First Use" is not nearly as unpopular a policy among the American and European populace as is often imagined. See Russett and DeLuca (1983), and Yankelovich and Doble (1984).

References:

Adams, Ruth, and Susan Cullen, eds. (1981). The Final Epidemic: Physicians and Scientists on Nuclear War (Chicago: Educational Foundation for Nuclear Science).

Ball, Desmond (1981). "Can Nuclear War Be Controlled?" Adelphi Paper 161 (London: International Institute for Strategic Studies).

Blackaby, Frank, Josef Goldblat, and Sverre Lodgaard, eds. (1984). No First Use (Stockholm: SIPRI).

Blair, Bruce G. (1985). Strategic Command and Control (Washington, D.C.: Brookings).

Blechman, Barry, and Stephen Kaplan (1978). Force with-out War: U.S. Armed Forces as a Political Instrument (Washington, D. C.: Brookings).

Bracken, Paul (1983). The Command and Control of Nuclear Forces (New Haven: Yale University Press).

Brown, Harold (1985). "Is SDI Technically Feasible?" Foreign Affairs, Special Issue on America and the World, 64, 3: 435-54.

Bundy, McGeorge (1969). "To Cap the Volcano," Foreign Affairs, 48, 1 (Spring), p. 10.

----------------, George Kennan, Robert McNamara, and Gerard Smith (1982). "Nuclear Weapons and the Atlantic Alliance," Foreign Affairs, 60, 4, (Spring): 753-68.

Chivian, Eric, ed. (1981). Last Aid: The Medical Dimensions of Nuclear War (New York: Freeman).

Erlich, Paul, Carl Sagan, Donald Kennedy, and Walter Roberts (1984). The Cold and the Dark: The World after Nuclear War (New York: Norton).

European Security Study (1983). Strengthening Conventional Deterrence: Proposals for the 1980s (New York: St. Martin's).

Gottfried, Kurt, Henry W. Kendall and John M. Lee (1985). "No First Use of Nuclear Weapons," in Bruce Russett and Fred Chernoff, eds., Arms Control and the Arms Race: Readings from SCIENTIFIC AMERICAN (New York: Freeman).

Howard, Michael (1984). "Reassurance and Deterrence," Foreign Affairs, 61, 2 (Winter): 309-24.

Huth, Paul (1986). The Dilemma of Deterrence: Credibility vs. Stability (New Haven: Yale University, Ph.D. dissertation).

-----------, and Bruce Russett (1984). "What Makes Deterrence Work? Cases from 1900 to 1980," World Politics, 37, 4 (July): 496-526.

-----------, and Bruce Russett (1986). "The Escalation of Extended Deterrence Crises to War," paper presented to conference on accidental nuclear war, University of British Columbia, Vancouver, B.C., May.

Kaiser, Karl, George Leber, Alois Mertes, and Fran Josef Schulze (1982). "Nuclear Weapons and the Preservation of Peace: A German Response," Foreign Affairs, 60, 5 (Summer): 1157-70.

Kincade, W. H. and J. D. Porro, (1979). Negotiating Security: An Arms Control Reader (Washington).

Leng, Russell (1983). "When Will They Ever Learn? Coercive Bargaining in Recurrent Crises," Journal of Conflict Resolution, 27, 3 (September): 379-419.

Mearsheimer, John (1983). Conventional Deterrence (Ithaca: Cornell University Press).

McNamara, Robert S. (1968). Statement on the Fiscal Year 1969-73 Defense Program and 1969 Defense Budget (Washington: U.S. Government Printing Office), p. 47.

-------------------- (1983). "The Military Role of Nuclear Weapons: Perceptions and Misperceptions." Foreign Affairs, 62, 1 (Fall): 59-80.

Riordan, Michael, ed. (1982). The Day After Midnight: The Effects of Nuclear War (Palo Alto, CA: Cheshire).

Rogers, Bernard W. (1982). "The Atlantic Alliance: Prescriptions for a Difficult Decade," Foreign Affairs, 60, 5 (Summer): 1145-56.

Rosenberg, David Alan (1983). "The Origins of Overkill: Nuclear Weapons and American Strategy, 1945-1960," International Security, 7, 4 (Spring): 3-71.

Russett, Bruce (1983). The Prisoners of Insecurity: Nuclear Deterrence, the Arms Race, and Arms Control (New York: Freeman).

--------------- and Donald R. DeLuca (1983). "Theater Nuclear Forces: Public Opinion in Western Europe," Political Science Quarterly, 98, 2 (Summer): 179-96.

Schelling, Thomas C. (1966). Arms and Influence (New Haven: Yale University Press).

Steinbruner, John (1981-82). "Nuclear Decapitation," Foreign Policy, 45 (Winter): 16-28.

229

---------------- (1985). "Launch Under Attack," in Bruce Russett and Fred Chernoff, eds., Arms Control and the Arms Race: Readings from SCIENTIFIC AMERICAN (New York: Freeman).

----------------, and Leon Sigal, eds. (1983). Alliance Security (Washington: Brookings).

Wallace, Michael, Brian Crissey, and Linn Sennott (1986). "Accidental Nuclear War: A Risk Assessment," Journal of Peace Research, 23, 1 (March): 9-28.

Yankelovich, Daniel, and John Doble (1984). "The Public Mood: Nuclear Weapons and the U.S.S.R.," Foreign Affairs, 63, 1 (Fall): 33-46.

Zuckerman, Sir Solly (1982) Nuclear Illusion and Reality (New York: Vintage).

THINKING THE UNTHINKABLE: UNILATERAL DISARMAMENT

Mulford Q. Sibley

INTRODUCTION

Although arguments for unilateral disarmament could obviously stress the moral and religious dimensions of the subject, in this paper the emphasis is utilitarian and pragmatic, as we contend that

1) Military power cannot defend or protect anything valuable and cannot deter war in the long run.

2) If military power cannot defend or deter, it is irrational to formulate policies which rely on it, even if other Nation States choose to do so. A consequence of this radical change in outlook would be unilateral disarmament.

3) The disarmament should proceed through planned phases and in the context of fundamentally changed economic and social priorities and policies.

4) Although we cannot be certain, unilateralism as conceived here might well lead to competitive disarmament. As a minimum, a unilateralist frame of mind or outlook would seem to be a prerequisite for a thorough going multilateral disarmament agreement.

5) Characteristic objections to unilateralism do not seriously impair the case for it.

I

Military power cannot protect or defend the United States nor will it deter war.

It cannot protect or defend in the sense that if it is ever used the destruction wrought would far outweigh any possible gain. Many "scenarios" have drawn up the indictment: 100,000,000 killed on each side; destruction of all health facilities; disintegration of communications; pollution on a large scale of the environment; a "nuclear winter." And we could go on and on. It seems clear, in other words, that if the weapons are used, the very continuation of

the human race is at stake.   This much is widely
admitted.

But it may be argued, we don't intend to use the
weapons but merely to threaten their use.   We stockpile the weapons for purposes of intimidation: if you
don't behave, we say, just remember that we have this
superiority in military power, which, of course, we
don't intend to use. Just how "credible" would such a
statement be to the "other side"?   Or its similar
statements to us?

Yet the defenders of military power would have us
believe that "deterrence" built upon such propositions
can in the long run be effective.   Arguments of this
order seem to be the basis of MAD--the doctrine of
"mutual assured destruction."   One need only state the
theory to see its limitations and its monumental
dangers.

In the long run, if we continue to rely on such
propositions, we are bound, either accidentally or
through   design,   to   bring   about   the   wholesale
destruction which we ostensibly seek to avoid.

Thus military power defeats its alleged objectives
if it is used and fails to deter the war which all
dread.

Even short of nuclear war, the very commitment to
mammoth military defense is changing the character of
American life to such a degree that the old values we
are presumably defending tend to fall by the wayside.
Years ago Erich Fromm pointed out that the continuing
arms race "creates certain psychological effects in
most human beings--fright, hostility, callousness, a
hardening of the heart, and a resulting indifference to
all the values we cherish."[1]

Moreover, the arms race, because it entails both
intensive   and   extensive   technological   development,
accentuates the tendency of modern Western culture to
transform the means (technique) into the central goal
of life itself.   Thus human beings become even more
than before robot-like in nature.   The "military
industrial-complex," against which President Eisenhower
warned us, continues to grow in influence and power
and, like a tornado, seems increasingly beyond control.
We become its victims.

232

In effect, with every dollar invested in military defense, we would seem to run an escalating risk of bringing about the antithesis of what we ostensibly seek. Indeed, arms races such as the one in which we are now engaged almost inevitably lead to the war which is the result of the "deterrence" espoused by most theorists of national defense. Just as the arms race before World War I made it difficult for politicians to avoid war, so arms build-ups today are likely to lead not only to utter destruction but also to militaristic transformation of the very nation that is supposedly being "defended."

Nor is this all. So costly are missiles and the other accouterments of war that their purchase bids fair to bankrupt the nations which rely on them. We may think that we are "defending" the United States by means of the latest technology but in reality we are weakening the nation through depletion of natural resources.

To be sure, we have had with us for years those who contend that the build-up of arms, including nuclear weapons, is necessary if we are to have multilateral arms agreements. We must have military budgets of the order of three hundred billions annually so that we can "negotiate from a position of strength." This has been a favorite argument of the Reagan Administration but has also been characteristic of proponents of the arms race for decades.

However, supporting evidence for such a position is hard to come by. Indeed, it would seem to be non-existent. A hard empirical examination would appear to show that possession of military might and development of the attitudes which always accompany it tend to increase our delusions. We seek a kind of refuge in the illusion that missiles make us more secure and discover that it is more difficult than before to give them up. We become attached to the murderous devices which we claim to wish to destroy. The very build-up which we allege would enable us to negotiate from strength imposes its own imperatives on us. We tend to spurn apparently reasonable proposals of "the other side" almost automatically; and again and again we have rationalized our rejections on the ground that the new scheme for disarmament or arms control would give the other side a few more missiles or other implements of war. Since we continue to believe that missiles can defend something valuable, the possession of any additional weapons by the "adversary" is regarded as dangerous.

In the context of the arms race, it is difficult to over-emphasize the faith commitment to which most of us seem to be pledged: we rarely question the premise that a nation with more missiles than its neighbor or opponent is "stronger" than a nation which possesses fewer missiles. When a given State promises to reduce its arsenal, it is said, therefore, to be "sacrificing" for peace. But from the viewpoint of this essay, and assuming that military weapons do not defend, protect, or, in the long run, deter, the surrender of weapons is not a sacrifice but rather a great benefit: it diminishes by that much our proneness to idolize military hardware--which is useless in any event--and frees us to think constructively.

Much of what we have been saying has been stated explicitly or implicitly by Walter Millis. In an essay which the late military historian wrote shortly before his death and which he called "The Uselessness of Military Power," he spelled out his view that, in the context of the history of the past century and a half particularly, the employment of military force had become of no utility, whatever may have been true in earlier ages. "Real, effective national power on the modern world stage," Millis argued, "is no longer expressed accurately, if at all, by relative military strengths....The great military establishments which exist are not practically usable in the conduct of international relations."[2]

In general, Millis seems to be arguing that military devices in the modern world cannot be effectively employed as instruments of policy. Far from being "realistic," policies which rely on military threat and counter-threat are too dangerous, whatever their purpose, to be taken literally. Yet given the atmosphere of an arms race, we do find ourselves engaging in them, which can only lead to still greater irrationality. We need to be protected against ourselves, yet who is to do the protecting?

Military defense, at least in our day, does not defend, protect, or, in the long run, deter. Military power, to repeat Millis, is "useless," whether as an instrument of general public policy, as defense in time of war, or as long-run deterrence of the war which its existence tends to make more likely.

234

II

Once we are convinced that military power is "useless," we are driven to propose an alternative military policy along with drastically different emphases in economic, political, and social policies.

A policy which is "useless" must necessarily be reviewed in light of that uselessness. If we really believe that a policy based on military power lacks utility, then at a minimum the policy should be abandoned, however we formulate the alternatives. If our faith today is in weapons of mass destruction, then the judgment of military power as useless must somehow be connected with a radically different faith which no longer accepts the centrality of the military. This is what we shall refer to as "unilateralism." If commitment to military might is irrational, which we are arguing, then the nation which continues to rely on it in face of the evidence is pursuing an intellectually bankrupt as well as a futile policy.

Unilateralism is based in part on the proposition that just as the arms race began and is perpetuated through unilateral initiatives Washington builds up, Moscow responds, Washington responds, etc., so disarmament will be likely only when, through unilateral initiatives, one large nation radically transforms its faith in arms and regards them as obstacles rather than benefits. Once one side becomes convinced that the common faith in arms is without foundation and acts accordingly--though unilateralism-- the challenge and response pattern that now perpetuates the arms race will probably be used to undermine it.

To be sure, unilateralism as conceived here would entail a far more extreme initiative--no less than a renunciation of the central pillar of international politics--than that involved in the thrusts and counter-thrusts of the arms race. But the general principle would be similar in that in neither instance are multilateral agreements the instruments.

The nation first embracing unilateralism would in a sense be striking a blow for national independence. Insofar as the "super powers" are enslaved today by the shibboleths of arms competition and the delusive proposition that armaments protect something valuable, the Great Powers are dominated by a jealous and demanding task-master. The nation which first accepted unilateralism would not be subject to this serfdom but would be striking out on its own. Thus if the United States were the first unilateralist nation, it would not worry unduly if the "adversary" continued to build arms, for it would conclude that its international rival was simply acting irrationally and would unfortunately have to pay the price for its continued reliance on arms.

But, more explicitly, what would be the general pattern of a unilateralist policy?

III

First of all, a considerable body of opinion would have to reach the conclusion that military power is useless. Without the support of public opinion, in other words, unilateralism would be still born. But given a public sentiment in agreement with the policy in general, the details could be worked out with relatively little difficulty. Here we outline a possible unilateralism, keeping in mind that there are also other methods of implementing it.

The policy, then, might consist of publicized gradualism; widespread public education; and unilateral disarmament spread over, perhaps, six or seven years.

Publicized gradualism would entail a publicity campaign stating the contents of the new policy and announcing that international relations would from now on be carried out in the full glare of publicity. The CIA would be abolished and its staff transferred to the staff of the campaign for unilateralism. It would be repeated that in carrying out other aspects of the unilateralist policy the details would be based on the principle of utter disillusion with the efficiency of military defense.

By widespread education, we imply not only formal education but also much informal dialogue re-examining prevalent interpretations of American history. A new perspective on history might include one stressing the failures of military violence. The coming of the Civil War, as well as its long-run effects, might need re-evaluation. Wouldn't the world have been better off had Lincoln refused to fight Jefferson Davis? A re-examination of the Revolution might include a discussion of how the objective of independence could have been attained without the use of military

236

violence. In short, "education" would imply a serious questioning of many propositions now associated with the interpretation of American history, as well as careful statement of the case for unilateralism. Moreover, an effort would also be made to relate the proposed policy to the American and general Western religious heritage. The moral as well as practical implications of the new proposals would need to be examined.

Finally, to facilitate the many alterations in thought and practice that would be required, the full policy would be implemented over a period of six to seven years--a period brief enough to sustain the dramatic effect of the new policy yet long to permit the inevitable economic and social adjustments which would otherwise be too painful.

The plan might divide the six or seven years into three periods. In the first, of 12 months, the emphasis would be on the kind of education we have outlined. The second phase, of perhaps two years, would witness a complete dismantling of nuclear weapons. During the third phase, extending over the remaining time, the central concern would be "conventional" weapons of mass destruction. Each of the three phases would, of course, involve not only military policy in the narrow sense but also radically changed international and socio-economic commitments.

As we spell out the details of the three periods, we are not proposing a rigid blueprint but are rather attempting to illustrate the kinds of policies which might be envisioned. Actual experience from month to month might well alter the details and some aspects originally seen as falling into the earlier developments might be postponed to alter dates.

THE FIRST PHASE

Examples of what might be done during the first or educational phase (after a national referendum and act of Congress approving unilateralism) include dramatization of the new policy by political leaders; presidential press conferences; television and radio forums; debates with those who still have confidence in military defense; and reproduction in large quantities of the works of such persons as Mohandas Gandhi, Martin Luther King, and Walter Millis (particularly "The Uselessness of Military Power").

237

Fairly soon in this phase, the President would state that he had just appointed a committee to study plans for conversion from a war-preparing to a peace-building economy. The committee would work out detailed proposals for constructive use of resources now devoted to implementing faith in the military. Reports from the committee would be due early in the second phase.

In whatever disarmament or arms control conference was then in session, a unilateralist United States delegation would accept the latest Soviet proposals as a basis for negotiations, announcing incidentally that in any event it was committed to unilateralism as a principle. The problem of inspection and verification, whether on-site or off-site, it would go on, was far less important than before. Since the United States no longer had any faith in weapons as the way to security, the fact that the other side had them was its own misfortune. To be sure, the other side could still devastate the world with its weapons, but with the United States preparing for imminent unilateral disarmament, the general power to destroy would be drastically reduced. And the American delegation would invite the Soviets to initiate Soviet unilateralism. The Soviet Union would, of course, decline to do so at this time, calling the American proposal an example of "bourgeois sentimentalism." The Soviet delegation, the Soviet delegate might go on, demanded "deeds, not words."

To provide the deeds, the Secretary of Defense would proclaim that this country was withdrawing gradually from its military bases abroad. Within a year, all would be abandoned. Erstwhile military allies would be told that they could now participate in the non-violent defense being prepared as an aspect of unilateralism. The Secretary might add that, even from a military viewpoint, most of the bases were obsolete.

By the end of the first phase, no Nation State could afford to ignore the outlined and already partly implemented policy. Whether skeptical, angry, or favorable, foreign ministries and public opinion generally would have to develop responses to the American plans and actions. This would be particularly true in view of the stimulus to the American economy given by the first aspects of American disarmament: the stock-market would experience a minor boom, with a

238

major one predicted as the economy anticipated complete liberation from the burden of military power.

No longer would this country be simply reacting to the initiatives of others, including Moscow's; instead, it would be proposing its own radical course and demanding that others respond to its initiative. It would be far more "independent" than under the regime of arms competition.

THE SECOND PHASE

The President might initiate the second phase by announcing the formation of a Non-Violent Resistance Corps, which would constitute the leadership in any non-violent resistance to invasion. Trained in as rugged a fashion as past armies and navies, the Corps would build on the experience of the Civil Rights struggle, the Gandhi movement in India, and many other past "wars without violence." The Corps would become skilled, for example, in conducting strikes. At first a relatively small body--perhaps 50,000--by the end of the second phase this might reach 150,000, many of them former West Point, Annapolis, and Colorado Springs officers.

Meanwhile, the nuclear disarmament initiatives would have begun. The President would announce that all nuclear weapons were being destroyed and all establishments devoted to their manufacture were being diverted to other uses. All foreign governments would be invited to send inspectors to monitor the disarmament process.

At some point in this phase, the Committee on Utilization of Resources, which, it will be remembered, had been appointed during the first phase, would offer its preliminary report. It would recommend the principles to be followed in re-allocation of resources. Among these principles would be: (a) an emphasis on collective rather than individual and private expenditures (public transportation rather than money to buy more automobiles, for example), on the ground that the social sector desperately needs new capital. (b) American contributions to economic development abroad would gradually increase until by the end of the six or seven year disarmament period they would be in the neighborhood of possibly $85,000,000,000 annually. Training of skilled personnel would be a high order priority.

239

Purposes to which the former military budget would be committed might include reforestation, soil conservation, a gigantic environmental clean-up; several billions a year to subsidize educational institutions; a program of world scholarships on the order of $50,000,000,000 a year; and a housing scheme to provide dwelling places for millions of persons.

The theory behind expenditures of this kind would be that if we wish a peaceful world the resources hitherto used for war preparation must find a new outlet compatible with the works of peace. The sum mentioned here are merely suggestive or illustrative.

THE THIRD PHASE

By now the main lines of policy would have been laid down. Its outlines should be clear to the world and its formulators would insist on full publicity for every aspect of it.

The main tasks of the third phase would be to provide a schedule for "conventional" disarmament to match that for nuclear divestment; to develop even more extensive programs to retrain workers for peaceful pursuits; and to complete the organization and training of the Non-Violent Resistance Corps.

As the third phase proceeded, it should become increasingly clear that unilateralism does not mean a mere negation. Both nuclear and conventional disarmament would be seen as paving the way for a whole re-thinking of the purposes to which human labor and natural resources ought to be put. Unilateralism would entail a new value system and a new faith. The faith in arms, so characteristic of both the Soviet Union and the United States, would have given way to the faith in planning for human needs as the way to peace and security. Neither faith can, of course, guarantee "security." But the advocate of unilateralism in its broad sense believes that the faith upon which it reposes is much more likely to produce a large measure of security than the commitment to arms. Either way we are tied to faith propositions of some kind.

IV

What might be the response to this version of unilateralism?

240

Already we have suggested that the first reaction might be one of disbelief on the part of the "opponent" or "adversary." So unprecedented would the unilateralist policy be that political leaders would be hard pressed to formulate a response. We have said that the Soviet Union's characterization might be that the scheme was a bit of "bourgeois sentimentality." Other adversaries might claim fraud or deceit or trickery by the CIA--particularly because part of the proposal would include abolition of the CIA. The fact that all nations would be invited to send inspectors to examine first-hand the progress in unilateralism might at first seem to be utterly beyond belief.

In announcing the whole program, of course, the newly radicalized United States would remind the world that unilateral initiatives in the past had sometimes led to multilateral agreements. Thus before the Test Ban Treaty of 1963, there was an informal ban on the testing of nuclear weapons for three years which came about through the unilateral initiative of the Soviet Union and a reciprocal response by the United States. The unilateralist policy makers would no doubt hold out the hope that something of the same development might take place with their initiatives, albeit on a far larger scale and with a much more complex policy.

Nevertheless, the policy formulators would be prepared to go ahead whether or not there was any immediate reciprocal response by the other side. Unilateralism might hope for reciprocity but would not expect it immediately. At the same time the world would be reminded again and again that the arms race itself had been the result of unilateralism of a certain kind: the participants did not sit down and formulate a treaty establishing an arms race. Instead, one side initiated arms build-ups, the other side reciprocated, the first side went even higher, and so on: basically, the modern arms race is the result of unilateral initiatives and responses. Why, it might be repeated, could we not expect similar results through a well thought out unilateralism for disarmament?

But it is not a sheer fantasy, it might be asked, to assume that any Great Power could undergo so basic a change in outlook--a change comparable to a religious conversion? Of course. But it also seems to be true to say that, while such a fundamental transformation would be startling, only a dramatic change of this kind could provide the dynamic essential to cut through the

241

obfuscations and hypocrisies of previous disarmament efforts. For more than a half century we have worked within the old frameworks which assumed that, while dangerous, the possession of armaments defended valuable things. The radical unilateralists would simply be saying that it is now time for a basically different set of assumptions reposing on the proposition that military power is useless.

Although the initial response to unilateralism might be skepticism or cynicism, the world could not go on in the old ways with the greatest military power on earth renouncing its faith in military violence. At some point the pressures would mount for reciprocity or competition in disarmament. If one doubts this, imagine how the United States would react if the Soviet union should announce a complete program of unilateralism. Who can doubt that this would be a powerful impetus for the United States to follow suit? If it be replied that the Soviet Union is not the United States, the answer is that in many of the basic hall-marks of international politics the two super-powers are amazingly alike: thus they imitate each other in arms and in the ways they rationalize the arms race; state goals that are strikingly alike; and deeply committed to technological "progress"; and worship the sacred altar of bigness. We surely must take seriously the proposition that unilateral initiatives on a large scale could not be ignored by the Soviet Union any more than by the United States.

This conclusion is reinforced when we consider the domestic politics of the Soviet Union. For years there has been enormous pressure for more consumers' goods, and American unilateralism would be calculated to reinforce that pressure by removing any possible excuse for increasing the military. The Soviet Union presumably has its hard-liners who would now begin to be viewed as rigid, inflexible, and unrealistic--somewhat as Stalinists began to be seen after the revelations of Khrushchev.

Because the alternation in American policy would be so fundamental, we cannot assume that contemporary hostilities and fears would remain the same. Indeed, it is almost certain that unilateralism would tend to produce a radically different outlook in both the United States and the Soviet Union. Fear would be supplanted by hope and the whole set of "disarming" attitudes now created by the new policies would stimulate the imaginations of human beings who could no

242

longer rely on arms. Faith in arms tends to make for stupidity in policy making. Without arms, men and women would be compelled to turn to their wits in promoting national defense. Having seen the futility of defending anything valuable by arms, they would be forced to be clever. And utilization of intelligence could open up vistas for creative action that can only be dimly envisioned today.

It may be alleged, of course, that the adversary would simply use its great military predominance to "take over" the West. But this assertion is dubious. Even in the days immediately after World War II, when the West was relatively weak militarily, men like Ambassador Kennan doubted that a "take over" was the Russian purpose. Any attempt by Russia to "conquer" the West would simply complicate its own domestic problems and vastly expand its problem of control. The Soviet Union has had difficulties enough in controlling its East European satellites: to attempt to control the West could create problems of enormous magnitude both within the Soviet Union and in connection with its allies.

We must also remember that an integral part of unilateralism is recognition of non-violent resistance as an important part of "defense." While armaments would decline steadily over a period of six or seven years, organization for "civilian defense" would escalate. Increasingly, we are becoming acquainted with the great possibilities of non-violent resistance as one of our most effective tools against tyranny. Although the techniques are not fool-proof, the under-cutting of the power of violence through non-violence has been shown to be a "realistic" possibility, even in nations not specifically trained to use it (as in Norwegian and Danish resistance to Hitler). With training and discipline, the potentialities of non-violent resistance are almost endless, as Gene Sharp and others have maintained.

Military pressure from the outside (the United States versus the Soviet Union, for example) tends to solidify the governing classes. With obvious removal of the military threat, the tendency for the ruling class in the Soviet Union to split would be greatly enhanced. The way to bolster the governing class would be to confront it with the threat of military violence, as the United States is doing today. The removal of the threat of violence would tend to undermine the authority of the governing elite and to open the way to

243

a non-militarized adversary. Conflict would not, of course, be abolished but rather transformed into non-violent struggle.

Even if this relatively hopeful scenario did not come about, unilateralism would still produce a better world than reliance on armaments. Even assuming the worst (by some standards)--bombing by the Soviet Union of Western Europe and the United States--destruction would be far less extensive than in a situation in which the United States responded violently.

But it is difficult to imagine why the "adversary" would wish to bomb the United States or to maintain a huge military establishment in face of an unarmed America. The Soviet Union, along with others, would have peaceful access to a vastly expanded Economic Development Fund of the UN (due to American disarmament); it would share the fruits of unilateralism generally and the cost of Soviet armaments would be an enormous strain on the Russian economy. Unless Soviet rulers were more short-sighted than one can imagine, their self-interest would dictate their own unilateralism as a response to American disarmament.

Thus the two super-powers would find themselves in competition for disarmament.

V

Critics might offer a number of objections. Let us respond to a few of them.

POWER AND ITS PROBLEMS

It might be said that unilateralism ignores the central problem of power. But such is not the case. Unilateralism fully recognizes the centrality of power but argues that there are varieties of it far more efficacious than the military type. Unilateralism is an appeal from confidence in military power to commitment to the power of organized non-violence. Admittedly this is a shift of faith. But every policy ultimately must rely on a faith. Military power, as we have said, can no longer be effectively used to support public policies and unilateralism in all its manifestations would seem to be the alternative faith.

UNACCEPTABLE RISKS

It might be argued, too, that unilateralism is enormously risky. There is little if any precedent for it. Unilateralism would make the United States vulnerable not only in terms of physical safety but also in those of economic and social well-being.

Now there is little question that these are among the risks which must be accepted under unilateralism. But the question is whether these and similar hazards are likely to be fewer under unilateralism than they are under the contemporary policy of armed might. The answer would seem to be clear: with every new day under a policy of armed might we grow perceptibly closer to the obliteration of the human race. Only by radical surgery in policy can that day be averted.

POSSIBILITIES OF NEGOTIATION

It may be said that unilateralism reflects an unfounded pessimism about the possibilities of negotiation. After all, a test ban treaty and an Antarctic pact were negotiated. Why now a general disarmament pact? The critic raises a good question. But negotiating a general disarmament pact is of a different order from a test ban treaty. If the negotiations take place with the policy of armed might still intact, it is difficult to see why the disarmament conference might succeed when a dozen others have failed. At one end of the negotiating table would be an Intercontinental Ballistic Missile and at the other end an MX-type missile. So long as we continue to believe that the military can be an effective instrument of public policy, so long will we fail to reach an agreement for genuine disarmament: indeed, the negotiating atmosphere is likely to become worse with every new frustration.

But the unilateralist would hold out great hope for mutually resolving issues through negotiation if we should go into the negotiating conference with no hydrogen bomb in the room, so to speak, and with an outlook characterized by the conviction that military violence is useless. The fundamental change in attitude implied by unilateralism would be a condition for any true success.

REPUDIATION OF FORCE?

Hard-headed "realists" might contend that the principles of unilateralism repose on a rather naive attempt to reject the use of physical force. Gradually speaking, however, defenders of unilateralism do not ground their principles on repudiation of all force. The legitimacy of physical force depends on the context within which it is utilized and the spirit of the user. Saving a child from an onrushing automobile entails the employment of physical force, as does the bombing of a city. But surely the two acts must be placed in different categories, ethical or otherwise. There is a place for a genuine police force, but what does it have to do with weapons of mass destruction, nuclear or "conventional"?

CONCLUSION

Walter Millis, in the essay to which we referred earlier, argued that military power is "useless" for obtaining any legitimate public policy education and health budgets have to be cut in order to provide resources for still more weaponry.

Beliefs of this kind need a sharp challenge, somewhat like the child's "But the Emperor has nothing on?" in Andersen's The Emperor's New Clothes. The beliefs are so firmly fixed and so widely accepted by the supposedly sophisticated of this world that only the naive questioning of a child can undermine their credibility. It is the task of the unilateralist to become that child.

FOOTNOTES

1. "The Case for Unilateral Disarmament" in Donald G. Brennan (ed.), Arms Control, Disarmament, and National Security (New York: Braziller, 1961), p. 190.

2. Walter Millis, "The Uselessness of Military Power," in Robert A. Goldwin, (ed.), America Armed (Chicago: Rand McNally, 1963), pp. 37, 38.

MAKING CHOICES ON THE NORTH GERMAN PLAIN

Bruce D. Berkowitz

Even though the defense of Western Europe has probably been the single most important American foreign commitment since World War II, the fact remains that for most of the post-war era the United States has usually been ill-prepared to carry out the promises that it has made to its European allies. By almost any objective standard, NATO has been outmanned and outgunned from the time of its formation in 1949, a fact that has led the alliance from its earliest days to rely heavily on nuclear weapons in one form or another as a deterrent.

Many people have criticized NATO's dependence on nuclear weapons throughout the history of the alliance, but this criticism has reached a noticeable crescendo during the past decade. Some of the critics, of course, are people who object in principle to the use of nuclear weapons under any condition. Lately, however, critics of NATO's nuclear policy have also begun to include moderates from the political center. Some military officials wonder about the feasibility of fighting a war with tactical nuclear weapons without destroying most of West Germany in the process. European leaders have long doubted the credibility of a threat to use American nuclear weapons against Russian soldiers so long as the Soviet Union has the ability to retaliate against the United States. And American officials are increasingly coming to see the question of nuclear weapons as a divisive wedge that undermines the solidarity of the alliance. As a result, many writers lately have tried to find some alternative to the nuclear option.

So far they have not been successful. The dilemma for the United States is that, although many good arguments can be made that the best defense of Western Europe would rely on conventional military forces, deploying sufficient conventional forces within the immediate future -- say, within four or five years-- would be enormously expensive. Indeed, as we shall see, in order to deploy the forces necessary for a credible conventional deterrent, the United States would be required to raise defense spending to a level exceeding any that the American public has been willing to support during the post-World War II period.

247

Yet all of the "cheap" alternatives to deploying additional conventional forces present their own difficulties. Proposals such as relying more on high technology weapons, imposing reform on the U.S. military, reinstitution of the draft, and so forth all may have some usefulness, but none of them can solve the problem completely.

Thus, the problem of defending Europe is only in part a military problem. Largely the NATO dilemma is a political problem: how to defend NATO within the budget limits that the American public has imposed. This becomes clear when one considers some of the economic facts of life that have constrained U.S. defense spending since World War II.

American Defense Spending in the Post-War Era

In debates over the U.S. defense budget, hawks often claim that U.S. defense spending has fallen dangerously. Doves often say that defense spending has risen to unaffordable levels. Who is correct?

The simple answer is "both and neither." Figure 1 shows the amount of money spent annually on the U.S. defense budget since the beginning of this century (all budget figures in this essay are given in FY 1984 dollars, the most recent available). As one can see, before World War II, the United States spent little for defense, other than a blip that coincided with World War I. This trend reflected the American policy of isolationism from foreign affairs and the security afforded by two oceans, weak neighbors to the south, and a friendly neighbor to the north.

After a huge jump in defense spending during World War II, the American defense budget leveled off on a plateau in the early 1950s. This plateau was considerably higher than the pre-war spending levels, reflecting the new role the United States played in the world. World War II had drained the ability of Great Britain to provide defense and stability for the Western world, and events from 1945 to 1950 led most governments in the West to view the Soviet Union as a threat to their security. The United States assumed most of the burden, and this was reflected in the post-war level of defense spending.

Perhaps the most remarkable fact concerning U.S. defense spending in the post-war era is that it has remained so stable. American defense spending

248

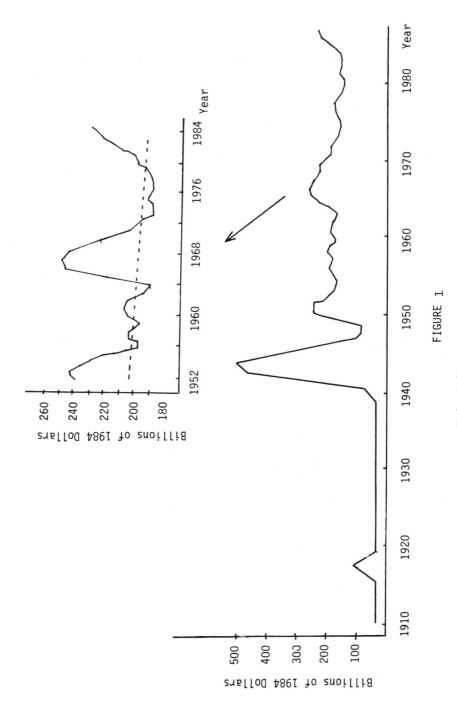

FIGURE 1

U.S. Defense Expenditures, 1910-1984

has, in fact, remained within a plus-or-minus 12% range, and until recently, there had never been more than four consecutive years in which the defense budget has grown or shrunk.

There is no absolute proof, but it is tempting to assume that this relatively stable trend reflects a broad consensus that has underlined American national security policy since World War II and the willingness of the American public to support a finite set of foreign defense commitments. Surveys of popular support for increased defense spending during the past four decades would seem to support this hypothesis. Most polls indicate that defense spending and support for defense spending are countercyclical: upturns in defense spending are soon followed by downturns in support for increased defense spending, while downturns in defense spending are generally followed by upturns in support for defense spending.

Witness, for example, the most recent cycle: As real defense spending declined throughout the 1970s, public opinion favoring larger defense budgets steadily grew; after this trend was abruptly reversed in the current defense buildup that was begun under the Carter Administration and accelerated under the Reagan Administration, public support for defense spending abruptly fell. It would seem that public opinion serves as an outsized counterweight constraining the defense budget to a relatively narrow range (though, of course, there are also other factors that contribute to this effect).

This is an important point to understand, because, if one improved NATO defenses so that after a four or five year program the alliance could repel a Warsaw Pact threat with high confidence, one would also greatly exceed the post-World War II norms for defense spending. It might make sense for NATO to depend so heavily on nuclear weapons; however, any alternative strategy needs to be politically feasible.

To see why spending limits would prevent a four or five year fix for NATO's conventional defenses, first consider by just how much NATO forces would need be improved.

The Current Balance on the Central Front

NATO forces are arranged, as the saying goes, in "layer cake fashion" along the inter-German border (see Figure 2). The southern half of the Central Front is divided into four corps sectors, two West German and two American. Together, these units are called the Central Group of Allied Forces, or CENTAG.

The northern half of the Central Front is defended by the Northern Group of Allied Forces, or NORTHAG. NORTHAG also consists of four corps sectors: one German, one Dutch, one British, and one Belgian. Most analysts believe that, if there is a weak link in NATO, it lies in NORTHAG. The British, Belgian, and Dutch forces are especially troublesome.

The equipment in these forces tends to be twenty to twenty-five years old; the British, for example, still field foot infantry, when most of the rest of the world has put its infantry in armored personnel carriers. Also, many of the so-called active forces of these corps are in fact manned well below wartime levels or are kept at a very low level of readiness. The Dutch, for instance, station only one of their six brigades in Germany; the others are stationed several hundred kilometers from the inter-German border and would require 2-4 days to come up to strength and move to the front. Half of the British infantry forces assigned to NATO are on duty in Northern Ireland and would require three days to return to their units in Germany. NORTHAG is also considered the Achilles' heel of NATO because of the terrain of the region, which consists mainly of flat, rolling plains -- just the kind of terrain suited to the kind of regimented, high-speed armor operations that the Soviet Army has practiced for thirty years.[1]

One saving grace for NATO is that it is not necessary for NATO to match the Warsaw Pact forces on a one-to-one basis; traditionally, defense has an advantage in military operations over offense, and almost all scenarios for a Central European war depict NATO as the defenders (this is even true in Soviet exercises, since Soviet military doctrine stresses offensive operations). One can easily see why this is so; attacking forces at some point must move across open terrain, during which time they are more vulnerable. Moreover, it is more difficult to aim and fire a weapon in a moving vehicle or on the run than it is from cover.

FIGURE 2

Sectors of Responsibility on NATO's Central Front

252

NATO planners believe that they can prevent the Soviets from establishing a breakthrough if the Pact can be prevented from massing more than a 3:1 advantage anywhere over the front.[2] Naturally, there is nothing sacrosanct about this ratio. The advantage that an attacker actually needs for success varies from situation to situation; mountain positions, for instance, are much more difficult to attack than are open field. But this rule is useful as a rule of thumb.

Thus, the problem for the Warsaw Pact is massing its forces at two or three points along the Central Front so that it has the advantage necessary for a breakthrough. Conversely, the problem for NATO is to detect a Warsaw Pact mobilization quickly enough so that it can mobilize its own forces in time to meet the attack at the border, and shifting its limited, outnumbered forces along the border so that it is can avoid being overwhelmed at any one approach.

The key question is, at what point does the overall imbalance become so lopsided that, even after redeploying along the front and taking advantage of the terrain, NATO would be unable to plug all of the gaps in the line? According to the Defense Department, NATO can hold the Pact in an "elastic defense" so long as the Pact forces do not have more than a 1.5 to 1 advantage over the entire front (just how these force ratios are measured will be explained in a moment). If the imbalance is greater than this, then the Warsaw Pact would be able to mass its troops at two or three corps, so that it had the advantage that it needed for a breakthrough.

It should be kept in mind, however, that an "elastic defense" means only that NATO would be able to keep the Warsaw Pact forces from utterly rupturing NATO lines and proceeding to take territory at will. An elastic defense would surrender some territory to the Pact, and the disadvantages that caused NATO to lose the territory in the first place would make it unlikely that it would have the ability to retake the land. A "steadfast defense," in which little or no territory would be conceded to the Pact, would require lowering overall force ratios to 1.2:1.

Recently two studies have been published that examine how the balance on the Central Front in fact shapes up today, and how much NATO would have to spend

253

to bring the imbalance within acceptable limits. One of these studies was written by the Congressional Budget Office (CBO), the non-partisan office that analyzes the costs and effectiveness programs proposed by the President to Congress (in this case, CBO was analyzing the Reagan Administration's proposal to modernize the U.S. Army's ground forces).

The other study was written by a panel selected by the Union of Concerned Scientists (UCS). The UCS had recommended for many years that NATO adopt a policy a "no first use" of nuclear weapons and had acknowledged that this policy would require NATO to strengthen its conventional forces, This study was one of their first serious attempts to estimate how much these improvements would cost.[3]

The CBO and UCS studies are interesting because, even though each makes different assumptions about how a war on the Central Front would evolve, they both reach similar conclusions: currently NATO is at a disadvantage on the Central Front, and, although correcting the situation is not impossible, it would require a substantial amount of money.

Both the CBO and the UCS study used an accepted measure of military capability called the "armored division equivalent," or ADE. Comparing NATO and Warsaw Pact forces on a one-to-one basis would be comparing apples and oranges, as the weapons and organization of each tend to be quite different and an analysis based on such a comparison would be meaningless. Therefore, for example, Soviet divisions tend to be smaller than their NATO counterparts, and they usually are more heavily armed. On the other hand, NATO military equipment is usually agreed to be more lethal. As a result, The ADE was developed by the Defense Department in order to avoid this problem.[4]

The capability that NATO and the Warsaw Pact would have on the battlefield in a given stage of the war would depend on how much time each side required to move each of its units from the rear to the front lines. As each side was able to deliver another unit to the front, it would tilt the overall ratio of forces toward its favor.

The chart given in Figure 3 portrays the CBO and UCS estimates for the fluctuations that would occur in the overall ratio of forces on the Central Front as each side mobilized (in both studies, these ratios were

254

calculated using ADEs as described above). So, for example, according to CBO, in 1987 the Warsaw Pact would have about a two-to-one advantage over NATO a day or so after it began to mobilize. This advantage would then diminish for a few days to about the critical 1.5:1 level (this would occur as U.S. reinforcements arrived from North America), and then climb back up to about 1.7:1 about thirty-five days after mobilization had begun (this would reflect the arrival of Soviet cadre divisions, which are manned and equipped at minimal levels and which would require several weeks to mobilize).

According to the UCS study, the Warsaw Pact would actually be at a disadvantage immediately after it mobilized; it would then gradually build up a 1.8:1 advantage seven days later, and finally level off at about 1.6:1 thirty days after mobilization began.

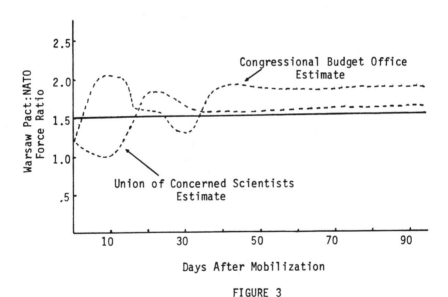

FIGURE 3

Warsaw Pact - NATO Force Ratios on Central Front,
0-90 Days After Mobilization

255

The two studies differ because each makes different assumptions about how a European war would evolve. The UCS study assumes that NATO would immediately detect the Warsaw Pact as it mobilized and would react promptly; the CBO study assumes that the Warsaw Pact would be able to camouflage its early preparations and that this, along with some indecision on the part of NATO leaders, would give the Soviet Union and its allies a four-day headstart. Also, CBO assumes that the Pact can mobilize more quickly than the UCS analysts assume, and that the Pact will be able to draw on the thirty divisions based in their Southwestern Theater of Military Operations (mainly from Hungary), bringing the total number of divisions that the Pact would ultimately deploy in the first three months of the war to 120 (versus the 90 assumed in the UCS study).[5] In either case, however, both studies conclude that the Soviets would be able to deploy more than the number of forces necessary for Soviet military leaders to believe that they had a good chance of breaking through NATO lines.

Both studies describe the additional forces that would be necessary to bring the force ratios to acceptable levels throughout a possible war.

According to CBO, in order to bring the imbalance within more manageable levels, the United States would need to authorize $75.8 billion over five years. Of this, $37.6 billion was the Reagan Administration's originally-proposed plan to modernize existing U.S. forces committed to NATO; $7 billion was additional funding that would be used to accelerate procurement of the proposed forces; and $31.2 billion was funding that would have to be used to add two new divisions, their equipment, and the ships necessary to transport them to Europe in 14 days. Stretched over five years, these improvements would have totalled an annual increase in U.S. defense authorizations of $15.2 billion in 1982 (when the study was written). In 1984, the cost would be slightly more -- $17 billion per year.

Although the willingness of our allies to increase their own defense budget is too complicated an issue to discuss here, it is worth noting that the other NATO members would collectively need to match this spending in order to strengthen their own forces if a conventional defense were to succeed (i.e., for the entire alliance, we are talking about an additional $34 billion a year in defense spending).[6] Remember, however, even these improvements would provide only the capability necessary for an "elastic defense." A "steadfast defense" would cost about twice as much.

According to the UCS study, NATO as a whole would need to spend $97 billion over six years; the authors do not indicate whether this would provide an elastic defense or a steadfast defense. This money would be spent on tank obstacles and fortifications; increased combat stocks and supplies' improved pre-positioned equipment for U.S. troops stationed in North America; increased sealift capacity; and nine new divisions (five American, three Allied). Assuming that the United States would pay for these additions in the same proportion as the additional manpower that it would be contributing (i.e., five-eighths), then the total U.S. expenditures over six years would be $60.6 billion. The annual increase in U.S. defense expenditures would be $10.1 billion per year for the six years.[7]

Now, what would this additional funding mean in terms of the overall defense budget? In either case, it would seem as though the cost to the United States for its share of a non-nuclear defense of Europe would be in the neighborhood of $10-$17 billion in additional annual defense spending over the next five to six years, resulting in defense outlays ranging from $269 billion to $289 billion in present dollars -- well above the historically acceptable levels.

Whether or not these additional expenditures are desirable is a political question of priorities. However, they certainly are affordable. The burden of government spending is not so much its absolute size, but its size in relation to the growth of the economy; if government spending increases faster than the economy as a whole, then the result would likely be (a) an increase in taxes, leading to possible distortions in investment and a decline in the performance of the economy; (b) an increase in interest rates, as the government borrowed the money in the marketplace, with the possible result being a similar dropoff in the economy; (c) inflation, as the government creates the money necessary to cover its expenses by fiat; or (d) some combination of the above.

One might argue that defense spending can readily be increased with little or no harm because the burden it has placed on the economy has actually diminished in recent years. Defense spending has remained relatively

257

constant, as we have seen, and because the economy has grown during the post-war period, the percentage of the gross national product consumed by defense has steadily diminished since the mid-1950s. The problem, of course, is that whatever economic slack that has been created by this trend -- and more -- has been consumed by the growth in other government spending. So again a problematical choice appears: a conventional defense of NATO is, strictly speaking, economic feasible -- but not if we continue to hold other government spending at its current level.

There is, of course, nothing sacred about the historical limits on defense spending that have prevailed since World War II. However, one should keep in mind that betting that we can afford the forces necessary for even a marginal conventional defense of NATO is betting against thirty years of experience.

Alternatives to Financing a Non-Nuclear European Defense

One of the frustrations of dealing with the question of how to provide a conventional defense of Europe is that a number of "easy" solutions have been proposed. These proposals are beguiling because they lead one to believe that it is only the lack of wisdom or foresight that is responsible for the problems of NATO. In fact, there is little or no evidence that should lead one to believe that any one of them would be a cheap cure-all. Let us consider some of the most often-cited proposals.

Suggestion I: Gutting the Strategic Weapons Budget. Some writers have suggested that the money for conventional European forces could be obtained by eliminating some American strategic nuclear forces from the U.S. defense budget; the UCS writers, for example, make this recommendation. Such individuals would be especially willing to forego such weapons systems as the MX missile and the B-1B bomber. Many of these writers also support strategic arms control treaties for the same reasons.

Eliminating the MX and the B-1B would save money, but the savings would still fall well short of freeing the funds necessary for an effective conventional European deterrence. According to one recent study, the annual savings produced by cancelling the MX would average only $2.8 billion over five years. Cancelling the B-1B project would save even less; much of the B-1B

258

program was adopted in the form of long-term contracts in order to save money. Because of these multi-year contracts, termination fees would have to be paid to the contractors and this would offset many of the savings that would be obtained by cancelling the program. Even in 1983, before many of these long-term contracts were made, it was estimated that the annual savings from cancelling the B-1B would average only $2.6 billion annually over five years.[8]

Thus, even eliminating two of the most costly programs in the current strategic modernization program would not yield enough money to cover the costs of the American share in a non-nuclear NATO defense. This may seem surprising, considering the amount of attention that strategic programs such as the MX and B-1B receive. In fact, however, strategic forces have, on average, accounted for only about 15% of the defense budget. General purpose ground forces, on the other hand, have accounted account for about 40% of the budget. Indeed, considering the large amounts of manpower that ground forces require in comparison with strategic forces, and understanding that people, not equipment, consumes most of the defense budget, this fact should not be so surprising. The net result is that there probably is not enough money in the strategic budget to fund an improved American contribution to NATO.

Suggestion II: Conscription. Many analysts, such as Senator Sam Nunn of Georgia (one of the leading defense specialists in Congress), have advocated reinstitution of the draft in order to reduce the manpower costs associated with a non-nuclear defense of Europe. Unfortunately, the savings produced by a draft would be minuscule and would not solve the most important manpower problems of a conventional defense. Moreover, almost any draft instituted today would be inequitable, inefficient, or both.

The most pressing personnel problem that the Defense Department has faced in recent years has been the difficulty of retaining experienced technical specialists and non-commissioned officers. A draft, of course, would bring in only new recruits, so naturally it would offer little or no relief from the retention problem. The government could use conscription in order to pay new soldiers artificially depressed salaries, but the retention of trained soldiers depends entirely on the government's ability to compete with the private market.

Moreover, a draft would impose new costs. Because the government would be paying wages below what its recruits could command in the market (otherwise there is little rationale for a draft), retention would necessarily fall. As retention fell, personnel turnover would rise, and so training costs would presumably rise, too. Just how much retention would fall would depend on how much the government depressed the wages of its conscripts; as it paid lower and lower salaries, it would need to spend more and more money on training as retention fell. To some degree, the savings from depressed salaries would be proportional to the losses of additional training costs. According to the Defense Department, the net savings resulting from reinstitution of the draft would amount to only $600 million per year.[9]

One reason why economics do not favor the draft is that demographic characteristics of the American population have changed. During the 1950s, the ratio of the total 18-year old male population to those males who served in the military was 1.5:1 or less, i.e., there were at most only three men who did not serve in the military for every two who did. During the 1970s, this ratio rose to almost 4.4:1; for the rest of this decade and through the 1990s, the ratio will hover in the 3.5:1 to 4.0:1 range. In other words, while the market for eligible males in previous years was tight, the market price for their labor was high and the government could "save" a lot of money by simply conscripting the individuals. Today, however, it is a buyer's market because there are so many males of military service age in comparison to the actual number of males that are needed. Because the buyer of 18-year-old-male labor today has so much leverage in the market, conscription does not offer the government much of a discount on new recruits.[10]

Of course, even these "savings" would be illusionary. Although the expenditures reflected in the federal budget may be lower, in fact the additional manpower costs of a conventional European defense would still exist; they would simply be borne by a smaller group of people, whose payments would not be reflected in official government figures, i.e., they would be borne by the conscripts.[11]

Yet not only are the economic benefits of restoring the draft dubious; because of the current demographic situation, there would also be serious questions of equity. In the 1950s, no matter what other harms the draft may have represented, one still might claim that the system was at least equitable, insofar as a large proportion of young men were required to serve in the military. Today, however, there are so many more young men in the population than the government needs for military service that, if the draft were reinstituted, some means would have to be found to select those who will serve from those who would not. In the early 1960s, this was done primarily through various deferments (e.g., student, medical, etc.). Naturally, this system was inequitable to those young men who could not avail themselves of such deferments. Moreover, this method seemed stacked against low-income individuals, blacks, Hispanics, and other minorities.

The "deferment method" of choosing conscripts by default was replaced by a random lottery. However, this system had its own inequities. Although all 18-year old males theoretically had an equal chance to be caught in the draft, the costs to all who were drafted was not the same. Military service represented a greater "opportunity cost" for some than for others. For example, an 18-year-old laborer might lose $10,000 a year in wages (at current prices) by being drafted, while a pre-med student who was required to postpone his career in order to serve in the military might lose $30,000 a year.

Some individuals (e.g., writer James Fallows and former Congressman Pete McClosky) have suggested that uniform national service may be a way to avoid the equity problems that any selection system would present. However, uniform national service would still pose the problem of different individuals having differing opportunity costs. Moreover, uniform national service would be extraordinarily costly. Because only one out of four 18-year old males would be needed to serve in the armed forces, some other work would need to be found for the other 75% of the male population (88% of the total 18-year old population, if one believes that women should also be required to serve). Even if these conscripted workers were paid the minimum wage, the salaries, training, and administration of such a program -- which would include 1.7-1.8 million individuals -- could cost as much as $30 billion a year. One can also imagine the tug-of-war between politicians who would fight over the political plum that such a program would represent.[12]

Suggestion III: High Tech Weapons : The final two proposals -- deploying more high-technology weapons (also known as "emerging technology" or "ET") and improving American military strategy (i.e., "military reform") -- are more speculative than those that have been discussed up to now, and thus are more difficult to evaluate; little hard evidence exists on which to base a judgment.

Several studies have been put forward in recent years suggesting that NATO can avoid much of the cost associated with conventional defense by deploying greater numbers of "precision guided munitions" (PGMs), the so-called "smart munitions" that use sophisticated electronic guidance systems in order to achieve remarkable probabilities of destroying their targets. Such munitions would supposedly multiply the lethality of each soldier at a modest cost.

For example, one study that received a good amount of attention in the late 1970s was written by the "Boston Study Group" (BSG). Among other recommendations, the BSG proposed eliminating large numbers of traditional conventional weapons used by the Army, such as tanks and armored personnel carriers, etc. By restructuring these units around advanced PGMs rather than around heavy armor, the group expected to save substantial amounts of money; when combined with cutbacks in American commitments abroad and sharp reductions in strategic and naval forces, the BSG expected to be able to cut defense spending by 42%.[13]

A study that is probably taken more seriously by the mainstream of defense analysts was published by the European Security Study (ESECS) in late 1983. ESECS specifically intended its proposal to be an alternative to the reliance on tactical nuclear weapons by NATO (though the group recommended that NATO should continue to deploy tactical nuclear weapons in order to deter the Soviets from using their own nuclear weapons).[14]

The ESECS study proposed a $20 billion program for medium-range ballistic missiles that would have the capability to destroy Warsaw Pact transportation choke points and military units deep behind enemy lines. The missiles would be armed with high-technology munitions such as Skeet, a heat-seeking warhead that would zero in on the engines of Soviet tanks. As a result, NATO would have the ability to disrupt the reinforcements (the "second echelon") necessary for a successful Warsaw Pact offensive. The ESECS writers believed that, after the Warsaw Pact's reserves had been decimated and its lines of communications disrupted as a result of the deep attack, the Pact advance would bog down enough to give NATO an opportunity to regroup and secure its defensive lines.

The difficulty in evaluating proposals such as the ESECS plan is that there is insufficient evidence to confirm or contradict whether PGMs would perform as hoped under battlefield conditions. Anti-tank submunitions have indeed performed well in tests against tanks, but these tests were conducted under well-controlled conditions. For example, in the test trials for Skeet, the tanks in the target area were arranged in a uniform pattern with their engines running; the tests were held in the desert, so there was no foliage obscuring the targets; and the locations of the tanks was known to the missile crew, simplifying the task of acquiring the targets. Battlefield conditions would not be so hospitable; Europe is heavily forested (masking the heat from tanks and trucks), battlefields tend to be packed with hot, burning objects (any of which might distract a heat-seeking guidance system), and, in any case, the Soviets often ship their tanks to the front on trucks (meaning that there would be no engine heat from the tanks to attract heat-seeking munitions). No one knows for sure just how much this would degrade the performance of Skeet.

Smart munitions have been used in the Yom Kippur War, the Vietnam War, the Falklands War, and the recent battles between Israel and Syria in Lebanon. Yet the evidence on the performance of the weapons is decidedly mixed. For example, the writers connected with the BSG study cite a debacle in the Yom Kippur War in which more than 130 Israeli tanks were destroyed in a few hours by Egyptian infantrymen using Russian-built Sagger missiles. On the other hand, other analysts, who have examined the same incident more closely, point out that the Israeli commanders in that battle committed several unpardonable tactical errors that left their units in an unusually vulnerable position (for example, the Israeli tanks went into battle with no infantry or artillery support, which most experts believe tanks need in order to defeat PGM-equipped infantry).[15]

Overall, sometimes it appears that PGMs let down their users at key moments, while at other times PGMs allowed an outnumbered force to fight and win. The lesson seems to be that PGMs have their uses and that they can be a valuable asset in some situations, but they are not a panacea that would automatically allow one to solve the problems of manpower.

Suggestion IV: Military Reform. Even more difficult to evaluate than PGMs and ET is the "military reform movement" that has materialized in the United States during the past ten years. These writers argue from several different viewpoints, but a common theme that runs through their work is that the United States puts too much emphasis on sophisticated equipment and firepower, that the U.S. military is too stultified and orthodox in developing its strategy, and that the U.S. military bureaucracy itself is too stifling and inefficient to perform effectively.[16]

Most of the points made by the military reform movement are obviously valid: organizations should not be so big that they cannot operate efficiently in changing conditions, technology should not be so complicated that it is unreliable on the battlefield, equipment should not be so expensive that it cannot be bought in adequate numbers, and tactics should not be so stultified that they are predictable and inflexible. The issue, however, is not be whether these qualities are desirable, but where the tradeoffs lie. For example, no one wants a military organization that is over-bureaucratized; but, on the other hand, no one wants an organization that is so informal that all of the efficiency that is gained by having standard operating procedures is lost, either. Empirically, it seems that at least as many wars were lost by rag-tag irregulars who could not master the basics of traditional military practices as have been lost by Colonel Blimps.

Many military reformers assert that a conventional defense of Europe would be feasible with innovative doctrine and tactics, but until they are specific in their arguments and offer more supporting evidence, it is difficult either to judge their views or implement their policies.

Conclusions

The Soviet Union has invested a tremendous amount of money during the past two decades in both its nuclear forces and its conventional forces. This two-pronged program has had the effect of (a) rendering the traditional NATO policy of relying on tactical

264

nuclear warfare incredible, and (b) escalating the costs that NATO would have to bear in order to meet the Soviet threat.

Unfortunately, though the United States is capable of meeting this threat by quickly building up American forces over four or five years, the historical record suggests that the American public most likely will not support such a program. Moreover, the most often-heard alternatives to such an expensive program -- a return to the draft, high technology, military reform, etc. -- are not the "quick fixes" that they are often made out to be, either.

In sum, there are no easy solutions -- only difficult choices. Short of rethinking its commitment to NATO, probably the only alternative left to American leaders is a combined approach, in which American defense officials manage to press U.S. defense spending up toward the upper limits of what the American political system can support for eight or ten years. Taking advantage of whatever technology or tactical innovations that come along would help, too, as would considering the long-run costs of strategic forces and their drain on commitments that are more important to day-to-day events. However, it seems to be a matter of political reality that the correlation of forces on the Central Front is going to marginal for the next several years.

References

1. See Pat Hillier, <u>Strengthening NATO: Pomcus and Other Approaches</u> (Washington, D.C.: Congressional Budget Office, 1979).

2. See, for example, FM 100-76, <u>Operations</u> (Washington, D.C.: Department of the Army, 1976).

3. See Nora Slatkin, <u>Army Ground Combat Modernization for the 1980s: Potential Costs and Effects for NATO</u>, (Washington, D.C.: Congressional Budget Office, 1982); and Kurt Gottfried, Henry W. Kendall, and John M. Lee, "'No First Use' of Nuclear Weapons," <u>Scientific American</u> (March 1984), pp. 33-41.

4. An ADE is calculated by first weighting each piece of military equipment that would be used in a NATO-Warsaw Pact war according to its lethality (e.g., a certain Soviet tank might be considered to be four-fifths as effective as a certain American or British tank. One than calculates the total military capability by then summing each unit's order of battle, using the adjusted units of effectiveness.

5. The CBO assumptions concerning the rate at which the Warsaw Pact forces could mobilize and the four-day headstart that they would enjoy over NATO are consistent with assumptions that the Defense Department makes in its own planning. On the other hand, the assumption that the UCS study makes in positing that the Pact will ultimately be able to mobilize 90 divisions is consistent with Defense Department studies.

The UCS authors believe that the 30 additional divisions envisioned by CBO would not be used on the Central Front because they are stationed in Hungary and Rumania, and would thus need to cross neutral Austria in order to reach the fighting. The Defense Department makes no explicit assumptions about how these forces would be used in the scenarios that it studies, but apparently simply lists them as "unassigned." Presumably the Defense Department assumes that these forces would be used to protect the southern borders of the Soviet Union. CBO believed that these borders would be protected with fewer units and that the Soviets would commit as many units as possible to the

Central Front because of its overriding importance.

See Pat Hillier and Nora Slatkin, U.S. Ground Forces: Design and Cost Alternatives for NATO and Non-NATO Contingencies (Washington, D.C.: Congressional Budget Office, 1980).

6. The actual inflation-adjusted cost of the program in 1984 would be $16.4 billion. However, only part of the Reagan Administration's ground force modernization program was actually adopted in 1983. The Administration reduced its proposal so that 24% of the M-1 tank program and 5% of the Bradley Fighting Vehicle program were deleted, while it also added funds to enlarge the AH-64 helicopter program by 16%. To catch up to the originally projected force levels, the United States would need to authorize and additional $2.4 billion over the remaining four years of the program, assuming that no additional cuts are made. This would bring the total necessary annual authorization to $17.0 billion in 1984 dollars.

7. The UCS authors do not explain how they arrived at their estimates. Interestingly, their costs estimates are within a reasonable range of other studies, but the forces that the authors believe that they could buy with this money are considerably larger; CBO, for example, estimates that the Army could recruit and equip only about half as many new units for the amount of money the UCS study allocates for additional forces.

Though most of the empirical findings of the UCS study are not very different from those of the CBO analysis, its authors tend to reach conclusions that are more optimistic. One reason for this is that the authors of the UCS study assume the Warsaw Pact would requires 2:1 overall advantage in order to defeat NATO; most other analysts believe that the critical level is around 1.2:1 to 1.5:1. Also, the UCS authors believe that the Pact would have only a 3:1 or 4:1 advantage against any one NATO corps sector after full mobilization most other analysts believe that the Pact could have a 5:1 to 6:1 advantage if they have a chance to mobilize and get an adequate jump on NATO.

8. See Lawrence J. Cavaiola and Bonita J. Dombey, Modernizing U.S. Strategic Offensive Forces: The Administration's Program and Alternatives (Washington, D.C.: Congressional Budget Office, 1983), p. xxii; and Cavaiola and Dombey, An Analysis of Administration Strategic Arms Reduction and Modernization Programs

(Washington, D.C.: Congressional Budget Office, 1984), pp. 47-58.

9. See Testimony of the Honorable Casper Weinberger in Hearings Before the Committee on Armed Services, United States Senate (2 February 1982), 97th Congress (Washington, D.C.: USGPO, 1982): 97.

10. See Richard W. Hunter and Gary R. Nelson, "The All-Volunteer Force: Has It Worked, Will It Work?" in Martin Anderson, ed. Registration and the Draft (Stanford, Cal.: Hoover Institution Press, 1982): 287.

11. To his credit, Weinberger appreciates this point; in answer to a question from Senator Strom Thurmond, he said:

> A return to the draft may result in little or no savings to the Federal Government and, in certain circumstances, could be more costly. It would merely transfer part of our manpower cost from the Federal budget to an unbudgetted tax on those we would draft...

See Weinberger, ibid.

12. For some of the proposals for uniform national service that have been made, see Pete McClosky, in Anderson, op. cit.:177-178; and James Fallows, National Defense (New York: Random House, 1981): 138 (Fallows, it should be noted, severely underestimates the rate at which the pool of 18-year olds would dwindle). For estimates of the cost of a national service, see Richard V.L. Cooper, "Military Manpower Procurement: Equity, Efficiency, and National Security," in Anderson, op. cit.

13. See Randall Forsberg, Nartin Moore-Ede, Phillip Morrison, Phyllis Morrison, George Sommaripa, and Paul F. Walker, The Price of Defense (New York: Times Books, 1979); and Morrison and Walker, "A New Strategy for Military Spending," Scientific American (October 1978), 239: 48-61.

14. See Robert R. Bowie, ed. Strengthening Conventional Deterrence in Europe (New York: St. Martin's Press, 1983).

15. See Morrison and Walker, op cit, for their favorable evaluation of the Sagger's performance; see John J. McGrath, "The Battle of El Firdan," Armor (May-June 1983) 42: 9-13, for his analysis discounting

the key role of the Sagger in the same event. For other views on PGMs (both pro and con), see Fallows, _op cit._: 35-106; James Digby, _Precision-guided Munitions_, Adelphi Paper No. 118 (London: International Institute for Strategic Studies, 1975); John Mearsheimer, "Precision-guided Munitions and Conventional Deterrence," _Survival_ (March/April 1979) 21: 68-76; Daniel Goure and Gordon McCormick, "PGM: No Panacea," _Survival_ (January/February 1980) 22: 15-21; Robert Kennedy, "Precision ATGMs and NATO Defense, _Orbis_ (Winter 1979) 22: 897-927; and, for the Soviet view on the question, C.N. Donnely, "Soviet Tactics for Overcoming NATO Anti-Tank Defenses," _International Security Review_ (July 1979): 1099-1106.

16. Two good summaries of the military reform movement are Paul Bracken, "Defense Organization and Management, _Orbis_, (Summer 1983) 27: 253-266; and John Mearshiemer, "The Military Reform Movement: A Critical Assessment," _Orbis_ (Summer 1983, 27: 245-268.

AN ENTANGLING ALLIANCE:
NATO, U.S. POLICY, AND PUBLIC OPINION

By Paul M. Cole and Dunbar Lockwood

Crises in the North Atlantic Treaty Organization (NATO) are nothing new. Since its founding in 1949, the rumors of NATO's death have been often greatly exaggerated. In each instance the institutional structures of the alliance and the disposition of public opinion have been strong enough to endure even prolonged problems such as the intermediate-range missile deployment debate, the Nunn amendment controversy, and the split between the United States and some NATO governments over ballistic missile defense. These disputes have been interpreted by some as the symptoms of irreconcilable differences within the alliance; to the critics these pressures are new and forebode the end of NATO.

This chapter examines these pressures, and also looks at the role of the U.S. public. A pro-NATO consensus among the American people may not endure repeated crises. Whether NATO has a "next generation" depends to a large extent on the desire and ability of the federal government to sustain public support for the alliance. Without such support in the long run, political pressure will build, especially if budgetary constraints become tighter, to end or reduce the U.S. commitment to NATO. This chapter asks the question: Does U.S. public policy actively contribute to an Atlantic-oriented, pro-NATO defense policy, or is the survival of NATO a by-product of current public policy?

Sources of Tension

Multiple sources of tension exist within NATO. One of the more visible and perhaps the most insoluble issue is burden-sharing. In a collective security arrangement the division of costs will always be one of the most politically charged questions. Who provides the money, who provides the soldiers and where the next war will be fought are fundamental issues that may never be completely resolved. The division of NATO's budget is neither static nor politically insulated. Events and policy can change the way the burden is divided. Perceptions and politics will influence the way member nations think the burden should be divided.

In June 1984, Senator Sam Nunn (D-Ga.), the ranking minority member of the Senate Armed Services Committee with an established pro-alliance record, introduced an amendment in the U.S. Senate. The so-called Nunn amendment was an ultimatum: If the European members of NATO failed to increase defense spending, then the United States would begin to withdraw troops from Western Europe. The question Senator Nunn asked was, why should the United States take defense of Europe more seriously than the Europeans do? General Bernard Rogers, Supreme Allied Commander in Europe, has also expressed Senator Nunn's concern. He has made public appeals for increased allied support for conventional forces, saying that the Europeans must make substantial spending increases in this area. [1]

Other Americans have joined in with similar comments, analyses, and demands. Columnist William Safire, and defense analysts Jeffrey Record and Robert Hanks have openly criticized U.S. policies which have required the United States to pay a high percentage of the burden for defense of "prosperous economic competitors." [2] James Schlesinger, former U.S. Secretary of Defense, has argued that the European allies do not provide an adequate amount of support for their own defense. The perception that the United States carries too much of NATO's defense burden is echoed by the American people. In 1983, a Harris poll showed that a majority of Americans (66 percent) felt that the U.S. share of the NATO defense burden was excessive. [3]

In spite of it all, the United States maintains a strong political-military commitment to NATO. Two recent studies show that between 55-58 percent of the U.S. defense budget for FY 1985 was allocated to NATO. [4] But whether this is a disproportionate share depends on how the question is analyzed. If burden sharing is defined as the percentage of a nation's GNP allocated to NATO, then the U.S. portion falls behind the U.K., France, Greece, and Turkey. But if per capita defense spending for national defense budgets is compared, the result is very different. In 1983 per capita defense spending in the United States was $920, compared to $450 for the British, $360 for the West Germans, and $310 for the French, according to the International Institute for Strategic Studies. For the Americans this represented nearly 10 percent of per capita income, three times the amount paid by the Europeans. [5] When analyzed in this way, it becomes clear that the United States "spends more in total and per person to defend West Europe than nations there spend to defend themselves." [6]

The American public has also expressed a deep commitment to NATO. In 1984, public opinion polls showed that 70 percent of the American people were willing to support NATO, while 55.7 percent expressed a willingness to increase U.S. defense spending if the increase would permit the United States to reduce its reliance on nuclear weapons. [7] The latter figure suggests attitudes consistent with the U.S.government's goal of strenghtning NATO's conventional forces. This augurs well for continued support for the alliance. The United States remains prepared to act in the defense of Western Europe, but this commitment is threatened by, inter alia, the U.S. perception that the European NATO allies are not paying their "fair share" for defense.

In an age of nuclear parity, regional military balances become incrementally more important. Among some quarters in Europe, the discussion has focused recently on two related issues. First, what should NATO do about the USSR's effort to achieve clear superiority in one class (intermediate-range) of nuclear weapons? Second, how can NATO reduce its reliance on nuclear weapons in general? The answer to the first question took the form of the nuclear modernization program that was initiated in part by former West German Chancellor Helmut Schmidt in 1977, and adopted by NATO in 1979 as the modernization/ negotiation "dual track" decision. The answer to the second question is deceptively easy to state in theory yet nearly impossible to translate into NATO policy. In order to reduce NATO's reliance on nuclear weapons, large increases in conventional forces need to be made. But this solution is vast, complicated, difficult to implement, and expensive. Since conventional forces are more costly than nuclear weapons, the burden-sharing issue will become more acute if conventional forces begin to grow. Who should pay to augment and improve conventional forces in Western Europe?

Another source of constant tension is the question of how to deal with the Soviet Union? To what extent should NATO act on trade issues? As the pipeline controversy demonstrated, the United States tends to take a maximum position, extending the struggle against the Soviet Union into non-military fields. The

272

Europeans, due partly to their geographic proximity, tend to minimize the scope of the East-West conflict. Their general preference is to restrict confrontation to a narrow field of issues, excluding economic and cultural relations with the Soviet Union from NATO's agenda. Yet even when the agenda is very narrow, burden-sharing and the question of the Soviet challenge to Western interests remain. The current debate demonstrates that the U.S. commitment to NATO is not open-ended. There are limits to U.S. willingness to support a NATO strategy dominated by European policies, as illustrated by the U.S. effort to modernize chemical weapon inventories.

The list of unfavorable trends includes a number of issues that have been identified by prominent Americans who were at one time instrumental in the formulation and execution of U.S. foreign policy. Henry Kissinger, former U.S. Secretary of State, has stated that not only does NATO lack a coherent strategy, the alliance is in a precarious state and may not last until the end of the century. [8] After the French government refused to allow American planes to fly over France's air space during the U.S. bombing raid on Libya in April 1986, Kissinger suggested that American troops should be recalled from Europe. Lawrence Eagleburger, former U.S. Undersecretary of State for political affairs, has identified three trends that are undermining the alliance. First, U.S. trade with the Pacific Basin and Japan now exceeds U.S. trade with Europe. In addition to this, the United States and Japan are leaving Western Europe far behind in the field of high technology. Second,

> American demographics are shifting the political and economic center of gravity of the United States westward, away from the regions most historically attuned to the trans-Atlantic relationship. [9]

Third, Eagleburger argues that Western Europe is becoming preoccupied with its own problems. The product is an "inner-directedness" that is inconsistent with the more global view of the United States. He cites two examples to support this; the U.S.-European argument about the divisibility of detente, and the Western European reaction to the U.S. intervention in Grenada. [10]

The United States does not have a monopoly on discontent within the alliance, however.

273

Dissatisfaction has been growing on the other side of the Atlantic as well. Helmut Schmidt, in a speech given in Brussels in January 1984, articulated some of the main European grievances with U.S. behavior. In this speech Schmidt brought forth five major complaints related to U.S. policy toward NATO. First, Schmidt argued that U.S. policy is inconsistent and lacks a coherent strategy, citing the positions held by the Carter and Reagan adminstrations as an example.

> There has not been a continuity of aims or plans vis-a-vis the USSR, nor has there been any consistency of military plans, or of posture on arms control diplomacy, or of behavior vis-a-vis the Soviet Union. [11]

Second, Schmidt contended that the United States frequently acts unilaterally without consulting its European allies. He cited the grain embargo and the gas pipeline embargo as examples. A further example of this is the fact that the United States did not consult its European allies before taking action in Grenada.

A third grievance of the European allies, expressed by Schmidt, is that the United States generally lacks understanding of the Soviet Union. The former chancellor implied that certain U.S. ideas concerning the USSR are simply incorrect.

> Ideas of economic warfare against the Soviet Union or of a full scale arms race in order to strangle them economically are grossly invalid. [12]

A fourth matter which grates the European allies, according to Schmidt, and which addresses the primary American misgiving is the constant U.S. complaint that European defense spending is too low. Schmidt feels that this allegation is unjustified. He argues that wars are not won primarily by increasing military budgets, but rather by mobilizing, motivating, training, and educating soldiers. These factors, Schmidt suggests, should be given higher priority than trying to increase defense budgets. In support of this point it should be noted that certain military comparisons can be misleading. Most European allies have conscription, which means that they get greater manpower "for the dollar." In addition to this, European countries provide a great deal of free real estate for U.S. bases, which, as well as being an enormous cost for the allies, reduces U.S. force projection costs and supplies a potential battlefield.

274

Schmidt asserts that because of these factors it is misleading to compare defense burdens on a strict index of defense spending.

Finally, Schmidt is convinced that the allies have been hurt by U.S. domestic economic policy. The huge U.S. deficit has caused high interest rates and a massive shift of capital from European countries to the United States. Obviously, European leaders are disconcerted by seeing capital investment that could serve to improve the living standard of their own countries directed to the United States. Schmidt complained:

> The present rather egotistical policies of by far the biggest economy in the alliance are certainly a danger to the future cohesion of the alliance. [13]

Public Opinion

Beyond politics, however, European bilateral relations with the United States must be assessed in terms of public opinion. Without friendly relations between American and West European people, as well as between their governments, the alliance can not hope to endure. For geographical, political, economic, and strategic reasons, the Federal Republic of Germany must be considered the European linchpin of the alliance. Thus to understand U.S./European relations it is helpful to examine some indicators of German attitudes toward both NATO and the United States.

Some analysts of U.S./German relations have pointed to growing anti-Americanism in certain demographic sectors of the Federal Republic. The West German media have recently reflected negative opinions of America. A deprecatory view of the United States became manifest in novels, movies, and television shows produced in the late 1970s. In 1984, numerous books were published in Germany about the United States, most of which cast the United States in an unfavorable light. [14] One such book portrays the United States as a "reeling, incalculable force from which Germans should keep their distance." [15] One editor of Der Spiegel has written that "nothing can be done (about German problems) as long as Germany is an occupied country." [16] Herman Piwitt the editor of Konkret, an illustrated monthly, has voiced what he believes to be the need for "cultural decolonization." [17] The West

German journal Englisch-Amerikanische Studien, which is used by school teachers to teach English, includes chapters entitled: "On the Ash Heap of History: Ronald Reagan's Crusade Against the Soviet Union," "An Analysis of Reagan's Programmatic Speeches," and "The C.I.A. in Grenada: Documentation and Analysis." [18]

West German intellectuals have also expressed discontent with the United States. Rudolph Bahro, a leader of the Left, has stated that the influx of American culture in Germany is analogous to the impact that the Spanish conquistadors had on the Incas. [19] Dorothy Solle, a professor of theology and an activist in the anti-missile movement, has referred to Europe's post-1945 history as a "Pax Americana based on exploitation and repression." [20] Gunter Grasse, who may be West Germany's best known author has said that the United States was disqualified from making moral judgements about anything. [21] In an article appearing in the New York Times magazine in 1984, John Vinocur wrote that following the lead of Grass many political writers in West Germany have depicted the United States as an "oafish bully." [22] In addition to these influential intellectuals, a number of politicians, including Petra Kelly of the Green Party, have spoken out against the United States and NATO.

Despite these undercurrents of anti-Americanism among the media, intellectuals, and the Greens, there are indications that the majority of the general public in West Germany has a positive opinion of both NATO and the United States. Public opinion polls suggest that the majority of the West German public advocates continued FRG membership in NATO and sees the United States as West Germany's best friend. A 1984 poll showed these results: When asked whether the Federal Republic should remain a member or withdraw from NATO, 72 percent responded that the FRG should stay in the alliance. [23] The positive response was consistent wihin every party except the Greens.

	Total Population	CDU-CSU	SPD	FDP	Greens
Remain a Member	72%	86%	68%	81%	28%
Withdraw	9%	2%	12%	8%	51%

When asked to name the country that is the best friend of the Federal Republic, 40 percent said the United States. The second place nation, France, was named by 15 percent, less than half of the U.S. total. [24] The trend was consistent on two additional points as well. The United States was overwhelmingly called the nation with which the FRG should seek the closest cooperation (79 percent) [25] and 53 percent said that they "liked" the United States. [26]According to a poll conducted in August 1983 by EMNID, a prominent opinion polling institute, there is strong support among West Germans for NATO and the presence of U.S. troops in the Federal Republic. EMNID reported:

88% of those questioned were in favor of Germany's staying in NATO,

86% believe that the West German Armed Forces make peace more secure,

45% consider the communist threat considerable or very considerable,

78% think the United States forces in Germany make peace more secure,

75% consider the U.S. presence indispensable or important, and,

73% are against any withdrawal of U.S. forces.

These data suggest that German public opinion is generally favorable toward NATO and the United States, but a look beyond basic attitudes and into more specific questions reveals emerging disagreements and contradictions, especially among the younger generation.

Polls have indicated that most Germans believe that the Soviet Union is becoming stronger militarily and that it is not necessary to do anything about it. [27] A poll conducted in early 1984 asked Japanese, French, British, and West German citizens to name the nations that will be important and powerful in twenty years. Only the West Germans answered that the U.S. position in the world would dwindle. [28] In another poll taken in England, Switzerland, and West Germany, people were asked about which nations they felt had a great deal of freedom. Majorities in the range of 70-80 percent in Britain and Switzerland said that their

countries and the United States had it, but in the
Federal Republic there was no consensus that West
Germans or Americans enjoy high levels of freedom. [29]
Finally, a public opinion poll taken in West Germany
among a group of 16-29 year olds showed that only 25
percent of those polled believe that democracy was
worth defending if the choice were between communism
and democracy. A "better red than dead" attitude was
also reflected as 56 percent of this group said that
they would avoid war at all costs, even if it meant the
Soviet Union taking over Europe. [30]

These various symptoms within German society point
out that the FRG continues to support NATO and to be
generally pro-U.S., but unfavorable trends on both
sides of the Atlantic threaten the cohesion of the
alliance.

Efforts to Sustain NATO

We have seen the rough waters through which the
alliance is sailing and the brewing storms which
threaten to sink the good ship NATO. The
precariousness of this voyage raises a few questions
for public policy seamanship: What steps are being
taken by NATO governments to produce public support for
the alliance, who is doing it, and is it working? Most
signs indicate that the European nation most active in
this area of pro-NATO public policy is the Federal
Republic of Germany. In the late 1970s, while the
debates over SALT II, the neutron bomb, and INF were
raging, U.S.-German post-war relations were dipping
toward the nadir. Chancellor Helmut Schmidt realized
that something needed to be done in order to rectify
the situation and commissioned Minister Hamm-Bruecher
to study the matter. The subsequent Hamm-Breucher
study concluded that more interpersonal contacts among
young people were necessary to improve German-American
relations. These increased contacts, the study
suggested, were required because the younger
generations in both countries have had limited exposure
to the highly productive German/American relationship
that flourished in the immediate post-World War II
years. During a visit to Washington in November 1981,
Mrs. Hamm-Breucher put forth a proposal to improve
German/American contacts to then-Secretary of State
Alexander Haig and certain members of Congress. This
initiative blossomed in early 1982 into the
Congress/Bundestag Youth Exchange Program wherein each
member of both legislatures would sponsor a teenager
from his or her constituency. On January 5, 1982 both

278

Chancellor Schmidt and President Reagan issued statements approving the new program.

In addition to the initiation of the Congress/Bundestag Youth Exchange Program, the West German government has taken further steps to strengthen ties with the United States. These steps have included not only verbal support for the initiation of new German/American contacts, but financial backing as well. In his first report on his office's achievements during the 1983 tricentennial year of German immigration to the United States, Berndt Von Stade, Bonn's coordinator for German/American cooperation, confirmed an increase in government funding of more than 25 percent; from DM 79.3 million (1984 $1=2.3 DM) in 1982 to over DM 100 million for 1984. [31] On June 25, 1983 Chancellor Helmut Kohl commented on a new program, the Youth Exchange Initiative, during a speech in Krefeld:

> The young generation, which has not experienced the start of close German/American cooperation in the post World War II period, is now assuming responsibility in our countries. I ask them to understand the history of the relationship between our nations in all its aspects and to make use of this insight in shaping our common future. The Federal government will try to the best of its ability to further the dialogue between those who belong to the successor generation.
> For this year (1983) and for 1984, the Federal Republic and the U.S. have made special efforts -- including financial efforts to expand youth exchange. We are aware that the schools and the media cannot take the place of the experience of getting acquainted with one another personally; that can at best be supplements. That is why the exchange of students will be expanded from 6,000 now to a future rate of 10,000 annually. [32]

Foreign Minister Dietrich Genscher also expressed his support for the program in a letter to Secretary of State George Shultz:

> The Government of the Federal Republic of Germany attaches the utmost importance to preserving and developing good German-American relations. Intensified exchanges between our peoples, especially between the young generations, is the best means of safeguarding these good relations in the long run. [33]

279

Another initiative, of a different vein, geared towards
U.S./German relations was proposed by Helmut Schmidt on
June 28, 1984, while speaking to the Bundestag.
Schmidt proposed increased Franco-German military
cooperation that he said might raise the "nuclear
threshold" and allow the United States to reduce its
force levels in Europe. [34]

Private initiatives in the FRG have also been
taken to enhance U.S./German relations. In early 1984
the Robert Bosch Foundation announced the establishment
of a new annual scholarship program, which will provide
funding for seven months of work and study in the FRG
for 15 future American leaders in the areas of
politics, economics, administration, and the media.

The program is designed to counter what the
foundation sees as a tendency of the two countries
to grow apart as a new generation of leaders comes
to the fore in the U.S. [35]

Elisabeth Noelle-Neumann, director of the Allensbach
Institute of Demographics, declared on March 30, 1984
that upon her death she will transfer the ownership of
the Institute to the University of Chicago. Ms.
Neumann said that this decision was intended to
stimulate increased German/American scientific
dialogue. [36] On June 15, 1984 the Krefeld society for
German/American relations announced that it would award
the Concord prize of DM 10,000 to President Karl
Carstens for his special contribution to
German/American friendship. In addition to awarding
this prize, which was established in 1983 on the
occasion of the tricentennial of German immigration to
America, the Krefeld society gave out 25 stipends to
young Germans for six week visits to America. [37]

The United States government has also made efforts
to ameliorate relations between the two nations. In
1982 the Inter-Agency Steering Committee for
U.S./German Contacts was created. This new structure,
made up of 23 federal agencies ranging from the
National Endowment for the Arts to the Department of
Defense, was established with the intention to organize
government-wide participation in the contacts
initiative. The director of USIA, Charles Z. Wick, was
appointed as coordinator and chairman of the steering
committee, and Richard Burt, the Assistant Secretary of
State for European affairs, was named deputy chairman
of the steering committee. [38]

In its first year the steering committee, which was established as a long term initiative, focused its energies on tricentenneal activities in which numerous government agencies participated. The International Trade Administration, a branch of the Department of Commerce, devoted its October issue of Business America to the tricentennial. The Department of Energy helped fund a $30 million joint project with German industry. The National Park Service conducted approximately 40 different tricentennial programs in 1983. NASA was an active participant in the tricentennial festivities. During this time the first non-U.S. citizen ever to fly on a U.S. space shuttle mission was Dr. Ulf Merbold of the FRG. A "conference call from space" among the spacelab astronauts, President Reagan and Chancellor Kohl was carried live on German television. It is estimated that 18-20 million Germans either saw the telecast or read about it. The National Endowment for Humanities devoted the issue of their November 1983 magazine, Humanities, to the tricentennial and also gave 30 awards totalling nearly $500,000 for exchange programs for 25 cooperative research programs and a number of seminars. The U.S. Postal service jointly issued with the FRG a stamp commemorating the 300th anniversay of the sailing of the first German emigration boat, the Concord. During 1983 160 million of these stamps were circulated in the United States and around the world. [39] A total of 45 states (plus the District of Columbia) participated in over 1,000 tricentennial events in 1983. One such event was the establishment of a national monument, the German-American Friendship Garden, which was dedicated in Washington, D.C. on the mall in the fall of 1983. [40]

Another effort begun by the Reagan administration to improve U.S./German relations is the President's International Youth Exchange Initiative, which was created in May 1982. This program, which is directed by the USIA, has allocated $400,000 for bilateral, short-term academic youth exchanges with the FRG. The aforementioned Congress/Bundestag Youth Exchange, which also falls under the auspices of this program, will eventually have 536 American participants and 520 German participants, has a budget of approximately $2.5 million and brings the total of new American funding for youth exchanges with Germany to approximately $2.9 million. The FRG has matched this total. Other USIA programs with West Germany include exchanges with vocational workers, young political leaders, journalists, and staff legislators. Further programs

include Fulbright scholarships, the International
Visitors program, and the American participants or
speakers program. The Fulbright program in the Federal
Republic is one of the largest in the world and West
Germany traditionally has the largest American
participants program in the world. In 1984 the
speakers program scheduled 106 speakers to visit West
Germany for talks on a wide variety of topics
including: "the successor generation," East-West
relations, arms control, the role of women in society,
and religion. These and other USIA programs are not
only targeted at youth, but at the general public.
Some programs are directly targeted at teachers,
teacher education programs, and text book publishers.
These include seminars for high school teachers and
exchange programs for authors, publishers, and editors.
The USIA also is responsible for the distribution of
booklets explaining U.S. foreign and domestic policy.

There has been a substantial increase in the
amount of money that is allocated by both the FRG and
the United States to youth exchange programs over the
last three years. An approximate total of $5.8 million
was added to these programs. In addition to this, great
efforts were made by both sides during the
tricentennial year to promote improved U.S./German
relations. This increase in funding and in effort
indicates that many people are concerned in the United
States, or are at least interested in being perceived
to be concerned, about the tensions and strains within
NATO.

Conclusion

Thus far we have looked at two issues. One is the
tension that exists among members of the Alliance.
This type of tension is created by conflicting
governmental policies and can be alleviated by changes
and compromises in governmental policy only. The
second issue is the perception that the pro-NATO
consensus in the United States and Europe is
diminishing. Stated another way, there appears to be a
danger that the trans-Atlantic defense orientation on
both sides of the Atlantic is perhaps becoming a thing
of the past. Thus there are three parts to the
problem; governmental policy towards the alliance,
solutions to short-term problems, and efforts to
sustain the alliance over the long-term.

A clear distinction must be made here. The Reagan
Administration recognizes the importance of NATO.

Within the alliance the United States, is taking firm, skillful, and forward-thinking action designed to avert disagreements over policy and strategy. This is not the focus of this critique. The problem is that there is a significant imbalance between the effort to work within NATO and the effort to sustain a pro-NATO consensus in the United States. The U.S. commitment to the defense of Europe rests ultimately on the will of American people as it is expressed through their elected representatives. The perception that the United States is "not wanted" in Europe, once established, will be erased only with great effort. The Reagan administration is not adequately confronting the present, though admittedly inchoate, trend of anti-NATO feeling in the United States.

The administration's policy toward NATO may be successful on a government-to-government level, but efforts to build a public consensus have not been equally successful. President Reagan's visit to the Bitburg cemetery in May 1985 may have strengthened relations between Bonn and Washington, but it stirred up some anti-German sentiments among the American people. Two recent, unrelated developments also help to illustrate this dichotomy. Decisions by various NATO governments to participate in the President's Strategic Defense Initiative (SDI) research program reflect strong cooperation at the policy level, but the American public vehemently resented the negative reaction of the European people to the U.S. bombing of Libya in April 1986.

In simple terms, the American people will not wait to be thrown out of Europe by "ungrateful" allies. Americans will not, as Senator Gary Hart (D.-Colo.) has stated, stay in Germany for 300 years like the Romans. They will instead support and perhaps demand congressional action that will "get us out" before we are pushed, particularly if it is perceived that bringing troops home will save money and reduce the military budget. It is true that in 1984 the Nunn amendment failed but if the measure had been introduced in the House of Representatives it would have most likely passed with ease. In 1986 and 1987 the Nunn amendment, in some form will probably be on the shelf ready to be reintroduced if the European allies do not conform to U.S. expectations. 1986 Gallup and Harris polls indicate that the American people favor lower defense spending. Thus the most fundamental crisis confronting NATO is not the U.S.-European disagreement over policy; rather it is whether the

American people will continue to believe that it makes a difference whether the United States remains in NATO.

The Congress-Bundestag Youth Exchange Program should help promote understanding between the young generations in the United States and the FRG, but these teenagers will not become political leaders for another 15 to 25 years. Short-term problems, if not addressed with assertive action by the United States, may become so acute that the alliance will not last long enough to enjoy the fruit of efforts like this exchange. The critical period in U.S.-European relations, if not here already, is certain to occur before current exchange programs pay off. If the alliance is to endure for another generation then the United States must take steps to enhance it relations with its allies. But there must also be a vigorous effort to build a public consensus on the necessity of maintaining the alliance. What is being neglected more in the United States than in West Germany are the measures that build such a domestic constituency.

Each dispute among the NATO countries, until now, has been resolved before it destroyed the alliance. One worrisome point, however, is the cumulative effect of the "permanent crisis" on public support for NATO. If present trends continue the American people may support moves to diminish the U.S. role in NATO even if the alliance is in robust condition on the official level.

It is not novel to conclude that the federal government waits until a problem becomes a domestic crisis before taking action. The risk in this case is that the damage created before this problem becomes a crisis may not be easily repaired. The security element of U.S.-European relations cannot endure without wide-spread, popular support among the American people. Waiting until the signs are unmistakable that popular support has eroded beyond the critical point will guarantee that official policy will follow; sooner or later, but it will follow. The American people could lead the United States out of NATO for reasons that have little to do with U.S. security interests.

Under present conditions the survival of a pro-NATO consensus in the United States appears to be a by-product rather than an objective of current U.S. policy.

NOTES

1. "General Rogers Says Europe is Heedless of His Arms Advice,"by Richard Barnard, <u>Defense</u> <u>Week</u>, July 2, 1984, 5.

2. "Standing Guard Over Europe," by Ted Carpenter, <u>Reason</u>,August 12, 1984, 43.

3. <u>Survey</u> <u>on</u> <u>National</u> <u>Defense</u> <u>and</u> <u>Economic</u> <u>Issues</u>, by Abt Associates, (Cambridge, MA), taken October 4-10, 1984, 15.

4. "Burden Shared," <u>The</u> <u>Economist</u>, August 15, 1984, 38.

5. "Europe Called Main U.S. Arms Cost," by Richard Halloran, <u>New</u> <u>York</u> <u>Times</u>, July 20, 1984.

6. "Europe Called Main U.S. Arms Cost."

7. <u>Survey</u> <u>on</u> <u>National</u> <u>Defense</u> <u>and</u> <u>Economic</u> <u>Issues</u>, 15-16.

8. "The NATO Alliance After 35 Years," by Lee Hamilton, <u>Christian</u> <u>Science</u> <u>Monitor</u>, August 13, 1984.

9. Lawrence Eagleburger, remarks at the John Davis Lodge International Conference on "The State of the Union," January 31, 1984.

10. "The State of the Union."

11. "Leadership in the Alliance," by Helmut Schmidt, in <u>Grand</u> <u>Strategy</u> <u>for</u> <u>the</u> <u>Western</u> <u>Alliance</u>, (Boulder, CO: Westview Press, 1984), 29.

12. "Leadership in the Alliance," 34.

285

13. "Leadership in the Alliance," 37.

14. "Post Pershing Germany," by Walter Laqueur, The New Republic, March 5, 1984, 22.

15. "Europe's Intellectuals and American power," by John Vinocur, The New York Times Magazine, August 29, 1984, 60.

16. "Post Pershing Germany," 22.

17. "Post Pershing Germany," 23.

18. "Post Pershing Germany," 23.

19. "Post Pershing Germany," 22.

20. "Europe's Intellectuals....," 70.

21. "Europe's Intellectuals....," 70.

22. "Europe's Intellectuals....," 60.

23. Die Politische Meinung, by Gerard Nerdegen and Elisabeth Noelle-Neumann, January-February 1984, 11.

24. Die Politische Meinung, 6.

25. Die Politische Meinung, 6.

26. Die Politische Meinung, 5.

27. "Post Pershing Germany," 22.

28. "Europe's Intellectuals....," 72.

29. "Europe's Intellectuals....," 72.

30. "Europe's Intellectuals....," 72.

31. The Week in Germany, (Published by the German Information Service), April 27, 1984.

32. See chapter 8 of the Final Report of the Presidential Commission for the German-American Tricentennial: Contacts Initiatives, (Washington, D.C.: United States Information Agency, 1984).

33. Final Report, 6.

34. "Helmut Schmidt's Good Idea," by Robert Komer, Washington Post, August 26, 1984.

35. The Week in Germany, February 3, 1984.

36. The Week in Germany, April 6, 1984.

37. The Week in Germany, June 22, 1984.

38. See Chapter 9 from the Final Report.

39. Final Report, 6-29.

40. "The German-American Connection in Years Ahead: A U.S. Government Perspective," a speech at Sweet Briar College by H. Alexander Wise, Jr., October 8, 1983.

RAPID DEPLOYMENT IN LIEU OF ENERGY POLICY?

Martin W. Sampson III

Although Americans devoted little effort to
worrying about the reliability of energy supplies in
the mid 1980s, energy is a national security topic.
The first part of this chapter argues that the apparent
amelioration of the U.S. energy situation since the
late 1970s in fact masks underlying characteristics of
dependence that are durable and worrisome. The second
section discusses major policies, public and military
of the Reagan administration's first five years in
regard to energy security. The final section assesses
these policies and concludes that the various public
policy and military policy pieces fit together poorly,
strikingly so considering the Reagan administration's
emphasis on national security.

The Situation

The remarkable flux of the oil market in the past
fifteen years has proved difficult to accurately
anticipate and predict. Its gyrations and surprises
confounded knowledgeable people who doubted that
exporting nations could muster any leverage over the
oil market, that the price rises of '73-'74 could be
sustained, that a subsequent jump in prices would occur
in the same decade, that conservation efforts could
make much progress in the U.S., or that OPEC would find
itself with vast unused capacity in the mid-1980s.
Projecting the energy status of the Soviet Union has
been a similarly difficult endeavor; expectations
stated in the 1977 CIA report that the Soviet Union
would in a few years cease to export petroleum
generated extensive discussion and left those
forecasters, who were wrong for many of the right
reasons,[1] amid the large number of others who had
hazarded erroneous projections of what the oil
situation would be within the next five or ten years.

It may be that so much has been learned about oil
forecasting that the next 15 years will be more
predictable and devoid of the major shocks of the
recent past. That, however, is dubious. It is dubious
in part because the catalysts for the two major shocks
of the 1970s were political events: an Arab-Israeli
war, which erupted with little obvious warning, and a
revolution in Iran, which differed from earlier kinds

288

of political change in the post-World War II Middle East. As was the case in the past 15 years, during the next 15 years political events may have effects on the market that the most skilled analysts of normal patterns of oil supply and demand cannot anticipate.

Various Presidential policy proclamations suggested that this second 15 years from 1985 to 2000 could be more predictable and less ominous for the United States. President Nixon proposed Project Independence, and President Carter's energy program called for effort on behalf of the moral equivalent of war. Nixon's idea succumbed to Watergate; Carter's idea included the unpopular news that the answers were expensive, long term, and would require personal sacrifice. The country did not resonate to that message, although increasing numbers of people began to recognize energy as a serious problem. During the 1980 Presidential campaign, candidate Reagan took a different tack by arguing that removing government from the energy field and allowing oil companies to proceed more freely would result in increased discovery of crude oil in the United States, higher levels of production, and the end of 1970s style oil shocks. His policies after the election were no surprise.

Although philosophically different, common to all these perspectives was a shared objective of greater U.S. energy independence. Also common to them is that none produced the desired results. Consumption and conservation patterns did change, largely a reflection of high oil prices and economic recession. Those are transient factors, yet, curiously, there was by the mid-1980s a sense in the country and the rhetoric of the Reagan Administration that the energy security problem had dramatically eased if not vanished. All the obvious kinds of evidence that a successful Project Independence might have produced by the mid 1980s seemed in place. Gasoline lines were non-existent; prices were dropping; the news was full of reports of intractable intra-OPEC turmoil; and auto companies with 'obsolete' large models still in production were doing much better than the companies, such as AMC, that concentrated on small cars. All of this was happening, moreover, without excruciating, nation-wide changes that Carter's warnings seemed to anticipate for the lifestyle or standard of living among the employed, prosperous people.

Unfortunately, this happy perception of the mid-1980s is at variance with some -- but not all -- of the underlying features of the oil situation. As oil prices began to ease and the economy began to strengthen in the mid 1980s, oil consumption in the U.S. rose slightly. More importantly, by that turning point the vast increase in the price of crude oil during the 1970s and early 1980s had not produced sizeable reductions in U.S. oil demand compared to 1970, an increase of U.S. oil production or an expansion of U.S. proved reserves.

U. S. PETROLEUM[2]

	Consumption	Production	Proved Reserve
1970	14.4 mbd	11.3 mbd	39.5 bb
1984	15.7 mbd	8.7 mbd	27.3 bb

Consumption, which peaked in 1978, has risen during the past 15 years. U.S. production of crude oil has been relatively stable at less than 10 mbd for over 10 years, despite dramatic increases in the United States. Exploration in this economic environment has not provided any major increase in the proved reserves of the U.S. In short, the U.S. is a long way away from the degree of self sufficiency that it had in an earlier era when oil sold for less than $2.00 a barrel, an era that Presidents Nixon, Carter, and Reagan hoped to revive, at least in regard to American energy security.

Even if the U.S. were experiencing a return to the kind of consumption/reserves or consumption/ productive capacity ratios that it had in the 1960s, there would still be reason for concern about the energy vulnerability of the economically linked western alliance. Throughout a decade of high oil prices the underlying characteristics of the Western European and Japanese oil situations have proved discouragingly durable. Prior to 1970 those areas did not produce much oil and were in a disadvantageous and dependent situation. In the early 1970s their dependency became even more disadvantageous, partially because the ability of the Western Hemisphere to replace oil imported from the Middle East had diminished. The 1970s decade of high prices produced some change but less than might have been hoped. During much of the 1970s oil consumption increased in Western Europe and Japan, with large proportions of that oil coming from the Middle East. European consumption rose more in the 1970s than oil production in the North Sea. There were oil production increases in Norway and Britain after 1980, but those increases were modest compared to the productive capacities of the major Middle East nations. In 1980 the level was 2.2mbd; in 1984 it was projected as 3.5mbd,[3] a difference that is slightly less than the production capacity of Indonesia. Nor were there sizeable new sources of oil in other locations outside of the Middle East that could enable these members of the Western alliance to forget about Middle East oil. The total 1980-1984 oil production rise in non-OPEC third world nations was expected to be 2mbd, mostly from Mexico,[4] and again a relatively modest amount considering the levels of consumption in Japan and Western Europe. As stated in the Joint Chiefs of Staff FY 1984 United States Military Posture,

> "The economies of many industrialized countries, particularly those of Western Europe and Japan, depend on continued access to adequate supplies of oil from the Middle East....The close interrelation of Western economies makes it extremely unlikely that the United States or its major allies could insulate themselves from the loss of Middle East oil.[5]

According to a 1984 statement by Secretary of Energy Hodel, the sources of surplus oil productive capacity available outside the Gulf region could replace only 3-3 1/2 mbd compared to the more than 8 mbd that was being sent through the Persian-Arab Gulf.[6] A statement by Melvin Conant to the U.S. Senate Committee on Energy and Natural Resources was more ominous. Looking ahead, Conant asserted that "with signals accumulating of declining production for exports from nearly every OPEC member outside the Middle East, a few years from now...as much as 90% of international oil trade will come from the Middle East Gulf."[7]

At the time these statements were made, crude oil cost more than $25 a barrel. The economic incentives for searching for new sources of oil -- or alternative kinds of energy -- resulting from such price levels did not produce staggering increases in American or world proved reserves. What market-induced opportunities for such changes had existed prior to winter 1985-86 ceased as the price per barrel dropped below $20 and then in mid 1986 threatened to stay at a level lower than $10.

291

These low prices may persist during the rest of the
1980s. Hard pressed for income after a few years in
the early 1980s of holding production levels down, some
Middle Eastern leaderships might decide to resume the
sizeable levels of production they had a few years ago.
Although they are reluctant to accept lower prices for
their oil, leaderships that need finances, whether for
warring against one another or for domestic
expenditures that help maintain themselves in power,
are even more reluctant to lose power. During the rest
of the 1980s it is probable that some will choose to
produce at high levels, keeping the price of crude oil
relatively low and further destroying the economic
incentives for development outside the Middle East of
new oil sources or alternative energy technologies.
That oil production costs are lower in the Middle East
than some other regions suggests that one of the
implications will be a forced reduction in output of
some oil fields elsewhere.

This conjecture offers a glum assessment of the
1980s as a time for progress on the problem of Western
energy security. Progress was disappointing in the
first years of the decade despite a supportive
environment of high oil prices; the latter part of the
decade may be a time when the incentives for
alternative energy discovery and development that would
benefit the western alliance are more anemic than at
any time since the early 1970s. That possibility
suggests that it is appropriate to consider whether the
U.S. has moved beyond the reasons for worrying about
energy security that surfaced in some of the studies
done in the late 1970s and early 1980s. Those studies
warned of serious possible situations, presumably at
probability levels that could be taken more seriously
by governments than by the private sector.

A 1979 Congressional Research Service study
predicted that a one to two million barrel a day
disruption could result in real declines in U.S. GNP of
between .1 to .2% in 1980 and 2.3 and 3% in 1981.[8] In
the Fall 1980 Foreign Policy, J. S. Nye asserted that a
one year cutoff of oil from the Gulf would cost Europe
23.3% of its GNP, Japan 27.3% of its GNP, and the
United States 17.6% of its GNP.[9] The Department of
Energy's 1979 Petroleum Supply Vulnerability study
projected that in 1985 a 75% a disruption of petroleum
exports from the Gulf would deprive the U.S. of between
4.7 mbd and 6.3 mbd.[10] In a Spring 1983 International
Energy Agency practice that used a scenario based upon

1981 world supply and demand data the price of oil rose to $98 a barrel.[11]

Subsequent studies considered the U.S. situation after oil demand began to drop in the early 1980s. A Congressional Research Service study on U.S. vulnerability in 1980 and 1982 concluded that reduced consumption of oil in the U.S. by 1982 had made a difference. In the earlier period a disruption of oil production would push prices to between $94 and $297 a barrel; in the latter period a disruption would push prices to between $66 and $128 a barrel.[12] An Office of Technology study entitled "U.S. Vulnerability to an Oil Import Curtailment" states that sustained disruption of all Gulf oil exports would reduce U.S. supplies by 5 mbd in the conditions of 1981, 3 mbd in the conditions of 1984.[13] That study foresees a 3 mbd disruption driving oil prices to between $50 and $70 a barrel,[14] and, depending upon the U.S. response, causing between a 1.3% and a 5.2% drop in GNP over a period of years. Comparing these figures to the '81-'82 recession the study observes that the 1.3% figure is toward the outer limit of U.S. historical experience and 5.3% is "well outside it."[15] The study also observes that a tighter oil market of the 1990s could make the U.S. more vulnerable than it was in the 1970s because U.S. production is expected to decline.[16]

As noted above, predicting the oil market is a hazardous task. Yet there are indications of less contrast between the era of the 1970s and the 1980s than is often assumed. If the experience of the first half of the 1980s is to justify a relaxed attitude toward oil security issues, that justification cannot be based upon a dramatically new pattern of oil supply and consumption. Overall there is no dramatically new pattern that has the requisite features of enhanced U.S. self-sufficiency and sharply increased proportions of world oil reserves outside the Middle East. The low prices of the mid 1980s, moreover, reflect a market that would seem to thwart progress toward such a pattern. Instead the optimism would have to be based on conclusions that the worries about supply interruption in circumstances of dependency were alarmist and can now be eased.

Two points are relevant here. First, many of the studies cited above incorporate scenarios that have only a partial shut-off of oil from the Gulf, not the 100% blockage that Nye discussed. The IEA simulation exercise, for example, stipulated only a 50% drop in

293

Gulf production coupled with a 75% reduction in Nigerian oil production. Thus these studies have typically not incorporated the worst case of a total cessation of oil exports from the Gulf.

Second, the Iran-Iraq war has provided some insights into the difficulties of effecting substantial disruptions of oil export from the Gulf, but the activities of that war by January 1985 hardly exhaust the possible ways to disrupt oil shipments. Picking off tankers in the northwest area of the Gulf that are bound for Kharg Island does not constitute the most serious threat. Some observers have argued that Iraq was reluctant to attack Kharg Island because Arab states of the Gulf region did not want to trigger an Iranian reprisal that would affect shipments of oil throughout the Gulf.[17] The most serious threat would have to focus on Saudi Arabia and would involve sabotage or other damage to production and exporting facilities rather than piecemeal disruption of tankers. The effects of such an event could be long-term. The success of suicide sabotage missions elsewhere in the Middle East is not reassuring evidence that sabotage is easy to prevent. The oil events of the early years of the 1980s, therefore, are not a complete basis for dismissing the possibility of supply interruptions.

As noted earlier, this situation does not mean that the western alliance is on the verge of a major energy disruption or that a major disruption in the coming 15 years is inevitable. It does underscore, however, that the apparent calm of the mid 1980s is misleading. There is still a potential for serious disruption (again, at probability levels that are low enough to interest government officials worried about national security more than the private sector). As energy exploration and production outside the Middle East decline because of anemic economic incentives, this potential may increase rather than decrease. For that reason energy matters should be of interest to people who worry about national security, particularly those who worry about what the U.S. can and cannot do in regard to the Arabian Peninsula.

Recent U.S. Policies

The policy measures that the Reagan administration has adopted toward the energy security situation can be grouped into three categories. They are military expenditures for a Rapid Deployment Force, expenditure to build up the strategic oil reserve, and reliance upon market mechanisms for other aspects of energy security. The first two are continuations of policies set down by the Carter administration; the third is a dramatic reversal of the kinds of initiatives that the Carter people favored.

Rapid Deployment Force.

The key military effort is the rapid deployment force that President Carter first set up in March 1980 under a joint command. During its first term the Reagan administration enlarged this force to 220,000 and indicated that it ought to be further expanded.[18] With some Congressional prompting the Reagan administration also altered the leadership arrangements so that the rapid deployment force now has its own command, CENTCOM, rather than a temporary, joint command. The force has been billed as a group that can go anywhere, but the concern about the Gulf is evident from CENTCOM's territorial responsibility for nineteen countries in East Africa and Southwest Asia. CENTCOM's headquarters are at MacDill Air Force Base in Florida, and it is the only command whose physical location is outside its area of responsibility.[19] That is not attributable to the go-anywhere nature of the RDF, because if used in a different area the RDF would be placed under the control of the U.S. military command for the affected region.[20] Instead it would seem that CENTCOM's mission can only be addressed with mobile forces because nations in its area are sensitive about U.S. military activities inside their borders.

Planning and development of the RDF in the Carter and Reagan administrations has focused on the Soviet Union as the overriding military threat to the security of the Gulf and hence to the continuation of oil supplies. The 1980 Carter Doctrine stated that "an attempt by any outside force to gain control of the Persian Gulf region will be regarded as an assault on the vital interests of the United States...". As Cecil V. Crabb, Jr. notes, "the context of his message left no doubt that his warning was aimed primarily at the Soviet Union."[21] Secretary of Defense Casper Weinberger commented in a September 1981 Congressional hearing that the Soviet threat in Southwest Asia is more serious than the Soviet threat to NATO or to Northwest Asia.[22] At the hearings for the 1983 budget, Assistant Secretary of Defense for International Security Affairs, Francis J. West, stated that the primary mission of the rapid deployment force is the goal of limiting Soviet military influence and leverage

in the region. Soviet control of oil, he noted, would
change everything, and it is crucial to deny the
Soviets a blitzkrieg triumph over control of oil in the
Gulf.[23]

The transcripts of four years of Congressional
hearings on the Rapid Deployment Force harbor two
interesting themes in regard to the objectives and
appropriateness of the force. One theme is the tension
between focusing on the Soviet Union as the worst-case
disrupter of the Gulf and, on the other hand,
recognizing that intra-Middle East or intra-Gulf nation
instabilities are a more probable cause of disruptions.
General Kingston, the first commander of CENTCOM,
stated in the same 1983 hearing where West testified
that the most serious threat would be Soviet invasion,
but the most likely would be subversion of the kinds
now evident in the region.[24] Intriguingly, he also
noted that:

> "usually it is inappropriate to associate
> U.S. forces with the most likely threat
> because regional states do not request
> that."[25]

To Senators' probes as to whether the RDF should
be shaped to deal with the most likely instead of the
most serious threat General Kingston responded that
"it's not an either/or situation."[26] Numerous officers
testified that worst-case preparation also addresses
other, less serious contingencies. In a slightly
different vein at a 1984 hearing General Klein observed
that planning focuses largely on possible Soviet moves
but "in the recent past there has been a significant
shift, the planning for a lesser case interregional
scenario," such as the defense of Saudi Arabia against
a regional threat.[27]

The 1983 Congressional Budget Office's Rapid
Deployment Forces offers an instructive glimpse of some
of the military parameters of preparing for worst-case
versus tailoring the force to the threat that stems
from regional instabilities. The CBO report considers
three sizes of RDF: the current 220,000, the Reagan
administration's projected force size of 440,000, and a
reduced size of 165,000. The largest size would impose
a drain on NATO defenses (unless budget increases
provide for large forces in both areas), implicitly
raising basic questions about the net gain in security
against Soviet threats if chaos in the Gulf forces a
depletion of troops in Europe. Moreover, given Soviet

capability around its own borders, "even as large an RDF as envisioned by the administration might have trouble against a determined Soviet invasion of Iran".[28] In contrast, the report finds that the current RDF could probably serve successfully in support of friendly Arab states involved in regional conflicts..."[29] The smallest RDF considered in the report might also be adequate because it "would still equal or exceed the size of many Mideastern armies." Such a force could, however, "offer almost no resistance against a Soviet invasion."[30] The CBO conclusion would thus seem to be that during its first term the Reagan administration purchased a force size that is adequate for regional challenges.

Unfortunately, the size of the force is not the only criterion that affects the effectiveness of the force. A second theme in the Congressional hearings is the clear implication that the unwillingness of major nations in the Middle East to provide the force with bases of its own is a regrettable and serious handicap. Centering communications and command in Florida is an obviously less than optimal arrangement. Considering that the limited infrastructure of the area requires more material and personnel than would be required in, for example, Europe, there is also a shortage of relevant places to locate the needed supplies. Eighteen ships anchored around Diego Garcia hold some supplies, and Oman has also agreed to the pre-positioning of some supplies there. Beyond the combination of large supply needs and few locations to place those supplies is the basic point that there are few relevant places to station troops prior to the outbreak of hostilities. The situation is summarized by the October 1984 Armed Forces Journal International list of "potential USCENTCOM contingency bases."[31] The list includes Diego Garcia, and nine countries, of which four are outside CENTCOM's region. Of the five in CENTCOM's region only Oman welcomes a standing U.S. force, albeit a small force. The U.S. has an access agreement with three (Oman, Kenya, and Somalia) and has negotiated, apparently unsuccessfully, with Egypt. U.S. military officials who are charged with protection of the oil producing areas confront an asymmetry between the help available from regional nations and the importance of the problem.

Strategic Petroleum Reserve.

A second element of the Carter/Reagan policies is the strategic petroleum reserve in the U.S.

Established during the Ford administration by the 1975 Energy Policy and Conservation Act, this reserve was originally intended to have 500 million barrels of oil by 1985. During the Carter administration the target rose to 1 billion barrels by 1985,[32] but the Carter administration was cautious about filling the reserve, in part because of a Saudi threat to raise prices if the U.S. proceeded to stockpile large amounts of oil.[33] In spring 1980 the Strategic Petroleum Reserve thus held 91 million barrels[34] and by December 1980 it held 100 million barrels.

The Reagan administration moved more aggressively in building up that reserve than did the Carter administration. Within a year and half it had reached 200 million barrels, rose to 385 million barrels by late 1983, and was supposed to reach 430 million barrels by the end of 1984.[35] In early winter of 1985 the Reagan administration announced as a cost-cutting measure that it would stop adding petroleum to the strategic reserve in order to reduce the budget deficit. That announcement echoed an earlier proposal, opposed in Congress, to delete funds for filling the Strategic Petroleum Reserve from the FY '85 budget.[36]

Other matters.

The third overall element of the Reagan administration approach is its reliance on market mechanisms for virtually all other aspects of its energy policy. This approach contrasts with the Carter policy of using market mechanisms in certain ways but attempting to achieve other results that would not be sustained in the short run by market forces. Indeed, the major tactic of the Carter administration was government intervention in a sometimes reluctant marketplace; the main tactic of the Reagan administration has been to leave such matters to the market place. In Kash and Rycoft's view, the Reagan administration displays a "categorical opposition to all government efforts to enforce energy conservation or efficiency."[37]

In the Reagan administration there has been no enthusiasm for government stimulation of energy production. As noted earlier, much of the progress made on energy conservation and possibly even energy development in the Carter administration was a response to market forces rather than a response to government programs. The actual high price of energy and increasingly widespread expectations that energy prices would not decline persuaded many businesses to move rapidly on energy conservation because it was economically advantageous to do so. That kind of stimulus was in fact the central argument that the Carter administration used to justify the decontrol of oil prices: oil prices at high levels would spur energy conservation.

The Reagan administration appears much less concerned with energy consumption per se. Its allegiance to decontrol stems from faith in the market, not from a calculation that the decontrol policy will enhance the incentives to invest in additional energy conservation or development measures. Thus the Reagan public policy leaves exploration and conservation to the market place.

The Reagan administration's allegiance to market forces extends beyond the realm of encouragement of new energy sources. The Reagan administration also clearly favors market forces as the appropriate mechanism to determine how government controlled oil should be distributed in times of emergency shortage. It allowed the allocation authorization to expire in September 1981, welcoming the end of what it viewed as an inappropriate governmental role. It vetoed a stand-by rationing program in 1982. The apparent presumption is that market forces best allocate oil supplies in the event of a crisis that forces sharp decreases of supply on the U.S. market and/or triggers panic behaviors among consumers. This presumption applies both to privately held stocks of oil, such as those owned by major oil companies, and to the government owned oil in the strategic petroleum reserve.

This approach also pertains to the administration's stance regarding the International Energy Agency. The International Energy Agency was established during the Ford administration as a coalition of industrialized oil importing nations that might in some respects counter the Organization of Petroleum Exporting Countries. The centerpiece of the IEA was an oil sharing agreement that involved pledges by member nations to assist countries that were experiencing large reductions of oil supplies. Various categories of shortage were established and responsibilities of member nations were assigned for each of the categories. The IEA also proclaimed an objective of cooperation with multinational oil companies, which were viewed as an essential source of information on the world oil market.[38]

The IEA has been criticized for various reasons, ranging from the argument that it is inappropriate for the U.S. to participate in arrangements that might require the U.S. to forego some of its oil imports to assist nations of the western alliance to, on the other hand, arguments that this kind of mechanism is too slow to be effective. It has also been argued that the IEA is the only organized effort by the western alliance to plan for the possible problem of oil shortages and that accordingly it is an important endeavor.

As noted above, in early 1983 the IEA conducted a simulation that was a trial run of the energy sharing agreement. The U.S. participated with other IEA members. Apparently the Department of Energy decided to comply with the energy sharing provision to reduce consumption by relying entirely on market forces, and in the exercise the DOE allowed the price of oil to rise to $98 a barrel, which in the U.S. would translate into gasoline selling for approximately $4 a gallon.[39] Congressional hearings note allegations that the DOE fabricated some of the information it supplied, further suggesting a lackadaisical attitude toward the IEA.[40]

The administration has also declined to establish a fair-sharing system or seek an anti-trust waiver for U.S. based multinational oil companies that would allow them to exchange information under emergency conditions and thus cope more effectively with the shortages.[41] The generally consistent stance is that market forces are the best means for dealing with energy shortages internationally as well as in the domestic market.

In conclusion, in the mid-1980s the U.S. response to the problem of energy security for itself and the western alliance has three basic components. There is a military aspect of a rapid deployment force, created for uses anywhere in the globe but devised with an emphasis on Southwest Asia. There is the non-market endeavor to put large amounts of oil into the strategic petroleum reserve, an effort that the White House recommended should end in 1985. Finally, there is an intense commitment to market mechanisms as the appropriate tactic for handling all other aspects of the energy situation, aspects including how the oil would be distributed from the strategic petroleum reserve and development of new energy supplies and technologies.

Analysis

Military Policies

Deterrence of the Soviet Union. An effective military deterrent requires at least two things. First, the targeted party has to recognize and understand the warnings and preparations that constitute the deterrent from the other side. Second, the party that is mounting the threat must have a substantial confidence that it can, if need be, carry through on the threat and obtain the outcome that it has expected. In regard to the Carter/Reagan policies for the defense of the Gulf against the Soviet Union it is reasonable to assume that the threat has registered and that the first requisite of deterrence is satisfied. Whether the second requisite is fulfilled is more problematic.

If the threat of a direct, large Soviet attempt to seize or obstruct the Gulf is to be taken seriously, and the Reagan administration's stand is that it is, 220,000 RDF troops cannot forestall such an invasion. Acquisition of sizeable bases in Saudi Arabia would not alter that fact, meaning that the defense of the Gulf as proclaimed in the Carter Doctrine relies upon a willingness to retaliate elsewhere against the Soviet Union.[42]

There are, however, intriguing questions about the effectiveness of such a deterrent that uses the rapid deployment force as a trip wire for retaliation elsewhere. A Soviet attack might be designed to damage oil installations, not designed as the Carter Doctrine envisioned to "control" any territory, or, as Reagan has feared, to turn Saudi Arabia into an Iran. Tripping the wire might also be the act of inflicting major damage, whose magnitude cannot be gauged by who eventually controls the territory. If large oil installations are disabled for long periods of time the result is a kind of economic damage that can be matched only by counter attacks on well defended areas of the Soviet Union. Do such areas qualify as locations more favorable to western military efforts? And what happens if the attack is by a third party surrogate force, whose connection with the Soviet Union is ambiguous?

Deterrence of Regional Threats. In some ways the direct Soviet threat is conceptually simpler than

301

purely regional threats. How the two requirements of deterrence mesh with the "more probable" but reportedly less dangerous regional threat to oil production is problematic.

Since President Truman's decision to recognize the State of Israel in 1948 there have been three major, identifiable objectives of U.S. policy toward the Middle East.[43] One is an effort to minimize Soviet influence in the region. Another is support for the State of Israel and nations of the region that support Israel. The third objective is maintenance of access to markets and raw materials, especially oil, in the region. Although U.S. administrations have made differing decisions about the priorities of these three objectives at various times, none has sought to abandon any of the objectives. Indeed, administrations that have focused excessively on any one of these objectives in the hope that the three objectives would condense into one have typically desisted because of the complexity of American interests in the region. (The Reagan Administration was not the first to discover this, but the fate of Secretary of State Haig's "strategic consensus" effort to muster an anti-Soviet alliance amongst the nations of the Middle East illustrates the point.)

These objectives are not logically consistent. Potentially, any two of the objectives are contradictory. For example American threats to seize the oil fields by force if necessary do not minimize the attractiveness of Soviet arms offers to Middle Eastern nations. Similarly, strong U.S. support for the State of Israel neither diminishes the willingness of nations such as Jordan or Kuwait for arms business with the Soviet Union, nor eases the objections within the region to stationing American troops on Arab soil to block possible -- but not likely -- Soviet invasions. Although the three objectives are deeply rooted in American circumstances, they are not a basis for a policy that is both simplistic and logical.

This background is a partial explanation of why the first requisite of deterrence is very difficult to muster against regional threats to oil security. In the Soviet case it is clear that the key U.S. objective is to minimize expansion of Soviet influence over the oil area, and presumably the Soviets can recognize that they are the target of that specific threat. In the regional-threat case, the U.S. deterrent is multi-faceted. It is a threat to those who oppose Israel, it

302

is a threat to those who court or cooperate with the Soviets, and it is also a threat to those who would disrupt oil supplies. The problem here is that the first threat is so broad gauged that it fits many nations of the region, meaning that states which cooperate too readily with the U.S. risk the consequences of appearing to side with an enemy. The second threat, though less broad, also splits a region of oil nations that have limited interest in the U.S./Soviet rivalry, particularly when the Soviets support militantly anti-Israeli forces in the region. The third aspect of the U.S. threat, for which the U.S. might willingly use troops, is unavoidably diluted.

Another, powerful difficulty in mustering the first requisite of deterrence is that the number of relevant targets is substantial. Deterring the Soviet Union is in this respect straightforward: there is only one target, the Soviet Union itself. Deterring regional parties that would consider interruption of the oil supplies is not a single-target exercise. Khomeini's regime is an obvious threat to the Saudi oil fields as well as to Arab oil fields elsewhere on the Gulf. The era of Iraqi belligerence to Saudi Arabia or Kuwait may be in only a temporary eclipse for the duration of the Iraq-Iran war. There are numerous other tensions in the Gulf, some inter-nation, some intra-nation, some religious. Protagonists include both nation states and a remarkable array of non-state groups, such as Palestinians, Arab Shi'ite fundamentalists, and dissident tribes in the Arabian peninsula. Circumstances can easily be imagined in which any of these groups might participate in efforts to affect oil flow.

Confidence that a deterrence threat, in for example the form of a rapid deployment force headquartered in Florida, has reached each of these groups should not be automatic. Confidence that a genuinely credible threat toward one target constrains rather than encourages or stimulates other group's activities ought not be automatic, either. Instead, threats against, say, Iran, may enhance the probability that another target, such as Shi'ite groups operating on their own, will attempt to cause damage. This point is not lost on Middle East leaderships that might welcome the protection of an RDF yet fear that its presence will stimulate politically dangerous hostility.

In a sense, then, a pair of underlying factors mars the deterrence effect of the RDF. There are too many targets, and U.S. foreign policy objectives in the region are too complex.

This point becomes much more serious in regard to the second requisite of deterrence, namely the capability to actually carry out the threat in the event that the target fails to be deterred. An aspect of this capacity is getting forces to places where they can deal promptly with an attack on oil installations, especially if the opponents do not give the U.S. the 30 days that are needed for a large build-up. A genuine capability would require troops and bases in the area. The reluctance of regional nations to admit U.S. troops, grant the U.S. broad basing rights, and the like is, however, a serious problem that relates directly to the triple-objectives of U.S. Middle East policy. Welcoming soldiers from the nation that is the key support for Israel is politically very difficult. Welcoming soldiers from a nation that might respond to a future rise in oil prices by threatening coercion, as the U.S. did during the Ford/Kissinger era, is also difficult politically. Given these two factors, a regime in the Arab world that is friendly to the U.S. and takes some steps in the direction of accepting U.S. troops creates issues and opportunities for its adversaries. Excessive U.S. military visibility in Saudi Arabia may well erode rather than strengthen the security of the Saudi government. Thus the prospects for the U.S. to markedly improve its basing situation seem poor.

Even if a government is directly threatened, it still might not request RDF help. The Saudi leadership, as a pertinent example, might refrain from requesting adequate assistance from the U.S. government because doing so is an unambiguous admission of inadequate credibility. Libya is a curious precedent in this regard. During the summer of 1967, when resentment against the Libyan government's lackadaisical attitude toward the 1967 June War was intense and the country remained under martial law for many months, the government did not request assistance from U.S. military forces that could be brought in through the large U.S. air force base in Libya. Two years later a rapid coup ended the monarchy, and the new leader, Qaddafi, was acclaimed by many Libyans for his subsequent success in terminating the U.S. air force base. This political dynamic is hardly a relic of the 1960s, even if leaders in power would like U.S.

assistance. An active policy of providing that assistance may well weaken the regimes that the U.S. is trying to help.

Even, however, if the RDF can muster adequate force and even if key regional nations change their policies and enable U.S. forces to station supplies and troops on site, there may be kinds of threats that the RDF cannot effectively prevent. A pessimistic 1975 study by John Collins updated in 1979 by Collins and Clyde Mark acknowledges the seriousness of inadequate U.S. forces in position, but continues to discuss additional problems, particularly sabotage, the difficulties of coping with numerous simultaneous fires, and the problems of operating the oil fields without the cooperation of local labor.[44] Howard Bucknell's 1981 Energy and the National Defense also notes the dangers of sabotage, including the possibility that "oil extracted from the Persian Gulf region could be rendered radioactive by covert chemical treatment and thus made useless at the ports of debarkation in Europe, Japan, and the U.S."[45] The sabotage item hardly seems less serious in the mid 1980s, given the simplicity of techniques utilized against U.S. embassies and Marines in Lebanon and the formidable difficulties of controlling populations so effectively that it becomes impossible for saboteurs to operate. Pipelines, oil collecting stations, pumping stations, and loading devices are very difficult to guard adequately. In the event of damage to major installations, the lead times for repair of that equipment so that oil production can resume may also be substantial, a point noted in the Collins studies. Inherent, then, in the task of the RDF is the prevention of damage, a more difficult and subtle task than deterring hostile occupation of territory. A splendid defense of turf could succeed at the same time that costly damage is done to the oil producing system, which is what the RDF is supposed to protect in the event of the "more probable" but "less costly" threat by regional forces.

Conclusion. The deterrence effect of the RDF is severely handicapped for reasons that are unrelated to the size or expertise of its force. A Soviet move that seeks destruction of oil producing equipment or, for example, loading facilities at Ras Tanura rather than occupation of parts of the Gulf could be much more rapid than the deployment of a force that has few base facilities in the area. Once the damage occurs the west could experience serious disruptions even though others retain, as the Carter Doctrine put it, control of the area.

Threatening retaliation against the Soviet Union elsewhere rather than engaging the Soviet force in the Gulf may be a relevant deterrent against this kind of threat. Against the same threat posed by regional groups, however, there is not necessarily a parallel answer. Palestinian or Shi'ite terrorism is unlikely to be deterred by threats of bombs on home areas, as the Israelis discovered with both groups. Even if there is some lead time for anticipating that kind of threat, the complexity of U.S. policy toward the Middle East severely complicates the tasks of adequately pre-positioning forces or encouraging regional leaders to seek help when they want help. Thus the Congressional Budget Office observation that 165,000 could be an effective RDF for dealing with regional threats should be regarded as a perspective that overlooks some crucial difficulties, difficulties that neither a 220,000 nor a 440,000 force level would address. There are then, very substantial defects in the RDF concept as a protection for oil supply from the Gulf region to the west.

Market Forces

Someone concerned about western security has ample reason to ask what kinds of policy initiatives accompany the RDF. Such policies could fall into two categories: endeavors that will mitigate the effects of large disruptions that the RDF fails to prevent and endeavors that help reduce western dependency on Middle East oil over the long run.

Emergency planning. The seriousness of the energy situation for Western Europe-Japan suggests why those governments would be concerned to find ways of coping with future energy shortages. One part of such an endeavor is preparation for months or years of less fuel and higher prices that accompany oil shocks. A second, related endeavor is to find any possible way to reduce the short-run speculation and panic that occurs when oil consumers begin to doubt the availability of supplies. In both the 1973-74 episode and the 1979 episode prices rose much more than could be explained by the availability of oil on the market. Panic buying coupled with economic incentives to retain inventories that would be worth more in the future were responsible for a substantial part of the increase.

306

The 1973-1974 OPEC embargo triggered a major endeavor: the establishment of the international energy sharing arrangements and the I.E.A. In some respects the actions of oil companies during the embargo demonstrated the usefulness of an effective oil sharing arrangement. The companies thwarted the OPEC attempt to target certain nations. Curiously, they did so without much regard for the then current market forces. Instead they pegged their deliveries to the amounts of oil provided certain customers prior to the onset of the crisis, regardless of what the market was willing to support under conditions of panic and chaos.[46] No nation suffered markedly more than other nations, and the effects of shortfall were distributed in an apparently reasonable way.

National governments had very little involvement in this process, and in some respects the I.E.A. energy sharing agreement is their plan to allocate oil supplies in an analogous fashion. Instead of leaving allocation to the market forces, the nation states, like the companies in 1973-74, would share oil so as to keep each country within a certain percentage of its previous supply of crude oil.

There are numerous problems. In their halcyon era when a few companies controlled most internationally traded crude oil, the companies had the market data, they controlled vast quantities of oil, and they could fend off the politicians, as they did in 1973-1974. Nation states have none of these advantages, and they are likely to move slowly. In Philip Verlegger's words,

> The problem with the IEA, or any organization designed to cope with an economic crisis, is that such organizations are, by their very nature, incapable of responding quickly.... Discussion among the IEA ministers would take place the first month or two after an interruption began while prices on spot markets were being pushed rapidly upward.... These price increases would set in motion the process of hoarding and stock building, which has been shown to worsen the crisis.[47]

In the 1980s the U.S. policy has been to continue American membership in the I.E.A., to allow price to regulate U.S. demand (in the I.E.A. simulation), and to dismantle domestic allocation controls. There is broad skepticism that the I.E.A. mechanisms would work under

307

conditions of major crisis. There is also a widespread malaise over the performance of allocation mechanisms in the U.S. during past times of oil shortage. A policy slanted heavily toward market mechanisms for coping with crises thus finds extensive support.

Yet studies by Verlegger and by Horwich and Weimer, among others, underscore a basic aspect of successful coping with oil crises. Verlegger observes that "banking and oil market disruptions have many identical characteristics, and the solution to banking panics will, if properly applied to oil markets, yield the same beneficial results."[48] The idea, then, is to counter disruptions by supplying oil to targeted parties so that panic, hoarding, and determined but cumbersome political interventions are not triggered. The Horich and Weimer study, which advocates reliance on the market for allocating energy supplies, argues that "an essentially free market response to an oil supply disruption can materialize only if it is preceded by a full-scale planning effort."[49] The market-allocation idea, then, does not hinge on governmental indifference to energy matters.

A policy of increasing the size of the Strategic Petroleum Reserve is a crucial aspect of an effective, market-oriented set of contingency plans for coping with disruptions. The progress during the first Reagan administration in filling the strategic reserve is a step in the right direction.

Yet that progress does not reflect an adequately aggressive policy. According to Horich and Weimer "regular sales of options for the purchase of SPR oil"[50] are important so that the oil stock is tapped promptly. That kind of policy has not yet happened. There are no clear statements that the strategic petroleum reserve would be used in this way. The Reagan administration has not been eager to even conduct tests of whether the oil removal and sale mechanisms actually work. Some Congressional committee members seem more interested in this matter than the administration people who have testified before Congress. Put differently, this concern is not among the national security items that have received aggressive attention from members of the administration. In early 1985 the administration declared that it would stop filling the reserve, implying further indifference to construction of the kinds of mechanisms that would allow a free market system to operate smoothly.

308

Progress toward lessened dependence on Middle East
oil. As noted above the Carter administration viewed
market mechanisms as a helpful incentive for new
exploration and production of crude oil as well as
other kinds of energy. The crux of Carter's effort to
decontrol oil was the expectation that allowing prices
to rise in a decontrolled market would spur energy
development. Indeed, at the beginning of the 1980s
there was a flurry of energy investment and exploration
in the U.S. Beginning in the late 1970s there was also
substantial investment, primarily among businesses, in
energy conservation measures, not because of Carter's
rhetoric about the energy issue being the "moral
equivalent of war" but rather because they were cost
effective. Rising energy prices, thus drove a search
for new energy and an effort to reduce energy
consumption. Both are the kinds of steps that reduce
U.S. as well as western reliance on Middle Eastern oil.

Focusing on the marketplace as the appropriate
incentive for conservation and investment in new energy
has in the Reagan years brought a result that inverts
the original rationale for price decontrol. During the
mid 1980s market forces have discouraged rather than
encouraged investment in new kinds of energy
technology, such as the synfuels program. Market
forces have slowed rather than strengthened the
momentum in conservation. An era that required
government incentives to compensate for weak market
forces has been an era of an administration that is
committed to the marketplace. From the perspective of
energy security one can ask if Reagan's policy was more
attuned to the Carter era and Carter's policy better
suited to the Reagan era.

The long-term dependency of the west on the Middle
East may be aggravated by continued declines in the
price of crude oil. Given that the RDF is not a basis
for expecting long-term security against energy shocks,
one could argue that the energy security of the western
nations justifies non-market incentives to stimulate
development of alternative energy sources, conversion
away from oil use, and exploration for oil outside the
Middle East. Such incentives might expire when the
price of oil rises, restoring the market incentives
that existed in the late 1970s. In the meantime,
however, reliance on anemic market forces decreases the
progress that can be made toward lesser dependence on
Middle East oil.

Conclusions

There is a clear dichotomy in the U.S. policy approach to a persisting and substantial energy dependence of the western nations and Japan. Many aspects of that dependency are consigned to the realm of market forces. Other aspects of that dependency are addressed through the non-market approach of building a rapid deployment force and putting oil into a strategic petroleum reserve. Unfortunately, the two elements of this dichotomous policy mesh poorly. The RDF has a major task and very thin political as well as logistical underpinnings for accomplishing that task. The real back-up for the RDF must be mechanisms for coping with oil disruption, not a threat of attacking some part of Russia or bombing perpetrators in the Middle East after oil production is disrupted. Market forces can be part of that back-up but only if security planners understand how to manipulate them in positive ways so that the market does not aggravate the problems of oil disruption. The apparent disinterest in further increases in the strategic petroleum reserve, the disinterest in testing the use of that reserve, and the confusion over how the reserve would be used suggest that market forces may be a poor back-up for the RDF in the event of threats to oil production. Worse, the market component does not, in times of slack energy markets, hasten the time when the RDFs importance for energy security can diminish.

As an administration determined to bolster America's defenses, the Reagan administration has overlooked some crucial aspects of the energy security by casting the issue as predominantly military rather than public policy plus military in nature. There is an enormous gap between the potential security importance of the energy situation to the Western alliance and the kinds of measures that are actually being taken. Crucial aspects of the energy situation are left to market forces as though they are indeed no more than a normal allocation component, while great attention is devoted to weapons programs because they are linked to the national security. Such a policy squares poorly with the intensity of concern about matching Soviet efforts in regard to arms build-ups so that the west can defend itself. One result is less security than would be possible in the mid 1980s. A second result is waste of years that could be used to enhance the security that can be possible in the 1990s. Such measures might also help to cushion a long-run

310

transition away from crude oil, which is an aspect of security for the next century.

These are largely critical comments. It should be noted that the energy security issue has an understandable, quite obvious political context. During the first half of the 1980s the probabilities of serious disruption dropped, the public began to forget about energy crises, and the issue therefore demanded little attention. Accordingly, Congressional support for energy matters, always a miserable task because of the complex uncertainty about costs, winners and losers, has now become more difficult to find. After all, President Carter in circumstances of much greater energy urgency had only limited success with the complexities of dealing with Congress on energy matters.

Politically, energy is a formidable issue that requires a great communicator interested in defense. It is ironic that the administration of a highly popular President fixated on national security has been indifferent to that task. Increasing the strategic petroleum reserve is an appropriate aspect of public policy on this issue. Leaving all the rest either to the market or the RDF masks a need that requires more imaginative public policy as an aspect of national security.

FOOTNOTES

1. Hewitt, Ed A. Energy Economics - Foreign Policy in the Soviet Union. Washington: Brookings, 1985. Pages 24-26.

2. The 1970 consumption and production data are from Stobaugh, Robert, "After the Peak," p. 18 in Stobaugh and Daniel Yergim, eds. Energy Future. New York: Random House, 1979. The 1970 proved reserves datum is from Blair, John, Control of Oil, New York: Vintage, 1976, p. 5. The 1970 figure includes the Alaskan North Slope. The 1984 consumption and production data are from Central Intelligence Agency, International Energy Statistical Review 29 January 1984, page 1 and 13.

The 1984 proved reserves datum is from "Middle East Oil and Gas," Exxon Background Series; Exxon, 1984, p. 3. See also Charles Masters, David Root, and William Dietzman, "Distributive and Quantitative Assessment of World Crude Oil Reserves and Resources," prepared for the U.S. Department of the Interior, Open-File Report 83-728, 1983, page 4a.

3. Mossavar-Rahmani, Bijan. "The War and the World Oil Market." Orbis 28:3, 1984, p. 452.

4. Ibid., p. 452. This figure is a projection.

5. Senate Committee on Armed Services. Department of Defense Authorization for Appropriations for Fiscal Year 1984, 98th Congress, 1st Sess., 1983. Senate Hearing 98-49, Pt. 1. P. 456.

6. Senate Committee on Energy and Natural Resources. World Petroleum Outlook - 1984, 98th Congress, 2nd Sess., 1984. Senate Hearing 98-752. Page 18. Page 80 of the same source quotes Anthony Cordesman as estimating that the ratio is 4 or 4^0 mbd excess capacity versus 8^0-9 mbd exported through the Gulf.

7. Ibid., p. 131.

8. Congressional Research Service. Macroeconomic Effects on the U.S. of a Major Disruption in OPEC Supplies: Illustrative Econometric Projections. Prepared by C. Brancato, E. Hull, and J. Brown, 1979. Page 3

9.   Nye, J.S. "Energy Nightmares". Foreign Policy #40. 1980. Page 132

10.   Department of Energy. Petroleum Supply Vulnerability 1985 and 1990, prepublication draft. 1979. Page 5.

11.   House Committee on Government Operations. Preparing for the Next Energy Crisis: DOE's Management of the Oil Sharing Test. 98th Congress. 2nd Sess., 1984. House Report 98-786. Page 23.

12.   Congressional Research Service. Western Vulnerability to a Disruption of Persian Gulf Oil Supplies. Report 83-24F. 1983. Page 42.

13.   Office of Technology Assessment. U.S. Vulnerability to an Oil Import Curtailment. OTA-E-243. 1984. Page 4

14.   Ibid., pages 143-146. This scenario assumes that the U.S. does what is possible (according to the report) to replace the lost energy, a task that would require five years.

15.   Ibid., page 147.

16.   Ibid., page 16.

17.   Mossavar-Rahmani. Page 453.

18.   Iungerich, Raphael, "U.S. Rapid Deployment Forces." Armed Forces Journal International, October 1984, p. 97.   See also Congressional Budget Office, Rapid Deployment Forces, 1983 p. xiii.

19.   Ibid., page 497.

20.   Congressional Budget Office, Rapid Deployment Forces, 1983, p. 5.

21.   Crabb, Cecil V. The Doctrines of American Foreign Policy. Baton Rouge: Louisiana State University Press, 1982. Page 330.

22.   Congressional Budget Office. Rapid Deployment Forces, page 8.

23.   Senate   Committee   on   Armed   Services.
Department of Defense Authorization for Appropriations
for Fiscal Year 1983. 97th Congress, 2nd Sess., 1983,
Part 6. pp. 3717-3719.

24. Ibid., page 3732.

25. Ibid., page 3733.

26. Ibid., page 3734.

27.   Senate   Committee   on   Armed   Services.
Department of Defense Authorization for Appropriations
for Fiscal Year 1984. 98th Congress, 1st Session.
Senate Hearing 98-49, Part 6. Page 3123.

28.   Congressional   Budget   Office.   Rapid
Deployment Forces. Page 13.

29. Ibid., page 6.

30. Ibid., page 18.

31. Iungerich, Raphael, page 99.

32. Horwich, George and David Leo Veimer. Oil
Price Shocks, Market   Response, and Contingency
Planning. Washington: American Enterprise Institute,
1984. Page 111.

33. Alm, Alvin, "Energy and Security: Act Two" in
Dorothy S. Zingerg, ed., Uncertain Power. New York:
Pergamon Press, 1983. Page 202.

34. Lieber, Robert J. "Cohesion and Disruption
in the Western Alliance" in Daniel G. Yergin and Martin
Hillenbrand, eds., Global Insecurity. Boston: Houghton
Mifflin Company, 1982. Page 336.

35. Subcommittee on Fossil and Synthetic Fuels of
the House Committee on Energy and Commerce. Hearings
on the Strategic Petroleum Reserve, 98th Congress, 1st
Session, 1983. Serial 98-63. Page 16.

36. Horwich and Weimer, page 123.

37. Kash, Don E. and Robert W. Rycroft. U.S.
Energy Policy. Norman: University of Oklahoma Press,
1984. Page 268.

38.   See, for example, Kohl, Wilfrid, "The International energy Agency" in J. C. Nurewitz, ed., Oil, the Arab-Israel Dispute, and the Industrial World. Boulder: Westview, 1976. Pages 246-257.

39.   Senate Committee on Energy and Natural Resources, World Petroleum Outlook 1984, page 11.

40.   House Committee on Gov. Ops., Preparing for Next Crisis, page 18.

41.   Senate Committee on Energy and Natural Resources, World Petroleum Outlook 1984, page 1.

42.   This point is evident in the testimony cited in footnote 22, especially page 3717. See also Wiley, Marshall W., "American Security Concerns in the Gulf." Orbis 28:3, 1984, p. 458.

43.   For discussions of these triple objectives see Quandt, William, Decade of Decision. Berkeley: University of California Press, 1978, and Brown, Seyom, On the Front Burner. Boston: Little, Brown, 1984. Pages 134-172.

44.   Collins, John and Mark Clyde, Petroleum Imports from the Persian Gulf: Use of U.S. Armed Forces to Ensure Supplies. Congressional Research Service Issue Brief 1 b 79046, 1979. Pages 12-13.

45.   Bucknell, Howard III. Energy and the National Defense. Lexington: University Press of Kentucky, 1981. Page 126.

46.   Stobaugh, Robert, "Oil Companies in the Crisis," Daedalus 104:4, 1975, pages 179-202.

47.   Verlegger, Philip K., Jr. Oil Markets in Turmoil. Cambridge: Ballinger, 1982. Pages 258-259.

48.   Ibid., pages 260-261.

49.   Horwich and Weimer, page 6. See also pp. 190-195.

50.   Ibid., page 193.

REFERENCES

Alm, A. 1983. "Energy and Security: Act Two: in Dorothy S. Zingerg, ed., <u>Uncertain Power</u>. New York: Pergamon Press.

Blair, J. 1976. <u>Control of Oil</u>. New York: Vintage.

Brown, S. 1984. <u>On the Front Burner</u>. Boston: Little, Brown.

Bucknell, H. 1981. <u>Energy and the National Defense</u>. Lexington: University Press of Kentucky.

Collins, J. and M. Clyde. 1979. <u>Petroleum Imports from the Persian Gulf: Use of U.S. Armed Forces to Ensure Supplies</u>. Congressional Research Service Issue Brief 1 b 79046.

Crabb, C. 1982. <u>The Doctrines of American Foreign Policy</u>. Baton Rouge: Louisiana State University Press.

Hewitt, E. A. 1985. <u>Energy Economics - Foreign Policy in the Soviet Union</u>. Washington: Brookings.

Horwich, G. and D. Weimer. 1984. <u>Oil Price Shocks, Market Response, and Contingency Planning</u>. Washington: American Enterprise Institute.

Iungerich, R. 1984. "U.S. Rapid Deployment Forces." <u>Armed Forced Journal International</u>, October.

Kash, D. and R. Rycroft. 1984. <u>U.S. Energy Policy</u>. Norman: University of Oklahoma Press.

Kohl, W. 1976. "The International Energy Agency" in J. C. Nurewitz, ed., <u>Oil, the Arab-Israel Dispute, and the Industrial World</u>. Boulder: Westview.

Lieber, R. 1982. "Cohesion and Disruption in the Western Allianace" in D. G. Yergin and M. Hillenbrand, eds., <u>Global Insecurity</u>. Boston: Houghton Mifflin Company.

Mossavar-Rahmani, B. 1984. "The War and the World Oil Market." <u>Orbis</u> 28:3.

Nye, J. S. 1980. "Energy Nightmares." <u>Foreign Policy</u> #40.

Quandt, W. 1978. Decade of Decision. Berkeley: University of California Press.

Stobaugh, R. 1975. "Oil Companies in the Crisis." Daedalus 104:4.

Stobaugh, R. and D. Yergin, eds. 1979. Energy Future. New York: Random House.

U.S. Central Intelligence Agency. 1984. International Energy Statistical Review 29, January.

U.S. Congressional Research Service. 1983. Western Vulnerability to a Disruption of Persian Gulf Oil Supplies. Report 83-24F.

U.S. Deparatmenta of Energy. 1979. Petroleum Supply Vulnerability 1985 and 1990. Prepublication draft.

U.S. House of Representatives. 1984. Committee on Government Operations. Preparing for the Next Energy Crisis: DOE's Management of the Oil Sharing Test. 98th Congress, 2nd Session. House Report 98-786.

U.S. House of Representatives. 1983. Subcommittee on Fossil and Synthetic Fuels of the House Committee on Energy and Commerce. Hearings on the Strategic Petroleum Reserve, 98th Congress, 1st Session. Serial 98-63.

U.S. Office of Technology Assessment. 1984. U.S. Vulnerability to an Oil Import Curtailment. OTA-E-243.

U.S. Senate. 1983. Committee on Armed Services. Department of Defense Authorization for Appropriations for Fiscal Year 1983. 97th Congress, 2nd Session. Part 6.

U.S. Senate. 1983. Committee on Armed Services. Departament of Defense Authorization for Appropriations for Fiscal Year 1984. 98th Congress, 1st Session. Senate Hearing 98-49, Part 1.

U.S. Senate. 1983. Committee on Armed Services. Department of Defense Authorization for Appropriations for Fiscal Year 1984. 98th Congress, 1st Session. Senate Hearing 98-49, Part 6.

U.S. Senate. 1984. Committee on Energy and Natural Resources. World Petroleum Outlook - 1984. 98th Congress, 2nd Session. Senate Hearing 98-752.

Verlegger, P. 1982. Oil Markets in Turmoil. Cambridge: Ballinger.

Wiley, M. 1984. "American Security Concerns in the Gulf." Orbis 28:3.

THE CONTRIBUTORS

JOHN ALDRICH is a Professor of Political Science at the University of Minnesota. He received his Ph.D. from the University of Rochester (1975), and was teaching at Michigan State University until 1981 before coming to Minnesota. His research is in the areas of American politics, positive political theory, and research methodology. Among his works are Before the Convention (1980) and numerous articles in the leading journals.

J. EDWARD ANDERSON is a Professor of Mechanical Engineering at the University of Minnesota. He has authored articles in many scientific journals besides those for The Bulletin of the Atomic Scientists and Strategic Review. Professor Anderson is a consultant to the Defense Department, and the inventor of several critical systems for military and commercial application.

BRUCE D. BERKOWITZ is a Professional Staff Member at the U.S. Senate. He is the author of American Security: Dilemmas for Modern Democracy (Yale University Press) and several articles concerning defense policy, intelligence, and international relations.

KENNETH E. BOULDING is Professor Emeritus at the University of Colorado and now works at the Institute of Behavioral Science. He is the author of numerous articles and books in the fields of international relations, political science, economics and defense policy.

PAUL M. COLE will commence his Ph.D. studies in international relations with the Johns Hopkins School of Advanced International Studies in fall of 1986. He is the author of numerous articles on national security policy, Scandinavian and West European politics, and U.S.-Allied defense policies. Mr. Cole is also a member of the Arms Control Association, and a candidate for a term membership to the Council on Foreign Relations.

319

RAYMOND DUVALL is a Professor of Political Science at the University of Minnesota. He received his Ph.D. in 1975 from Northwestern University, and taught for four years at Yale University. He has published his research on international and comparative political economy, and on processes of insurgency and state coercion in several journals and edited volumes.

JOSEPH RICHARD GOLDMAN is an Assistant Professor of Political Science at Augsburg College. He has taught at the University of Minnesota as a visiting scholar, and while there began American Security in a Changing World: Issues and Choices. Professor Goldman is the author of several articles and is conducting research on a monograph.

LAUREN H. HOLLAND is Associate Professor of Political Science at the University of Utah. She has published several articles on the MX Missile system controversy, and is co-author of The MX Decision: A New Direction in U.S. Weapons Procurement Policy? (Boulder, Colorado: Westview Press, 1985).

ROBERT A. HOOVER is Associate Professor and Dean of the College of Humanities, Arts, and the Social Sciences at Utah State University. He is co-author of The MX Decision, and author of The MX Controversy: A Guide To Issues and References (Claremont, Ca.: Regina Press, 1982) and Arms Control: The Interwar Naval Limitation Agreements (Denver, Co.: Denver University Press, 1980).

P. TERRENCE HOPMANN is Professor of Political Science at Brown University, where he is also Director of the International Relations Program and a Research Associate of the Center for Foreign Policy Development. From 1968-1985 he taught at the University of Minnesota. He is co-author of Unity and Disintegration in International Alliances (1973 & 1984), and co-editor of Rethinking the Nuclear Weapons Dilemma in Europe (1986), as well as numerous articles on topics in international politics such as alliances, the negotiation process, and arms control and disarmament.

320

DUNBAR LOCKWOOD is a graduate of the George Washington University's Master's program in Security Policy Studies. He took his B.A. in Government at Bowdoin College in 1982. He is originally from Boston and is currently living in Washington, D.C.

CHARLES W. OSTROM, JR. is an Associate Professor of Political Science at Michigan State University. He has authored articles that have appeared in journals like the American Political Science Review, and is working on a new book dealing with Presidential policymaking and choice.

EARL C. RAVENAL, a former official in the Office of the Secretary of Defense, is Distinguished Research Professor International Affairs at the Georgetown University School of Foreign Service and a Senior Fellow at the Cato Institute of Washington, D.C. He has been a Fellow of the Woodrow Wilson International Center for Scholars, the Institute for Policy Studies, and a Faculty Member of the Salzburg Seminar in American Studies. He is author or co-author of eight books on foreign and military policy, including, most recently, Never Again: Learning From America's Foreign Policy Failures, NATO: The Tides of Discontent, Defining Defense: The 1985 Military Budget, and Foreign Policy in an Uncontrollable World, and he has authored over a hundred thirty articles and papers.

BRUCE RUSSETT is Dean Acheson Professor of International Relations and Political Science at Yale University, Coordinator of the International Security and Arms Control Program there, and Editor of the Journal of Conflict Resolution. He has been President of the International Studies Association and the Peace Science Society (International), and is the author or editor of 17 books and many articles on international relations and strategic problems.

MARTIN W. SAMPSON III is an Associate Professor of Political Science at the University of Minnesota. He is author of a monograph that uses n-actor gain theory to analyze OPEC and other examples of international policy coordination, and his current interests include cultural influences on foreign policy decision processes.

321

MULFORD Q. SIBLEY is Professor Emeritus in the Department of Political Science at the University of Minnesota. He is the holder of several awards for scholarship and teaching. Professor Sibley has published numerous books in the area of political theory, world philosophy and peace studies. Among his works are: Unilateral Initiatives and Disarmament (1961), Political Ideas and Ideologies: A History of Political Thought (1970), Technology and Utopian Thought, and Nature and Civilization: Some Implications for Politics (1977). Professor Sibley has also taught at Stanford, Cornell and other leading universities over the years, in addition to consulting for programs at schools like Bucknell University and the University of Virginia.

DENNIS M. SIMON is an Associate Professor at Southern Methodist University. He taught at the University of Minnesota while publishing articles in journals like the American Political Science Review. Professor Simon is now engaged in research on Presidential behavior.

JUTTA WELDES is a graduate student in political science at the University of Minnesota. She is writing a dissertation which concerns the rhetoric of theories of international relations.